Avid Editing

Avid Editing: A Guide for Beginning and Intermediate Users

by Sam Kauffmann

Focal Press
Boston Oxford Auckland Johannesburg Melbourne New Delhi

Butterworth–Heinemann supports the efforts of American Forests and the Global ReLeaf program in its campaign for the betterment of trees, forests, and our environment.

ISBN 0-240-80421-X

The publisher offers special discounts on bulk orders of this book.
For information, please contact:
Manager of Special Sales
Butterworth–Heinemann
225 Wildwood Avenue
Woburn, MA 01801–2041
Tel: 781-904-2500
Fax: 781-904-2620
For information on all Butterworth–Heinemann publications available, contact our World Wide Web home page at: http://www.bh.com

10 9 8 7 6 5 4 3

Printed in the United States of America

For Katie, Allie, and Derek

"Our deepest fear is not that we are inadequate.
Our deepest fear is that we are powerful beyond measure."

— Nelson Mandela

Table of Contents

Preface

Editing is editing, whether it is done using analog equipment, such as a Steenbeck™ or a Sony edit controller, or a sophisticated digital system like the Avid™. Consider that more than 99 percent of all the films ever made were edited on analog equipment. Acclaimed films by directors from all over the world—Welles's *Citizen Kane*, Eisenstein's *Ivan the Terrible*, Kurosawa's *Rashomon*, Ray's *Pather Panchali*, Godard's *Breathless*, Kubrick's *2001: A Space Odyssey*, Bergman's *Persona*, Mambéty's *Touki Bouki*, Buñuel's *The Discreet Charm of the Bourgeoisie*, Fassbinder's *The Marriage of Maria Braun*, Wertmuller's *Swept Away*, Lucas's *Star Wars*, Babenco's *Pixote*, Beresford's *Breaker Morant*—were all edited before the words "personal computer" ever passed our lips. In fact, it wasn't until the 1990s that feature films and episodic television shows were edited with computers and digital editing software.

Obviously, film and television editors got along splendidly without Avids for almost a century. But the fact that a system works doesn't mean it can't be improved. And few would argue that the Avid isn't a vast improvement.

What is it like editing on a computer compared to an analog system? Can you remember typing on a manual or electric typewriter? Compare that experience to using a word processor loaded with scores of fonts, color capability, and a spell checker. The comparison is similar to the one between a Steenbeck and an Avid. In many ways an Avid is more like a word-processing program than a Steenbeck or KEM™. Want to move a paragraph in a word-processing program? You select and drag it. Voilà! Want to move a shot from one place in your show to another? Select and drag it, and it's done.

Some traditionalists will say that just because a system is faster, that doesn't make it better. I disagree. I believe an Avid *can* make you a better editor. Compared with a film or tape editing system, the Avid allows you to make changes quite easily. If you see that something isn't working, you're more likely to fix it, or try a different approach, with an Avid. And if it's easy to make a scene better, I think you'll make it better. Discovering how to make something better will make *you* a better editor.

Editing on an Avid is not only fast, but also gives you access to many sophisticated features not found on analog systems. Even the lowest-priced models allow you up to eight tracks of audio and advanced titling capabilities. And you can construct many versions of a scene, segment, or entire show and keep them all for comparison.

However, there is a price for all the Avid's speed and sophistication, and that price is not just in terms of dollars (or yen, rands, or euros). The Avid is much more difficult to master than an analog film or video editing system. Think about the typewriter analogy for a second. When you or, more likely, your parents bought an IBM Selectric™ typewriter (the hottest typewriter of the '70s) they probably never read the accompanying manual. They just plugged it in and started typing. Today, the user's guide for my word-processing program is more than 500 pages long. When you buy an Avid, it comes with nearly 1500 pages of documentation!

To put it another way, I teach film and video production classes, as well as digital editing classes. I can teach my film production students how to use a Steenbeck, a popular film editing machine, in about two to three class sessions. Yet I spend an entire semester, some 30 class sessions, teaching students how to use an Avid.

When I first started teaching the Avid, I searched for a textbook to assign to my students. I couldn't find one. Avid has some excellent workbooks that are part of Avid's training courses, but you have to pay close to a thousand dollars to get them. I searched everywhere for a book for the beginner and came up empty. So, with my students' encouragement, I decided to write my own.

This book is written for the beginning and intermediate Avid user. It's designed for producers, directors, editors—anyone who wants to learn the Avid—as well as for students enrolled in a college, university, or high-school editing course. For some, mastering a complex computer application might seem an impossible task. It's not. Just take it one chapter at a time, and you'll soon become the powerful Avid editor you knew you could be.

There will be frustrations. The Avid is software running on a computer, and as with any software on any computer, there are bugs—and sometimes those bugs can bite. Still, ask any film or video editor who uses an Avid if he or she would like to go back to an analog system, and I bet you'll hear a resounding, "No." When you reach the end of this book, I hope you feel that way too.

I have many people to thank for their assistance, none more so than the many students I've had the pleasure to teach during the past decade. There are too many to name, but all of them taught me as much as I taught them. My colleagues at Boston University have given me advice and encouragement throughout my teaching career, especially Bill Lawson and Mary Jane Doherty, who are inspired teachers and good friends. Bob Demers and Tim Kennedy offered invaluable technical assistance and helped my students over difficulties whenever I wasn't there. I also wish to thank Nancy Maguire, Ray Carney,

George Bluestone, Jim Lengel, Steve Geller, Chriss Williams, Charles Merzbacher, and Associate Dean Marilyn Root.

Thanks to Loren Miller, who is a great editor and showed me how to cut on an Avid, Michael Girard of Northeast Negative, Tom Ohanian and Michael Phillips of Avid, Don Wilkins of the Berklee College of Music, Adam Corey, Tony Gorman, Doug and Sandra Cress, Rose-Ann San Martino, Rick Coupe, Wes Plate, Bob Jones, David and Quinn Atherton, Jim Davidson, Hosea Gruber, and my siblings, Margaret, Louise and Bruce Kauffmann, who were my first friends and teachers.

Special thanks to Kate Shanaphy and Tim Eberle, who are Kate and Tim in "Wanna Trade."

This book could not have been written without Katherine Cress, who gave invaluable support and advice every step of the way.

Introduction

Think of this as a textbook, workbook, and user manual all rolled into one. It is written so you can read it at home, studying a chapter's contents, or while sitting in front of an Avid, following the book's step-by-step instructions.

Most colleges and universities divide their semesters into 16 weeks, so there are 16 chapters—one for each week. There are suggested assignments at the end of each chapter, which are there to encourage you to practice the techniques and skills explained in that particular chapter.

I believe you will learn to use the Avid more quickly if you start by editing a short narrative scene, rather than a short documentary project. With a script for the scene in front of you, you know where you are going; you can then concentrate on how to get there. To get you started, I've enclosed a short scene for you to edit. It's on the CD-ROM that comes with this book. Step-by-step instructions are provided at the end of Chapter 1 to guide you through the editing process. A two-page script for the scene is included as well.

Ideally, your professor, instructor, or teacher will mount the scene onto the Avid so you can begin editing after the first or second class. If you will be mounting the CD-ROM yourself, there are instructions in the section called "CD-ROM Instructions." It's really quite simple to install.

My goal is to get you editing as quickly as possible. The digitizing process is an important part of this book, but I've postponed it until Chapter 6. Once you've cut a scene, you'll find the intricacies of digitizing much more understandable.

The scene I've included is called "Wanna Trade." I wrote and directed it, using students in one of my Film Production II classes at Boston University as actors and crew. I am giving you permission to use this material for as long as you wish. If your instructor has material she or he is more comfortable with, then by all means use that material for the first assignment.

This book covers the Avid Xpress™ (Xpress) and the Media Composer™ (MC). Whenever techniques for the two products differ, I will offer instructions for both. Avids come on Windows NT computer systems as well as Macintosh systems. I've used both Macintosh and Windows screens to guide you through the instructions. Mac and Window screens are almost identical. The main difference between cutting on a Mac and cutting on a Windows NT computer is the shortcut keys you'll use. On the Macintosh the Command key, with its symbol ⌘, is the one I use most often in the book. If you are using Windows, substitute the Control (Ctrl) key every time you see the word Command. Windows users should also substitute Alt for Option. That's it. That's about the only difference between the Mac and Windows versions.

If you're new to the Avid, I suggest you read the chapters in the order they appear. Those of you who are intermediate Avid users may want to use this as a reference book, skipping those sections you have already mastered.

One caveat. Recent competition from other non-linear digital editing systems has forced Avid to offer powerful features on the Xpress that were once only offered on the more expensive Media Composer. Given this healthy trend, you may find that a feature I describe as exclusive to the Media Composer is, in fact, available on the latest version of Xpress. So if your cutting on an Xpress, learn the Media Composer features contained in the book. You may use them sooner than you think.

Getting Started

AVID'S ROOTS

Many of the people who designed the first digital editing systems were film-makers who found themselves doing a lot of videotape editing—and they didn't particularly like it. Still, there were things about video editing that they liked better than film editing. So they used the emerging power of personal computers to fashion a hybrid system that borrows the best from both worlds.

In order to understand the Avid, it helps to know a few things about film and video editing, because the Avid's roots run so deeply into both. In fact, so much of the Avid's terminology, and the way the Avid appears on the computer screen, comes from film and videotape editing, that if you know one or the other you already know a lot about an Avid.

Some editors come to the Avid with a film background, and some come with a television background. The first section of this chapter tries to give a brief overview of both film and video editing, in order to acquaint you with the side of editing you don't know. You'll be amazed at how many words and phrases used in this overview section will soon reappear as we discuss Avid editing.

Film and Tape Editing—The Old Way

The main advantage film editing has always had over video editing is that it is nonlinear. You can remove a shot in the middle of the film and put it at the beginning—or vice versa. It takes time to do all that unsplicing and splicing of polyester tape, but you can make changes at any time to any part of your film. Videotape editing is more automated and faster. You push buttons on a machine to set editing points, and the machine makes the edits. But videotape editing is linear—you can't switch shots around as you can with film. In video editing, after viewing your production tapes, you decide which will be your first shot, which will be the second shot, and so on, and then you build your show, one shot at a time. You do this by playing each shot on your source deck and recording the parts you want onto a second tape inside your record deck. If, midway through editing, you decide you want to change the order of shots, you must start over again.

Film editing is extremely flexible, but slow. Videotape editing is faster than film editing, but making changes is much more difficult. When the Avid was designed, the idea was to combine the speed of video editing with the flexibility of film editing.

Working with Picture and Sound

Films are made using a process called double system. A film camera photographs the images at a rate of 24 frames per second. The sound is recorded on a separate tape recorder. In the editing phase, the film is processed, an editing copy is made, and the sound is transferred to magnetic film stock. The picture and sound are synchronized on an editing bench or on a flatbed editing machine such as a Steenbeck or KEM. Because the film has sprocket holes and the sound track has sprocket holes, they can be played together in sync. Throughout the editing stage, the sound and picture are kept separate. An editor usually marks the film with a grease pencil to show where the film will be cut, and an assistant later cuts the picture and then the same amount of sound, so that everything stays in sync. The parts of the shots that are not wanted are cut off, or trimmed, and hung on a trim bin. Toward the end of the editing phase, other sound tracks are added, such as music, sound effects, and narration. In fact, by the time all the sounds are added, there may be 20 different sound tracks, all in sync with the picture.

In video productions, sound and picture are recorded on the same frame of videotape. Each frame of tape holds the picture *and* accompanying sound information. Sound and picture are already locked in sync.

The Editing Process

To save wear and tear on the original film or video, both film and video editors have developed systems that enable them to do all their creative work on a copy of the film or video, and not on the original. Then, after working on the copy, they make a clean master based on the work they did on the copy.

In film, a positive copy is made from the camera negative. This copy is called a *workprint*, and the editor does all her or his work on this copy. It often gets dropped on the floor, hung on trim bins, marked with grease pencils, and cut into pieces by a splicer. None of the resulting dirt or scratches are of any real concern because it is a workprint, after all, and the camera negative is safely stored in a film laboratory's vault. Once all the editing decisions have been made, the camera negative is taken from the vault and the negative is conformed, or cut, to exactly match the workprint. The system works by use of latent numbers printed on the edge of the original negative film. These numbers are placed on the negative in ascending order every foot. When the negative is processed with chemicals at the lab, those latent numbers—called *key numbers*—appear on the negative and are then printed onto the workprint. The job of conforming the negative to match the edited workprint is time-consuming but fairly straightforward. The edited workprint serves as an exact guide to splice together the camera original so that eventually thousands of projection prints can be made for distribution to theaters all over the world.

In video, a different system is used, but the effect is basically the same. Instead of key numbers, videotape uses a system called *timecode*. As sound and pictures are recorded onto the videotape, unique numbers, the timecode, are placed onto the videotape as well. There are approximately 30 frames of video per second, and each frame has its own timecode number. Whereas film's key numbers are based on the length of the film, timecode is measured in time. The first frame on the videotape is designated as 00 hours: 00 minutes: 00 seconds: and 01 frames. Or 00:00:00:01. The next frame is 00:00:00:02. Since video is based on 30 frames per second, after 29 frames, the 30th frame would be 00:00:01:00. Because each frame has its own unique address—its timecode—it is easy to keep track of them.

A production videotape, the master tape shot in the field, would often be transferred to another videotape—the copy. Not only would the copy carry the images and sound of the master, but it would also carry the timecode of the master. The process of editing the copy is called "offline" editing. The video editor would edit the copy, and after she or he finished editing the entire show, the video editing machine would create an EDL (Edit Decision List) that simply listed all the editing decisions—the places where the editor started a shot and ended a shot—listed by timecode. Now the master videotape could be put into an "online" video editing machine and, using the EDL, all the shots in the master would be selected, in the right length and in the right order, to make a finished video show.

AVID'S DIGITAL APPROACH

The Avid simply takes videotape, or film that has been transferred to videotape, and digitizes the images and sound so that you, the editor, can access the material almost instantly. Because all your pictures and sound are now 0's and 1's, they are truly at your fingertips. There is no need to wind and rewind through 20-minute tapes to find a shot, or to wind and rewind through 36-minute lab reels of film. If you're at the end of a 10-minute scene and you want to return to the beginning of that scene, simply push a button and you're there. You don't like what you did four cuts ago? Hit undo and it's undone. Think about it. You are in control of a very powerful machine.

Now that we have examined the Avid's roots, let's examine the computer hardware that houses the Avid software.

It's Just a Computer (with a Lot of Things Connected to It)

The Avid is like any other personal computer you may have used. At the heart of the system is the *CPU,* or central processing unit. For a number of years Avid's software would only work on an Apple Macintosh computer. Now, various Avid models, from the cheapest to the most expensive, are found on Windows NT computers. Whatever the system used, it must be fast, with substantial random access memory (RAM). Even the base systems require 192 megabytes (MB) of RAM. By comparison, an office computer with 64 MB is considered generously endowed. The CPU must also have slots for special audio and video capture boards.

The Avid software is mounted onto the CPU, just as a spreadsheet or word processing program would be mounted onto the CPU.

The CPU doesn't hold the digitized pictures and sound—a special *storage device* does that. Often Avids come with hard drives that are connected to the CPU through a SCSI (Small Computer System Interface) connector. Since you may be working on a film or show that is an hour or longer in length, you need

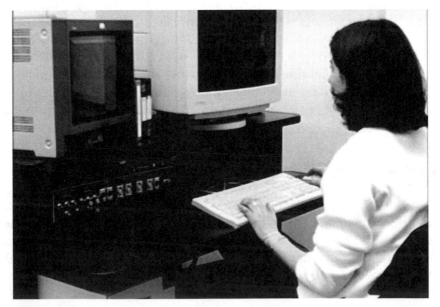

Figure 1.1   Everything you need is on a computer, like this Xpress system.

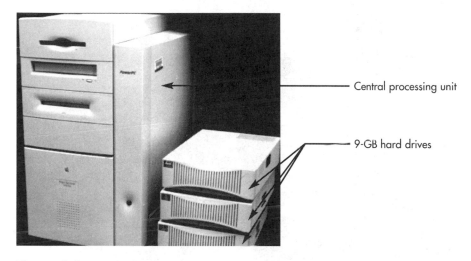

Central processing unit

9-GB hard drives

Figure 1.2

to digitize a lot of material. Many systems start with two 9-GB (gigabytes) hard drives, and as demand for more storage space increases, additional drives may be added. Systems with six 9-GB drives attached together to form 54 GB of storage are quite common. There are systems that allow several Avids to connect to a central storage device. In this way they can all share the same digitized material.

The Avid comes with a special keyboard, and it is attached to the CPU by way of a cable connected to a *dongle*. A dongle is like a bridge, and it sits between the CPU and the keyboard. Without the dongle, you can't access the Avid software.

Depending on the Avid, there are either two computer *monitors* or, in the case of the Xpress, one computer monitor. Usually the monitors are quite large, something like 20 inches. The monitor(s) is plugged into the CPU.

Two external loudspeakers transmit the sound coming out of the CPU for audio playback. There is often a television monitor that plays back the picture, using either an NTSC or PAL signal.

When you buy an Avid system, the dealer will require you to purchase an electrical backup device called a *UPS* (uninterruptible power supply). Because your work is important, and because you can't run a computer without electricity, common sense suggests that you plug the CPU, the computer monitor, and the hard drives into this backup system, which provides a stable electrical current and will keep everything running in case of a power failure. The idea isn't that you keep editing, but rather that you use the backup power to save all your work and then shut down your system.

Because you will want to bring into the Avid a whole range of sound and picture material, you will probably have a variety of input devices. The devices you might have include a Beta SP videotape player/recorder, a DAT tape machine, and a VHS deck. You might have a sound mixer to route the sound

Beta SP
videotape deck   DAT tape deck   VHS videotape deck

Figure 1.3   Input and output devices

through. And just as these devices will help you bring sound and picture into the Avid, you will also use them to output the work you have created on the Avid.

Because the Avid is different from a film or video editing machine, the way you organize your work is also somewhat different.

Avid Editing Workflow

1. **Gather tapes and files.** First, gather together all the picture and sounds elements that form the source material for your project. These may include:
   Videotapes: Digital Betacam, Beta SP, 3/4", VHS, Hi-8, DVC-Pro, Digital-S, or Mini-DV
   Film: Currently there is no way to input film directly into the Avid. Film is first transferred to videotape. (We will discuss this process at length in Chapter 15.)
   Audio: DAT tape, CDs, Nagra production tapes, and sound on a video-tape
   Picture and audio files: Computer graphics, animation, pictures, and audio files

2. **Create a new project.** When you start up the Avid software, it asks you to tell it which project to open. You might share an Avid with other students, or other editors, all working on different projects. If you're

beginning a new project, you click the new project button, name the project, and begin work on your new project.

3. **Digitize.** The Avid will open up the *project window* for your new project. You would now begin to digitize all your source material onto the Avid drives. As soon as you digitize something, the Avid creates two things: a *media file*, which is the digitized version of your picture or sound, and a *clip*, which is a virtual copy of the media file. Because it's a virtual copy, you can see it, hear it, and edit it a thousand ways and not affect the media file—the digitized picture and sound.

   Media files are stored on the Avid hard drives—like the camera negative that's stored in the lab's vault. One media file is created for each track of video and audio. If you have video and stereo sound, you would have three media files created for that digitized material. You don't edit, or work with, media files. You work with the clips. Think of the clip as a shot. You can edit the shot, duplicate the shot, flip the shot, and all those actions affect the clip, while the media file (the digitized picture or sound) stays safely on the hard drive.

4. **Create bins.** When you digitize your source material, you organize it into *bins*. You might have a bin for all the shots from tape number one, and a second bin for all the shots from tape number two. Bins are like folders on your home or office computer, but for people used to editing films, "bin" is a familiar name for a place to store material being edited. The Avid recognizes that you might be starting an ambitious project involving the creation of many bins, each holding hundreds of clips, and provides sophisticated search and find tools to help you locate just the shot you're looking for.

   The steps listed above are all about getting organized before you begin editing. If you're about to edit a feature film or an hour-long documentary, you'll appreciate how important the organizational steps are. Experienced feature film editors and documentary editors are among the most organized people on the planet.

   Now that you have organized the material, it is time to edit.

5. **Edit.** When you open up a clip (think of an entire shot from head to tail) and select a part of it to be included in your project, you are making your first cut. The Avid calls any material that is cut together a *sequence*. You create a sequence by editing together clips. In traditional film editing, the editor starts by putting together an *assembly*, which includes all the clips that might appear in the final film, spliced together in the right order. You could call your first sequence an "assembly sequence." Once you've assembled the material, the next stage is to create a *rough cut*, in which the clips are placed in the right order and trimmed to approximately the right length. You might call this a "rough cut sequence." Because the material is digital, sequences are easily duplicated. You

might create a sequence on Tuesday, duplicate it on Wednesday morning, and start making changes to it. At any time, you can open up the Tuesday version for comparison. As you get to the end of your editing, you are working on what is normally called a *fine cut*. Shots are trimmed to give each scene the right pace and timing.

6. **Add titles and effects.** Once you have edited your sequence, you can easily add titles and effects to it. The Avid has tools for creating multilayered effects and titles. Titles can be created and added to a sequence in minutes. Some effects, such as dissolves, take only a few seconds to create. Once all the titles and visual effects have been added, you have reached the stage called *picture lock*. No more changes are made to any of the picture tracks.

7. **Do sound work.** Once you have reached picture lock, it's time to add the many sound effects and music cues that will make for a rich and powerful sound track. The Avid can monitor between eight and twenty-four tracks, and using built-in tools, the sound editor can make intricate sound adjustments to any and all tracks.

8. **Output your project.** Finally, the end of the Avid workflow takes place when the final edited sequence is sent out into the world. There are three different output methods:
   a. Record the finished sequence onto videotape.
   b. Create an EDL (Edit Decision List) for an online videotape editing session.
   c. Create a film Cut List so a negative cutter can conform the original camera film to the Avid sequence.

With that overview behind us, let's turn on the computer, launch the software, and explore the work space the Avid provides us. Your system may be set up in a slightly different manner than what is described here, but all systems are fairly similar.

TURNING ON YOUR AVID

1. Turn on the power strip that is plugged into your UPS. The hard drives will turn on. If they do not, turn on the hard drives. Wait for them to spin up.
2. Turn on any peripheral devices not plugged into the UPS, such as the speakers and the NTSC monitor.
3. Press the Power key on the keyboard to turn on the CPU. Wait for the system to mount.
4. Windows NT users open "My Computer."
5. Double-click on the alias of the Avid Media Composer or Avid Xpress *application icon*. Wait for the software to mount.

6. The startup dialog box appears, containing columns for Avid Users/Avid Projects. Click on New User. Type in your first initial and last name.
7. Under Avid Projects, click on the project you have been assigned. If it has been mounted, choose "Wanna Trade."
8. Click OK. The project will open to the Project window.

THE AVID INTERFACE ON YOUR COMPUTER

The Xpress was designed for just one computer monitor, which contains both the Project window, containing all your bins, the Edit window, and the Timeline. You look for clips in the bins and edit those clips into the Timeline. Everything happens on one large monitor (Figure 1.4).

The Media Composer (MC) uses two computer monitors to do the same job. The monitor placed on your left is the Bin Monitor, and it contains the Project window and all the bins (Figure 1.5).

The second computer monitor is called the Edit Monitor as seen in Figure 1.6, and contains the editing window and the Timeline. All editing takes place here. The Source Monitor, on the left, contains the clips that will be edited into the project. The Record Monitor, on the right, shows the edited sequence. The Timeline presents a visual representation of the clips in the sequence.

Project window contains all the bins

Timeline

Figure 1.4 Avid Express

Project window contains
all the bins

Bins containing clips and sequences

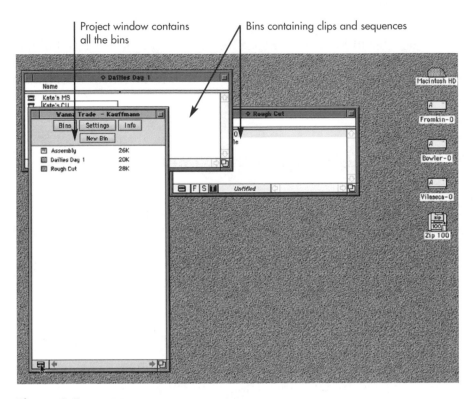

Figure 1.5   MC Bin Monitor

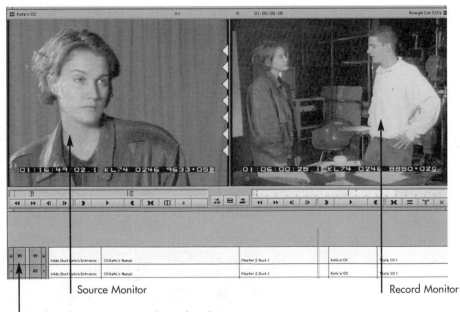

Source Monitor

Record Monitor

Timeline showing picture and sound tracks

Figure 1.6   MC Edit Monitor

As the price of computer monitors drops, more and more Xpress systems are being set up with two monitors, a Bin Monitor and an Edit Monitor, just like the Media Composer.

Now that you're looking at the Avid's interface, lets take a tour.

Project Window

It is like a home page. It lists all the bins. It must be open whenever you are working on a project.

Bins

You place the digitized material, the clips, into bins to help organize the material. You can name the bins anything you want. Common bin names are: Tape 001, Tape 002; or Dailies - Day 1, Sequences, Sound Effects, Music. Whatever makes it easiest for *you* to organize your material—that's the best system.

On the Media Composer, one of the two computer monitors is devoted to bins and working with bins, while the other monitor is for editing. Some Xpress models have just one monitor, which does double-duty.

The Clip icon. Double-click on the icon and it will open as a Pop-up Monitor, or go to the Source Monitor (MC).

Click inside the letters. They will be highlighted so you can type a new name.

Figure 1.7

If you double-click on the bin called Dailies - Day 1 (Figure 1.7), you will see it contains master clips and columns. This one has columns for the clip name, scene, take, duration, and starting timecode.

Clips

The clips in the bin contain different shots and different takes of a scene. The clip icon is on the far left. Next to it you see the name that I gave the clip, followed by important information about each clip. Clips don't take up hard drive space. Instead, each one is connected to the media file it represents. The media file is the actual digitized picture and sound, and it resides on the external hard drive. The clip contains all the timecode information (such as start and end timecode) about the media file. If your media file gets erased, the clip information still exists, but when you play the clip it will say "Media Offline."

Subclips

You can break up long master clips into smaller units, called *subclips*. You make subclips if doing so helps you organize the material.

Bins Views

You can look at the clips in the bin in several different ways.
Text View shows information in column form.
Frame View shows a picture of a frame from a clip.
You can change from Frame View to Text View simply by clicking on the T or F letter at the bottom of the bin.

The Media Composer has a third view called Script View. In this view you get a small picture of a frame, space for writing comments, and information in column form.

Mac users click here to close the Pop-up Monitor.

Picture window showing the position indicator and edit marks

Fast menu button

Button bar

Figure 1.8   Xpress Pop-up Monitor

Pop-up Monitor or Source Monitor

Depending on whether you're using an Avid Xpress or a Media Composer, when you double-click on a clip it appears either as a Pop-up Monitor or in the Source Monitor. (On the MC you can have Pop-up Monitors just as with the Xpress. If you hold down the Option key while double-clicking on a clip, you will get a Pop-up Monitor. For it to play correctly, drag it to the Edit Monitor.)

Beneath the clip window is a picture window with a position indicator, and beneath that is a button bar. The button bar contains buttons that carry out commands. Click a button with the mouse, and that command is executed. From left to right you'll see commands for opening a Fast menu and positioning a red indicator, and buttons for moving backwards and forwards one frame at a time. You also have buttons to place an IN edit mark, to play the clip, and to place an OUT edit mark. There are buttons that remove the IN and OUT edit marks. There's a button to place both an IN and an OUT, and a button that allows you to create a motion effect. The Fast menu, often called a hamburger because of its appearance, opens with a click to present you with even more editing buttons.

Mac users close the Pop-up Monitor by clicking on the close box in the upper-left corner. NT users click on the close button located in the upper-right corner of the Pop-up Monitor.

NT users click on the X box to close the Pop-up Monitor.

Picture window showing
the position indicator and
edit marks

Button bar

Figure 1.9   Source Monitor on the Media Composer

The Source Monitor on the Media Composer acts just like the Pop-up Monitor on the Xpress. It has a button bar that offers many of the same commands as the one on the Pop-up Monitor.

The Composer Monitor (Xpress) or Record Monitor (MC)

This monitor, which is called the Composer Monitor on an Xpress and the Record Monitor on the MC, shows you what is in your sequence; it shows what

Figure 1.10   Record Monitor - Media Composer

you have created by editing clips together. Just like the Source Monitor, it has a button bar and a window with a position indicator showing where you are in the sequence. There is a Fast menu between the Source and Record Monitors. It contains helpful command buttons.

The Timeline

It shows a graphic representation of the shots in your sequence, in track form: V1, V2, A1, A2, A3. The Timeline is like a sync block and splicing tool rolled into one. The Timeline has Source and Record track selectors, a blue position indicator, Zoom and Position bars, and Mark IN and OUT indicators.

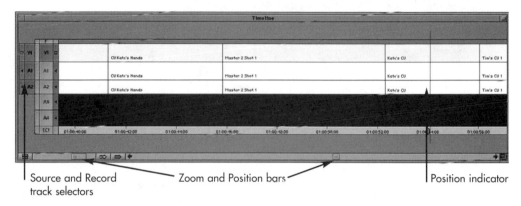

Source and Record   Zoom and Position bars   Position indicator
track selectors

Figure 1.11

Commands

You will instruct the Avid to do what you want through commands. Some of the commands are offered as buttons below the monitors, and some are hidden inside Fast menu buttons. Click and hold the Fast menu, and a palette appears. You can click and drag any palette and it will tear off, so you can place palettes anywhere you like. Once a palette is torn off, a click on its close button will send it back inside the Fast menu. Many commands are also offered as keys on the keyboard.

When you click on the
Fast menu a palette of
command buttons
appears.

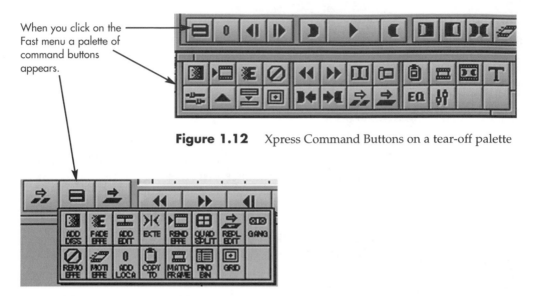

Figure 1.12   Xpress Command Buttons on a tear-off palette

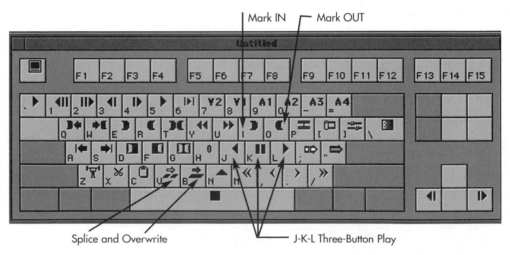

Figure 1.13   Media Composer Command buttons

The Keyboard

An important part of the Avid editing system. Many of the most important editing commands can be executed by simply typing a key on the keyboard.

The default or standard keyboard that comes with your system might be
slightly different than the one in Figure 1.14. Media Composer systems often
come with a default keyboard like the one shown in Figure 1.15. As you can see
the two keyboards are quite similar.

Figure 1.14   Standard keyboard

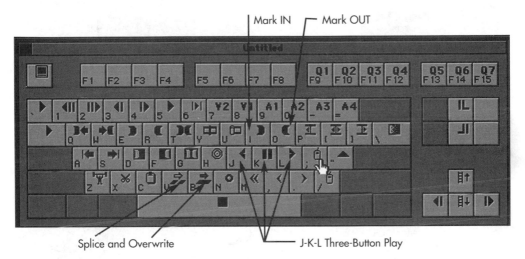

Figure 1.15 Media Composer keyboard

Three-Button Play

An extremely important keyboard combination involves the three letters on the keyboard J-K-L. Press the L key to play your clip or sequence forwards; the K is like a pause key, and the J key will play the clip or sequence in reverse. By placing three fingers of your left hand on those three letters, you have a wonderful controller. Many people call this the Three-Button Play. In fact you can use these keys to play the sequence at different speeds. If you press either the J or K key twice, it will play the clip or sequence at twice the sound speed. Click again and it will run at 90 frames per second, again and you're at 150, once more and you're at 240 frames per second. Hold down the K key while pressing either J or L, and the Avid will creep in slow motion.

Important Commands

Examine the list of some of the most important commands and their symbols (Figure 1.16). Most are available on the keyboard, as buttons on the computer screen, or in a Fast menu.

Two of the most import commands are Undo and Redo. To undo an action, simply hold down the Command key on the keyboard and press the keyboard letter Z.

⌘ - Z Undo
⌘ - R Redo, and you redo the action you undid!

You can go back and undo or redo up to 32 previous actions.

There are many more commands, and we'll get to all of them, but for now, let's practice what we've learned so far by starting an editing session. Granted

Splice and Overwrite

Play

Mark IN

Go to OUT and Go to IN

Mark OUT

Go to Previous Edit — Go to Next Edit

Mark Clip

Step Keys: Back and Forwards
One frame per click

Clear IN

Ten frames per click

Clear OUT

Lift and Extract

Clear IN and OUT

Figure 1.16   Commands

you'll be working at a handicap. You haven't been shown how to use many of Avid's most powerful tools. But you know enough to put together a rough cut of a scene. Just follow the instructions provided in the next section. They will guide you through your first edits and get you started. If you are cutting a different scene, and not "Wanna Trade," simply substitute your clip names for the clip names I provide in the instructions.

Before you make any edits, look at the script for the scene you'll be cutting, to get an idea of action and dialog. If you are cutting "Wanna Trade," you'll find the script on pages 25 and 26. Most of the action has been shot from several camera angles: a master shot and a closeup (CU) of each actor. Some of the action has more than one take. Your job is to make the scene come to life and to choose the best parts among the choices. Examine the performances and also determine which angle gives the audience the best vantage point for that part of the scene.

STARTING AN EDITING SESSION

The screen in Figure 1.17 shows the Xpress as it should look during an editing session. The Project window is in the upper left. Two bins are open: the bin containing the clips and the bin containing the sequence. One clip, a master shot of Kate and Tim, has been opened as a Pop-up Monitor. Several shots have been spliced into the Timeline, creating a sequence. The Composer Monitor is on the right-hand side and shows what's in the Timeline. We're looking at Kate's CU, because the position indicator in the Timeline is parked on that clip. Although some people like to put the Composer Monitor on the left, I think it's best to place it on the right, the way the Media Composer does it. Drag the windows and monitors to place them in the "correct" position.

The screen in Figure 1.18 shows the Media Composer's Edit Monitor as it would look during an editing session. Kate's CU is in the Source Monitor, and we're seeing a master shot of Kate and Tim in the Record Monitor because the position indicator in the Timeline is parked on that clip. The Bin Monitor is on a second computer screen (not shown) and contains the Project window and the bins.

The Source Monitor is like a holding tank. Every time you double-click on a clip icon, it appears in the Source Monitor. Click and drag on the name of the clip in the upper-left corner of the Source Monitor to see all the clips that are held there. Drag down and release to choose another clip from the list.

Making Your First Cut

Follow the step-by-step instructions that will lead you through your first editing session.

1. In the project "Wanna Trade" you'll see two bins: Dailies - Day 1 and Assembly Sequences. Double click on the Dailies - Day 1 bin icon.
2. When the bin opens, you will see a number of clips. You are probably in Text View. Switch to Frame View. Switch back to Text View.
3. Double click on the Clip icon for *Kate's Entrance - Wide Shot*. The clip appears in the Source Monitor or Pop-up Monitor. Media Composer users can also place clips in the Source Monitor by dragging the clips

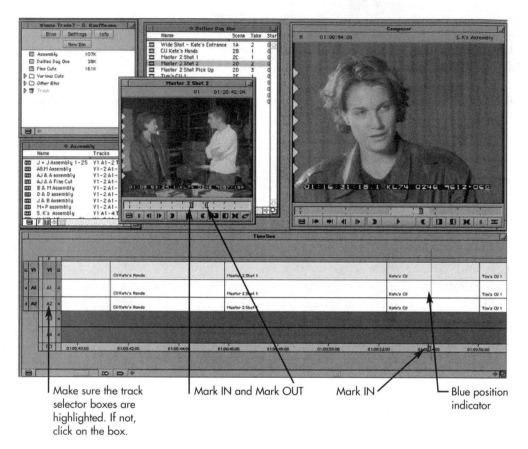

Make sure the track selector boxes are highlighted. If not, click on the box.   Mark IN and Mark OUT   Mark IN   Blue position indicator

Figure 1.17   Avid Xpress

from the bin and bringing them across to the right-hand computer monitor and then dropping them onto the Source Monitor.

4. Play the clip by selecting the Play key on the keyboard, or the Play button under the Source Monitor.

5. To move quickly through the clip, drag the blue position bar inside the position indicator window in the monitor.

6. On the keyboard press the J-K-L keys to move forward and backward. Hit J or L several times to go fast reverse or fast forward. Hold pause (K) while holding J or L to go backward or forward in slow motion.

7. Once you are familiar with the clip in the Source/Pop-up Monitor, choose your cut points. Mark an IN somewhere after the slate, and Mark an OUT after Kate is through searching for the papers on the desk.

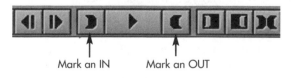

Mark an IN   Mark an OUT

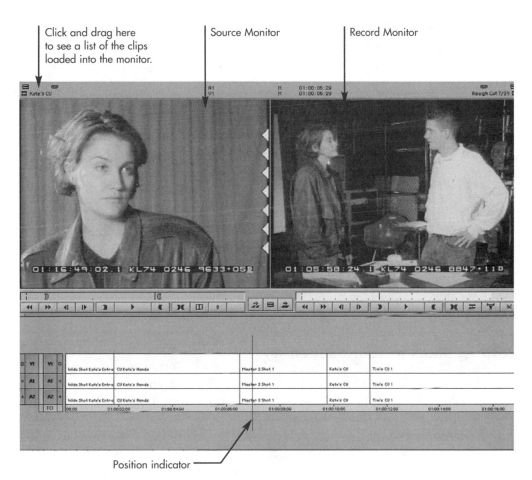

Click and drag here to see a list of the clips loaded into the monitor.

Source Monitor

Record Monitor

Position indicator

Figure 1.18 Media Composer

To make your first edit, click the Splice button. Presto! You have just created an "Untitled Sequence," and the Timeline will show you that the picture and tracks are spliced in your Sequence. (If there is no Timeline, press ⌘-0.)

Splice button

8. Find the "Untitled Sequence" in the Dailies-Day 1 bin and drag it to the Assembly Sequences bin.
9. In the Assembly Sequences bin, click on the "Untitled Sequence" letters (not the Sequence icon) so you can type a name, such as Assembly #1. If you're part of a class, add your initials so you can differentiate your work from that of others in the class. Make sure you do not close the

Assembly Sequences bin. Your sequence will disappear if you do. If that happens, double-click on the Assembly Sequence bin and drag the Sequence icon to the Record Monitor, and it will go to the Timeline.

◇ Wanna Trade? Bin		
Name	Tracks	Start
Untitled Sequence.02	Y1-2 A1-4 TC1	01:00:00:0

Sequence icon →

10. Those using Avid Xpress may want to close the Pop-up Monitor of *Kate's Entrance - Wide Shot*, by clicking in the close box.
11. Practice navigating the Timeline by playing the shot at various speeds using J-K-L, or by dragging the blue position indicator. Use the Home key and End key on the keyboard to jump to the head and tail of the shot.

Adding Shots to Your Sequence

1. You are ready to cut in the next shot. The clip you want next shows a closeup of Kate's hands searching the papers on the desk. The shot then tilts up to a closeup of Kate's face. Go to the Dailies - Day 1 bin and double-click on the *Kate's Hands, Face - CU* clip. You can either cut to her face or her hands—your choice.
2. Play through the clip so you know what your choices are.
3. Click anywhere on the Timeline. Navigate along the Timeline, looking for a spot to cut this shot of her hands (or a closeup of her face) into the wide shot of her searching the desk. Don't worry about where you'll come back to the wide shot. Just concentrate on finding the IN point.
4. In the Timeline, place your IN where you will cut to the closeup. Do this by placing the blue position indicator at the correct spot and clicking on the mark IN button, either on the keyboard or under the Composer/Record Monitor. This puts a mark IN tag on the Timeline.
5. Click anywhere on the Source Monitor or Pop-up Monitor to make it active and find a point in the *Kate's Hands, Face - CU* clip where you think the cut will work, and mark an IN. Go to the very end of the clip and mark an OUT.
6. IMPORTANT: It takes three "marks" to make an edit, and you now have three—an IN and an OUT in the Source/Pop-up Monitor, and an IN in the Timeline. Count to make sure you have three.
7. Now, you have two choices. You can select the Splice button or you can select the Overwrite button.

Splice and Overwrite

   The Splice button inserts material into the sequence at the IN mark, and pushes everything after that point to the right. The sequence gets longer.

   The Overwrite button replaces (writes over) what's already in the sequence with new material. The sequence remains the same length.

   In this exercise, I want you to press the Overwrite button.

8.   First, check the Timeline's track selection buttons to make sure the source and record tracks for V1 and A1 are selected (colored in). Click on them if they are not. Now, press the Overwrite button. The extraneous part of *Kate's Entrance - Wide Shot* has been replaced with the insert of her hands at the IN point you selected. Now play the entire sequence, to see if you like the way it works. If you don't like it, hit Command-Z (undo) and you will undo your last action; your overwrite is gone. Choose new edit points by clearing the IN or OUT in the Source Monitor, or the IN in the Timeline, and setting new marks.

9.   When you cut an assembly together, you are normally overwriting—in effect placing a new shot over the tail of the last shot in the Timeline.

10.   Now try cutting in a closeup of Kate's face (or her hands if you already cut to her face). Drag or play along the Timeline until you find a new point for your IN. Then return to the *Kate's Hands, Face - CU* clip. Xpress users, if the Pop-up Monitor is closed, reopen it by clicking on the Clip icon. If it is still open, select it by clicking anywhere on it. MC users, click on the Source Monitor. Now choose an IN and an OUT point. Return to the Timeline, select it by clicking anywhere on it, and then mark an IN. Hit the Overwrite button. You should now have three shots in your sequence.

11.   If you want to cut extraneous picture and sound out of the Timeline, mark an IN and then an OUT in the Timeline. Make sure all your tracks are selected—highlighted (colored). To lift, hit the Lift button. To cut out and shorten the sequence, hit Extract. Hit undo (command- Z) if there is a problem, and try again after correcting it.

Lift  Extract

   There are two takes of the *Master Shot Kate & Tim*. One covers the whole scene and the other is a pickup. There are several takes of Tim's closeup. Kate has a close-up and a medium shot. The medium shot doesn't cover the whole scene—just a few lines. Look at the performances, examine the choices, and continue cutting together the sequence. Leave your shots a bit long, and we'll trim them up later.

ENDING AN EDITING SESSION

1. Make sure your sequence is in the Assembly Sequences bin, with your initials added as part of the name.
2. To close your project, select the Project window. That's the window that contains all the bins. Click anywhere on it to make it active. Hit Command-S to save all your changes. Choose Quit (Exit) from the File Menu.
3. When you return to the main computer screen, go to Special Menu and choose Shut Down. When the computer shuts down, turn off the power to the speakers and the NTSC monitor, and turn off the power to the hard drives and computer monitors by pushing the power strip that is attached to the UPS.

Well done.

SCRIPT FOR WANNA TRADE

The two-page, lined script for the scene "Wanna Trade" can be found on pages 25 and 26.

1   INT. PHOTOGRAPHER'S STUDIO - NIGHT   1

A door slowly opens. Light pours into a darkened room. A
figure, in silhouette, enters cautiously. After a few steps
the figure is illuminated by moonlight coming from a high
window. KATE WINSLOW, attractive, in her mid-twenties, is
wearing jeans and a leather jacket. She turns on a desk lamp
and then crosses the studio in order to switch on a floor
lamp. She steps in front of a desk covered with papers and
begins rifling through it. Suddenly TIM HARPER steps from the
shadows. He is a fashion photographer and looks the part--
handsome, sleek, and self-satisfied.

                KATE
Geez, you scared me.

                TIM
What are you doing here?

                KATE
I was in the neighborhood and I thought
I'd drop off the jacket.

                TIM
Bull. You're looking for a small stack of
perfume-scented letters. Aren't you,
Kate.

                KATE
Yeah, I am.

                TIM
You figured, he doesn't need them any
more. I dumped the jerk, so . .

                KATE
Tim, we've been through this a million
times. . . .

                TIM
So why not break into his studio and
steal those juicy, embarrassing, and I-
can't-believe-I-ever-wrote-them love
letters.

                KATE
Where are they?

Tim looks down at the desk and starts shuffling papers.

                TIM
I guess they're not here.

                        (CONTINUED)

1   CONTINUED: 1C   1D Tim   1E Kate   2.

                    KATE
                 (outraged)
        Those are my letters.

                    TIM
        No, Kate. You sent them to me. They're
        mine now, and I can do whatever I want
        with them.

                    KATE
        Bastard.

    Tim is pleased. Kate turns and heads for the door. Tim grabs
    her arm and spins her around.

                    TIM
        Hey!

                    KATE
        What?

                    TIM
        That's my jacket. Give it here.

                    KATE
        No, Tim. You gave me this jacket.
        Remember? And I can do whatever I want
        with it.

                    TIM
        Jerk.

    Kate holds open the jacket, displaying it like a model.

                    KATE
        Wanna trade?

    Tim considers the offer. He dismisses her with a wave.

                    TIM
        Not a chance.

    Kate turns and exits.

                                        FADE TO BLACK.

Chapter 2

Basic Editing

EDITING RULES

Unfortunately, or fortunately, depending on your perspective, there are no editing rules. That is not to say there isn't an aesthetic at work, or that any ordering of shots is "correct." If that were the case, a trained monkey would be as good an editor as Michael Kahn, who won an Oscar for *Schindler's List*.

So what makes an editor good? When you're editing a sequence involving a number of different shots, many skills and talents come into play. First of all, you must be able to choose from among the choices given to you. To make the right choices you must understand the script and not just the storyline, but also the subjects' or characters' needs. If you don't know what motivates a character or subject, you can't really determine which shot or which take will work best. You also must judge performance, composition, screen direction, blocking, camera movement, lighting, and sound, for all those elements can help draw in your audience. The ability to judge the material is critical whatever the nature of the program you are editing, be it documentary, narrative, commercial, or experimental.

Once you have picked, from among the choices, the material that will work best, you must cut it to the right length and attach it to the right shot. And once you think you have done that, the most important skill of all comes into play. To be a good editor you must be a good watcher. It sounds simple, but it's not. Good editors can stop being editors and quickly transform themselves into good viewers. You have to be able to erase from your mind all your worries, hunger pangs, sore muscles, random thoughts, and anything else that could impede your concentration. And then you must really, really watch!

And as you watch, you are asking yourself one question: Does it work? Hopefully, you'll know the answer to that question by the end of this book.

STARTING YOUR SECOND EDITING SESSION

Follow the instructions provided in the first chapter for turning on your Avid (p. 19). When you reach the Project window, open the Dailies - Day 1 bin and the Assembly Sequences bin. Find your sequence, which you created during your first editing session. You probably named it Assembly #1; perhaps you added your initials to distinguish it from those of others in your class.

   If you are an Xpress user, select and drag your sequence from the bin to the Composer Monitor and release it. If you're a MC user, select and drag it from the bin all the way to the Record Monitor and release it. It will load in the Timeline, and you are ready to continue.

   What happens if you drag your sequence into the Timeline? If you're using a MC, nothing happens, but if you're an Xpress user, you'll create a new Untitled Sequence. Things get confusing if you do that. Remember, in order to load a sequence so you can continue to work on it, always drag it from the bin to the Record/Composer Monitor.

BASIC EDITING SKILLS

Let's review what we learned while cutting our first exercise at the end of the first chapter. Start by double-clicking on a clip to load it into the Source/Pop-up Monitor.

Marking Clips

Splice and Overwrite enable you to put your shots together in the order you want them to appear. They help you build your sequence. I suppose they are the most important commands at your disposal. But to use them, you must first select the material you want to splice or overwrite into your sequence. You select this material by placing an IN where you want to start, and an OUT where you want to end the shot.

   Click anywhere on the Source/Pop-up Monitor to make it active. Use the J-K-L keys to play through the clip, or click and drag the position indicator in the monitor's window. Once you are familiar with your clip, choose your cut points. Mark an IN and mark an OUT. You have just determined what will be spliced or overwritten into the sequence.

Mark an IN   Mark an OUT   Clear your IN and OUT

You can clear your marks by clicking the Clear IN and Clear OUT buttons.

Instead of using the buttons under the Source/Pop-up Monitor, use the Mark IN and OUT command keys on the keyboard to set your marks. It may be slower at first, but I think you'll find it faster in the long run. Use the ones just above the J-K-L keys.

Now you must determine where that material will go. Click anywhere on the Timeline to make it active. Play through the sequence. Using the keyboard, place a mark IN.

IMPORTANT: Remember, it takes three marks to make an edit, and you now have three—an IN and an OUT in the Source/Pop-up Monitor, and an IN in the Timeline. Count to make sure you have three.

Now, you have two choices. You can select the Splice button, or you can select the Overwrite button.

Splice and Overwrite

Splice and Overwrite

The Splice button inserts material into the sequence at the IN mark, and pushes everything after that point downstream. The sequence gets longer.

The Overwrite button replaces (writes over) what's already in the sequence with new material. Let's say your third shot, Kate's CU, is a bit too long. You can use Overwrite to trim the end of the shot while putting in the fourth shot. In Figure 2.1 the tail of Kate's CU is a bit long. I place a mark IN in the Timeline where I want the fourth shot to go. Overwrite will place Tim's CU right at the Mark IN and get rid of the tail of Kate's CU.

Kate's CU		Kate's CU	Tim's CU
Kate's CU		Kate's CU	Tim's CU
	0 00;36;00	4;00 01;00;36;00	01;00;38;00

Figure 2.1

SOURCE MONITOR MENU - MC

In the first chapter, we got an overview of the system. Now, let's dig deeper into the Avid's interface.

Xpress users view their clips in Pop-up Monitors, which open whenever they double-click on a clip icon. Usually, to save screen space, you'll want to close the old Pop-up Monitors as you open new clips. With the Media Composer,

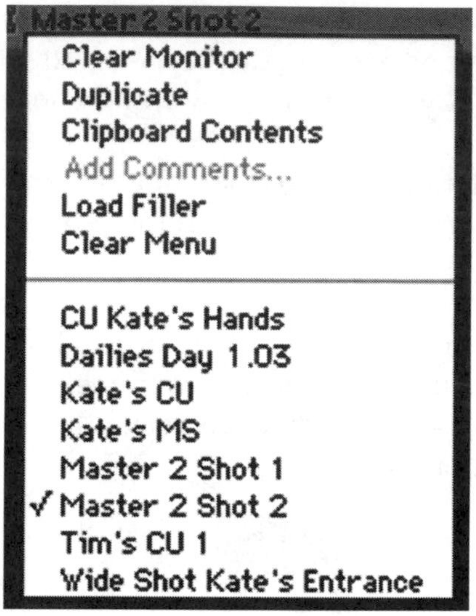

```
Master 2 Shot 2
    Clear Monitor
    Duplicate
    Clipboard Contents
    Add Comments...
    Load Filler
    Clear Menu

    CU Kate's Hands
    Dailies Day 1.03
    Kate's CU
    Kate's MS
    Master 2 Shot 1
  √ Master 2 Shot 2
    Tim's CU 1
    Wide Shot Kate's Entrance
```

Figure 2.2

you also double-click on clip icons to have clips appear in the Source Monitor. If you want to put more than one clip in the Source Monitor, just shift-click and then drag across a group of clips to the Source Monitor computer screen. Once clips have been loaded into the Source Monitor, they are available in the Source Monitor menu. Just press and hold the mouse on the clip name at the top of the Source Monitor screen. When the list comes down, drag and release the clip you want to open in the Source Monitor. Figure 2.2 shows all the clips loaded into the Source Monitor.

REVIEWING THE TIMELINE

As mentioned in Chapter 1, the Timeline is a graphic representation of the shots in your sequence. It is one of Avid's most intuitive and user-friendly features. It's easy to navigate the Timeline: either use the J-K-L keys, use the mouse to drag the blue position indicator, or press any number of keyboard buttons that will move you to various frames or edit points. Two Xpress buttons are particularly helpful:

Go to Previous Edit—Go to Next Edit

   Select the track whose cut points you want to navigate (select the track and deselect the other tracks). Press these buttons and you will jump to the cut points on the Timeline. On the MC, the Rewind and Fast Forward buttons do the same thing.

Home and End

Click anywhere on the Timeline to activate it and then press the Home key on the keyboard. You'll jump to the beginning of the sequence. Hit the End key, just below it, and you'll jump to the end of the sequence. If the Source Monitor or Pop-up Monitor is selected, home and end work there as well. This is a handy way to move to the beginning and end of your material using just one keystroke. (This feature somehow got dropped from early versions of Xpress 2.x, causing loud protests from every quarter.)

Moving with the Mouse

More often than not, you'll use the mouse to get where you want to go. The Media Composer lets you change the way the mouse behaves as you move around the Timeline. In Figure 2.3, you'll see two keyboard commands which are also available on the Command Palette (we'll discuss this in Chapter 3). The one on the N key is called "stepping" and the one on the semi-colon key is called "shuttling." Stepping (often called jogging) works just like the step one-frame key. If you move the mouse to the left, the Avid steps to the left, and if you move the mouse to the right, it steps to the right. Shuttling feels a bit weird at first. In the shuttle position, the mouse acts like the shuttle control on a video editing system. The further you drag the mouse left or right, the faster you move through the Timeline. To leave either shuttling or stepping, simply press the keyboard's spacebar. Some editors love them and others hardly ever use them.

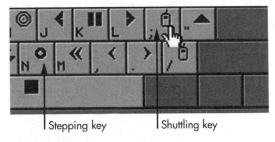

| Stepping key | Shuttling key

Figure 2.3

Snapping to Cut Points

So often when editing, you'll want to get to the end of a shot to mark an OUT, or go to the head of a shot in order to mark an IN. But getting the position indicator to quickly land on the beginning of a shot isn't all that easy. And if the position indicator in the Timeline isn't parked on the first frame, and you started splicing, you'll have little orphan frames hanging around. To quickly jump to the head of a shot or to snap to the tail of a shot in the Timeline, press the Command key or the Option-Command key while dragging the position indicator right or left (Figure 2.4).

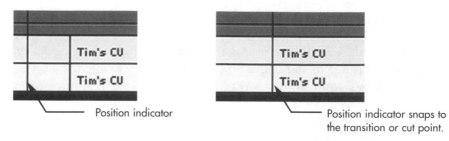

Figure 2.4

- *Hold the Command key* and drag the position indicator to the right— you'll snap to the head, or first frame, of a shot.
- *Hold Option and Command keys* and drag the position indicator to the left—you'll snap to the tail, or last frame, of a shot.

Practice this technique until it's automatic.

Selecting and Deselecting Tracks

The Track Selector panels are on the left of the Timeline. When you have a clip in the Source Monitor or Pop-up window, the Source Track Selector panel appears.

Before making any edits, always check to see which tracks are selected before splicing and overwriting. In Figure 2.5, the sound coming in on tracks A1 and A2 will not get edited with the picture on V1. Why not? Because the record tracks selectors for A1 and A2 are *deselected*. To *select* the record tracks for A1 and A2, simply click on the track boxes. If the Source track boxes aren't selected, the source material won't get edited in either.

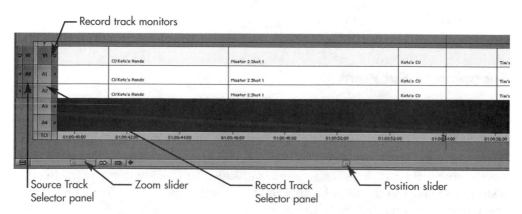

Figure 2.5   Timeline

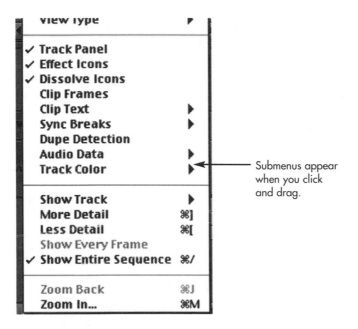

Figure 2.6 Media Composer Fast Menu

The Timeline Fast Menu

The Timeline has a Fast menu (bottom left), and it contains a number of options that allow you to change the Timeline's appearance and the view you have of your project. The Media Composer's Fast menu is extensive, allowing you to show or hide a great deal of information about your tracks. The Xpress Fast menu gives you fewer choices, but still gets the job done.

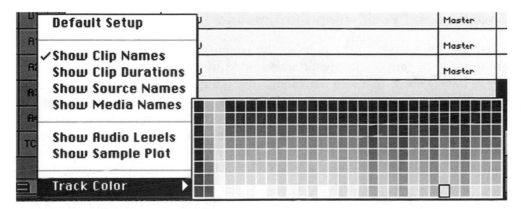

Figure 2.7 Xpress Fast Menu

One of the options available on both the MC and Xpress is the ability to choose the color of your tracks in the Timeline. To change the default color, select the track(s) you want to change, and then choose Track Color from the Timeline Fast menu, by holding and dragging the mouse to a color you'd like to see (Figure 2.7). Release the mouse and your track(s) will show you your selection. Normally, I keep stereo tracks, which go together, the same color. I'll have one color for V2, another for V1, a third for my sync tracks, a fourth for my music tracks, a fifth color for narration, and a sixth color for sound effects. The Media Composer allows you to change the color of the Timeline's background. You'll find it in the Track Color command.

Other options available in the Timeline Fast menu allow you to display clip names, source tape names, or the duration of clips in the Timeline. On many Avid systems the user can configure the Timeline in many different ways and then save the customized view by pressing the Timeline View button, choosing Save As from the pop-up menu, and typing a name. The view in the figure below is called "clip names." Until you save a name, the Timeline View button remains "Untitled." You can save a number of different views and select from among them the one appropriate for the type of work you're doing.

Timeline View button

The Xpress has a tiny "F" track just above the video track that displays individual video frames that represent the clips in your sequence. Enlarge the tiny "F" track and the frames become visible. Reduce that track and they disappear. Media Composer users can select the "Film" track from the Show Track submenu to display these frames. I'm hard pressed to provide an example of when you'd use this view. I really mention it so that if you inadvertently end up with these frames in your Timeline, you'll know what they are and how to get rid of them.

Zooming and Positioning the Timeline

There are times when you want to see the Timeline of the entire project, and there are times you want to view just the section you're currently editing. Obviously, if you have a show that's an hour long, involving a thousand cuts, showing the entire Timeline isn't useful for editing purposes. All you'll see is black lines. For editing purposes, you'll want to look at a specific edit point, or five or six shots. The ability to zoom in and out is obviously important. And once you've zoomed in, you may want to move ahead or back to another section of the project.

The Xpress and the newer version of the MC have two sliders along the bottom of the Timeline. The slider on the left is called the Zoom slider. It's sometimes called the Scale box on the MC. Drag the slider to the right and you're zooming in to look at just a few cuts—or even just a few frames. Try it and see.

Drag it to the left, and the Timeline compresses so you're looking at a much larger percentage of the sequence.

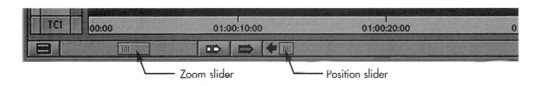

―――― Zoom slider   ―――― Position slider

The slider on the right is called the Position slider. It shows you a different section of the Timeline. When you drag the Position slider you are determining the section of the project to be displayed in the Timeline. If you look at the Record/Composer Monitor's window, you'll see that the part of the project that is viewed in the Timeline is white and the part hidden is gray.

The Xpress lets you use the keyboard's Up and Down arrows to Zoom in (up) and Zoom out (down). It's very fast.

Additional Timeline Controls in the Media Composer

The Media Composer's software versions 7.0 and up have the same Zoom and Position sliders as the Xpress, so resizing the Timeline is essentially the same.

Fast menu   Focus button   Zoom slider

The MC has additional means of controlling the Timeline view. The Focus button expands the Timeline on the frame in the sequence where the position indicator is parked. Click on it once to expand, and click it again to return to your view. The Timeline Fast menu gives you additional ways of controlling your view. There are keyboard equivalents for these commands, so you can quickly display different views of the Timeline with a few keystrokes.

Name in Fast Menu	Keyboard Strokes	Timeline Result
More Detail	Command-]	Shrinks the Timeline
Less Detail	Command-[	Expands the Timeline
Show Entire Sequence	Command/	Shows the entire sequence in the Timeline
Zoom In	Command-M	Then, using the cursor, make a box around the area in the Timeline you want to examine, and that area will fill the Timeline.

Name in Fast Menu	Keyboard Strokes	Timeline Result
Zoom Back	Command-J	This works with Zoom In. It restores the Timeline view that was there before you zoomed in.

Practice changing the Timeline View using all the choices.

Enlarge or Reduce Tracks

You can make the tracks in the Timeline larger or smaller. This is handy when you're working with more than four tracks. With six tracks, it's difficult to fit them all in the Timeline unless you make some of them smaller.

To change a track's size, select the track and press:

Command-L to enlarge

Command-K to reduce

If four tracks are selected, all four tracks change size. If one is selected, only that one changes size. You can also place the mouse pointer at the bottom line of a track selector box. On the Xpress, the pointer changes shape and becomes a *resize track cursor*. Drag this cursor down, and the track gets larger. Drag it up, and the track gets smaller. On the Media Composer you must hold down the Option key as you put the pointer on the bottom line of the track selector box. If the tracks take up more space than the Timeline has room for, a scroll bar appears on the right side.

Track Monitors

These buttons mean that the tracks can be seen and heard. If the box is empty you won't see or hear anything. The exception is when you have more than one video track. If the top video track has the monitor indicator, then all the video tracks beneath it will also be monitored.

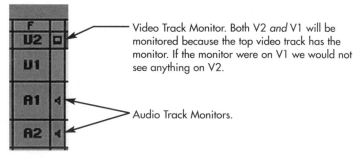

Video Track Monitor. Both V2 *and* V1 will be monitored because the top video track has the monitor. If the monitor were on V1 we would not see anything on V2.

Audio Track Monitors.

Figure 2.8

Click on the box, and the monitor indicator disappears. You won't hear that track. Click again and the indicator reappears, and you'll hear the track.

MARKING CLIPS IN THE TIMELINE

One of the most useful buttons at your disposal is the Mark Clip button. Often you will be working on your sequence and see that you want to get rid of a shot. One way to do this is to work in the Timeline and mark an IN at the head of the clip, then mark an OUT at the tail of the clip. But there's a much simpler way to do this.

1. Put the position indicator in the clip you want to mark. Make sure only the tracks containing material you want to edit are selected.
2. Press the Mark Clip button.

You'll see an IN mark at the head and an OUT at the tail of the clip. The entire clip is highlighted. Note, if you have tracks that are empty and they are selected, Mark Clip will mark the entire sequence. Deselect all empty tracks first!

Now we're ready to master two important command keys: Lift and Extract.

LIFT AND EXTRACT

Because these are such useful commands, you'll find them right on the keyboard.

Before practicing these commands on your sequence, *duplicate* it first, so if you get too excited by all the lifting and extracting and totally mess it up, you won't care because the original is still in the bin.

DUPLICATING A SEQUENCE

1. Go to the Assembly Sequences bin and find the sequence you've been working on.
2. Select it (click on the sequence icon and it will be selected) so it is highlighted.
3. Go to the Edit menu and choose Duplicate, or type Command-D.

Name	Start
▦ Assembly.Copy.01	01;00;
▦ Assembly	01;00;

You have created an identical copy of your sequence. The word *copy* is added to it so you can differentiate between the two versions.

Drag the copy version into the Record Monitor, and now you have a copy of the sequence to play around with.

Now, go to the third shot in the Timeline—Kate's CU. Use the Mark Clip button to select it.

Hit the Lift button. The clip is gone, and black *filler* is in its place (Figure 2.9). It's like black leader. Notice that when you lift, the length of your sequence does not change. The Timeline is the same length.

Hit Command-Z to undo the lift.

Now use the Mark Clip button to mark Kate's CU again. This time, hit the *Extract* button. Hey! The clip's gone and the Timeline has shrunk (Figure 2.10). This one can fool you sometimes, because it happens so fast you don't see it, and you wonder if you actually did anything.

If you want to see the clip return, hit Command-Z to undo.

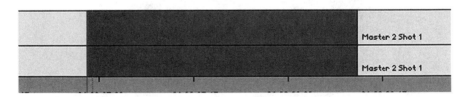

Figure 2.9   Kate's CU has been *lifted* from the sequence.

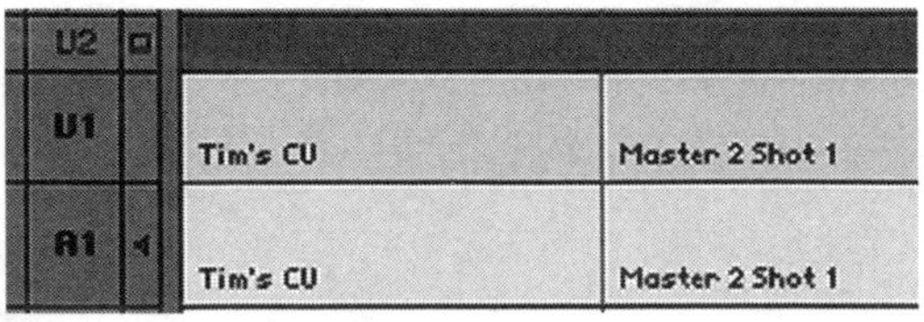

U2 ▫		
U1	Tim's CU	Master 2 Shot 1
A1 ◄	Tim's CU	Master 2 Shot 1

Figure 2.10   Kate's CU has been *extracted* from the sequence.

Now try lifting clips and extracting clips with the video track (V1) deselected. You'll see that the Lift button will take away the sound, leaving the picture and black filler where the sound used to be. In this example, I selected Tim's
audio track but not his video track, and then I hit the Lift button. His picture
remains, but his sound has been replaced by black filler.

Lift works without a problem. But watch out for the Extract button! By
extracting the audio and leaving the video clip in place, you shift all the audio
that comes after this clip!

Let's examine how Extract differs from Lift in this situation.

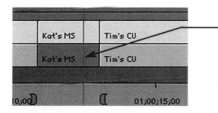

Select Kate's sound track and deselect V1. Now mark the clip. Only
the sound is marked.

As we've seen, if you *Lift* Kate's audio, the audio is removed and replaced
by fill. The audio downstream of this point isn't "pulled up" to fill in the space
left by the missing audio because there's something there—the black filler. But
with *Extract*, there is no filler. The audio rushes in to fill in the gap. Notice how
Tim's audio moves into the gap caused when Kate's audio is extracted, throwing
everything out of sync.

This is not something you want to do. Because you extract 62 frames of
audio, while leaving the video in place, the audio becomes 62 frames "out of
sync" everywhere after the extraction.

One nice feature of the Avid is that the Timeline shows you when you are out of sync and by how much. Plus and minus signs indicate the direction of the sync problem. The frame count indicates the extent of the sync problem.

Be careful when you use Extract. It's a great tool but only when all tracks are selected. Be prepared to use Undo to fix problems with Extract.

TRIM SHOTS USING EXTRACT

A common way to quickly trim the head or tail of a shot is to use Extract. Let's say the head of a shot that you cut into the sequence seems too long. Find the point where you want to cut it. Mark an OUT. Snap to the head of the clip (Command-drag the position indicator) and mark an IN. Hit *Extract* and the shot is trimmed to the desired length.

IT TAKES THREE MARKS TO MAKE AN EDIT

This is a rather simple statement of fact, yet when you really understand it, it makes profound sense. Whenever you make a splice or overwrite, you need to make three marks. There are only four possible choices. Look at the choices in the chart below. So far, we have concentrated on the first one. In the Source Monitor you mark the material you want to edit into the sequence with an IN and an OUT, and then you mark an IN in the Timeline where you want it to go. You've got three marks.

Source Monitor/Pop-up Monitor	*Record/Timeline Mark*
1. Mark IN and OUT	IN
2. Mark IN	IN and OUT
3. Mark OUT	IN and OUT
4. Mark IN and OUT	OUT

Let's look at the other three choices. They are most often used with the *Overwrite button*, whereas # 1 is used most frequently with the *Splice button*.

   #2.   This is useful whenever you want to replace a shot (or audio) that you've already cut into your Timeline with a better shot. Let's say you've cut a shot of a smiling baby into your sequence. Once you play the sequence you see that it would make more sense to use the shot of a crying baby. You like the length of the shot, but not the content. So you simply mark the clip (use the Mark Clip button) in the Timeline, and then find the clip of the crying baby in the bin. Play through the crying shot and mark an IN where you want the shot to begin. Now hit *Overwrite*. Now the shot of the smiling baby is replaced by the crying baby. The length of the sequence doesn't change. You've simply replaced one shot with another.

#3.   This is just like choice #2 except that it marks the clip in the Source/Pop-up Monitor from the OUT rather than the IN. Think about it. You mark the clip in the Timeline that you want to replace. Then you find the shot you want to put in its place. Perhaps the end of the shot of the crying baby is what makes it special. So you use a mark OUT, rather than a mark IN. You've got your three marks, and now you hit Overwrite. The shot of the smiling baby is replaced by the crying baby. The length of the sequence doesn't change. You've simply replaced one shot with another.

#4.   When I drove a truck for a living, I was told that 99 percent of all trucking accidents occur when backing up. That's the reason why you'll seldom use choice #4. With this choice, the material is backed into the Timeline and can end up erasing material you want to keep. However, this choice is handy whenever you're laying in music. Let's say you have music and you know the point in the sequence where you want the music to end. You mark the music clip in the Source/Pop-up Monitor with an IN and an OUT. Now you mark the point in the Timeline where the music will end with an OUT. You have your three marks. Hit Overwrite. You have "back-timed" the music into the Timeline.

LIKE A MANTRA

"It takes three marks to make an edit." Think about this simple sentence. Examine the choices. Imagine different situations in which you would use each of them. Try them out.

See what I mean? Profound.

USING THE CLIPBOARD

The Clipboard is one of the Avid's most useful tools. You can mark a section in the Timeline, with an IN and an OUT, and then place it into the Clipboard by pressing either Lift, Extract, or the Clipboard icon. You can also press Command-C for copy.

Unlike using Lift or Extract, which removes the material from the Timeline, when you press the Clipboard icon or Command-C, the material stays in the sequence and a copy of it, including all the audio and video tracks that you've selected, is saved to the Clipboard. This way you can take something you've done and place an exact copy of it elsewhere. You could even place it in another sequence.

To get material that you placed in the Clipboard, go to the Tools menu and select Clipboard Monitor. A Pop-up Monitor opens. Mark the material you want to cut into the sequence with an IN and an OUT, and then mark an IN in the Timeline. Now you can splice or overwrite the Clipboard contents into the Timeline.

The Clipboard holds whatever you have stored there only until you press Lift, Extract, or the Clipboard icon again. Then, whatever was there is gone—replaced by the new material.

The Media Composer gives you a way to save Clipboard contents throughout your editing session, by letting you hold the Clipboard contents in the Source Monitor as a clip, called "Clipboard Contents.n," which is available in the Source Monitor menu. When you close the project, it will all be gone. To save the Clipboard contents to the Source Monitor:

* Choose Clipboard Contents from the Source Monitor menu.

SUGGESTED ASSIGNMENTS

1. Duplicate your sequence. Change the name of the duplicate version to "Rough Cut" and add today's date.
2. Continue to work on the new version of your sequence until you have a rough cut of the entire scene.
3. Practice using all the commands discussed in this chapter.

The Project Window

STARTING A NEW PROJECT AND BECOMING A NEW USER

When you double click on the Media Composer or Xpress icon, you are launching the Avid software. Soon the Avid brings up a dialog box that asks you to let the Avid know who is going to be editing and on which project (Figure 3.1). The left-hand column lists all the editors who have registered as users, and the right-hand column lists all the projects that are currently in postproduction on this machine. Registering as an editor on the machine couldn't be simpler. Click the New User button and type your name. To select a project already on the Avid, such as "Wanna Trade" just click on the project name.

If you are going to start a new project, one that the Avid has never dealt with before, you will click on the New Project button and fill in the information that is asked for in the dialog box. The name of the project is often the title or working title; you just type the name. Before clicking OK, check to make sure that the other choices are correct. Is it a PAL or NTSC project? If you're working in the United States, it's NTSC. PAL is a television system common in Europe and many other parts of the world. There are many important differences between the two formats; the Avid can accommodate either one, as long as it knows which it is dealing with.

Depending on your version of Avid software, you might have other boxes to check. For instance, some Avid's are equipped with matchback software for those editing 16 mm or 35 mm film that has been transferred to video.

Once all the boxes are selected, click OK. You are returned to the User/Project window, and you select your name in the left column and the newly created project in the right column, and click OK. Now, the Avid brings you to the Project window for that project.

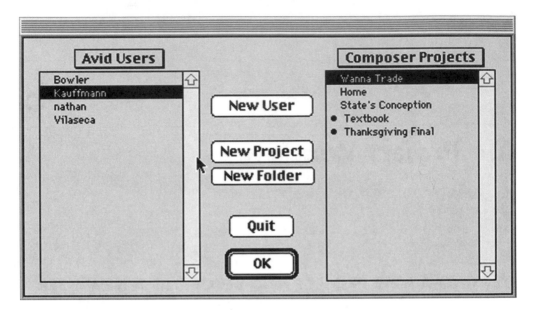

Figure 3.1

Since we have a project with media that we're already working on (either "Wanna Trade" or a project your instructor mounted), we'll continue working with that project.

MORE ABOUT THE PROJECT WINDOW

The Project window, as you recall from the first chapter, is like the home page of your project. In order to get you editing on the Avid as quickly as possible, we skipped some important information about the bins in the Project window; that information now needs our attention.

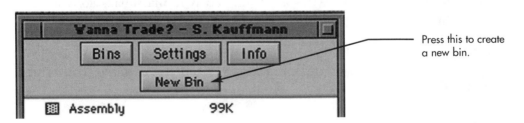

Press this to create
a new bin.

Figure 3.2

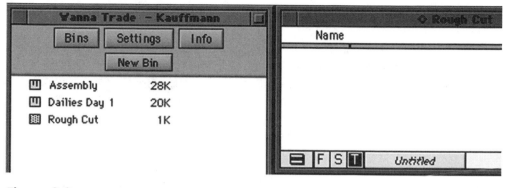

Figure 3.3

Creating a Bin

In the Project window there are four gray boxes. One says New Bin. Click on it, and a new bin is created.

Often, you will want to organize various categories of material, and the simplest way to do that is to create a new bin for each category. For instance, in addition to your video footage, you might have voice-over narration, music, animation, and titles. As you edit your footage, you might have a bin for your assembly sequences, one for your rough cut sequences, and as your work progresses, you might have a bin for your fine cut sequences.

Let's try creating a new bin and putting something in it.

1. In the Project window, click on the New Bin button, and a new bin will open. It will be titled "Wanna Trade bin 01." You need to give it a more helpful name.
2. In the Project window, click on the name "Wanna Trade bin 01" and type "Rough Cut."
3. Now simply click on the duplicate of your sequence in the Assembly bin, which you made while working on Chapter 2, and drag it into the Rough Cut bin.
4. You now want to change the name of the sequence from "Assembly copy. 01" to Rough Cut v. (version) and the date—Rough Cut v. 9/25. Just select it and type.

Remember, to duplicate a sequence, simply select it in the bin so that it's highlighted, and then press Command-D, or select Duplicate in the Edit Menu.

The process of duplicating a sequence is one of digital editing's most important features. In traditional film or video editing, making copies is expensive, time-consuming, or both. Get into the habit of making a new copy of your sequence every day. Give it the day's date to differentiate it, and then begin editing with the confidence that you can always go back to the old version.

ALL ABOUT BINS

The bin is like your project's library and card catalog all rolled into one. We'll spend much of this chapter learning about bins because that's where everything begins. Remember, to open a bin, double-click on it, or press Command-O. To close a bin, click in the close-box, or press Command-W.

Bin Views

Remember that there are three ways to view material in the bin. Text View, Frame View, and Script View (Xpress has just Text View and Frame View). Text View is the one you'll use most frequently. It's particularly useful when you want to organize and search through a lot of clips. As with any Windows or Macintosh software, you can easily select more than one clip by shift-clicking or lassoing. Command-A is particularly helpful because it selects all the clips in two quick keystrokes. Practice all these techniques.

Bin Headings

We're living in the information age. Billions of facts are available to us through the Internet. It makes sense, therefore, to have all the facts about your clips available to you. In Text View, look at the top of the bin and you'll see columns listed such as Name, Tracks, Mark In, Mark Out. There are something like 15 column headings, each providing specific information about each one of your clips. Stretch out the bin or scroll along the bin box to see all the columns. You'll notice that not all the columns are displayed. Some are hidden. To see all the choices, go to the top of the computer screen and pull down the Bin menu. One of the choices is *Headings*. Select it and you will get a dialog box.

You can select or deselect headings by clicking on them. Some headings are more useful than others, and you'll want different headings at different stages of editing. Having all the headings on display is more confusing than helpful. Select those you find useful and deselect those representing information you don't need.

Here are my choices for the early stages of editing:

Duration	It's helpful to know the length of a clip.
Start	Knowing the clip's starting timecode locates it on the source tape.
End	This is the clip's ending timecode.
Video	This is the resolution of the clip.
Tracks	This lists the video and audio tracks that are part of the clip.
Offline	This is helpful whenever you've erased media files.

Other column headings (shown below) will be more helpful later on, so for now, don't select them for display.

Creation Date	The date and time the clip was digitized (or logged)
Disk	The location of the media file on your storage drives
IN-OUT	Length of the segment you have "marked" with edit points
Mark IN	Timecode of your IN mark
Mark OUT	Timecode of your OUT mark
Project	Name of the project

If you have additional software, such as Avid's matchback software, other headings become available. We'll discuss those in Chapter 15.

Moving Columns

Once you have the columns you think you'll need, you can place them in any order. Simply click on the column heading (the entire column is highlighted), drag the column to a new location, and release the mouse. I wouldn't change the position of the Name column, since that's the most useful column and should be flush left, next to the icon. But you might want to set up your columns like this: Name, Start, End, Duration, Tracks, Video.

You can delete a column by selecting it and hitting delete. It's still available under Headings.

You can jump from column to column with Tab, Shift-Tab, Return and Shift-Return.

Sorting

Another really useful command is *Sort*. When you select a column and then choose Sort from the Bin menu, the Avid will arrange the column's contents in either alphabetical or numerical order. You can also use the keyboard to sort. Press Command-E.

Let's say you have a lot of clips in your bin, and you can't find the one you're looking for because you can't remember the name you gave it. However, you do know it came at the beginning of the source tape. Usually clips in the bin are sorted alphabetically by clip name, but since you can't remember the name, this column isn't helping you. You need to look at the names not in alphabetical order, but by each clip's starting timecode.

Click on the Start column and choose Sort from the Bin menu (or use Command-E). The clips in the bin now appear listed according to the starting timecode. Now, when you look at the names, you'll probably find the clip you're looking for, since it will be near the top of the list. To switch back to listing the clips by name, simply click on the Name column and choose Sort from the Bin menu, or use Command-E.

There are times when you may want to invert the order in which items appear.

To sort in descending order, hold down the Option key and press Command-E.

Frame View

Sometimes it's easier to edit material if you're looking at the choices as pictures rather than as columns of words and numbers. Frame view shows the clips in picture view.

Click on the *F* at the bottom of the bin, and all the clips will become frames from the clip.

- You can enlarge the frames by selecting Enlarge Frame from the Edit menu or pressing Command-L (think of enLarge).
- You can reduce the size of the frames by selecting Reduce Frame from the Edit menu or using Command-K.
- Repeat Command-L or Command-K, and the frames will keep getting bigger or smaller, respectively.

You can't enlarge or reduce just one frame; the command affects all the frames in the bin. But you can change the frame of the clip you're looking at.

Look at the previous picture. We have a frame showing a slate with an open clapstick. The sticks don't give us much visual information about the clip. By selecting the frame (just click on it) and using the J-K-L keys, you can play the clip. Whatever frame you stop on becomes *the reference frame*—the frame you'll see from now on. The reference frame of Kate's CU was once a slate, but I advanced it so that the reference frame shows the actual composition of the clip—much more helpful. You can drag the clips all around the bin, putting them in any order. If things get messy, go to the Bin menu and choose Align to Grid.

Another useful Bin menu item is Fill Window. When you select it, the frames are positioned nicely in the bin window.

STORYBOARD TECHNIQUE

One of the features that people like to play with, because it seems so powerful and impressive, is called the storyboard technique. It works best in Frame View. Simply put, you make the bin large enough so that there is space at the bottom. Then drag the clips in the order you think they might appear in the final version, creating a storyboard. A storyboard looks like a comic strip in a newspaper.

Xpress users can create an instant rough cut by selecting the clips in a storyboard (shift-click or lasso them) and then dragging them to the Timeline and releasing them. If you are an MC user, you can create an instant rough cut by selecting the clips in your storyboard (shift-click or lasso them) and then pressing and holding the Option key as you drag them to the Record monitor. To be honest, this is something that looks good and impresses people, but you'll hardly ever use it.

But, hey, let's try it. In Frame View, drag any three clips to the bottom of the bin, forming a storyboard (Figure 3.4). If you already have a sequence in the Timeline and you don't want to mess it up, start a new sequence. Go to the Clip menu (top of your screen). You'll see the first choice is New Sequence. Select it and you'll have a new, untitled sequence. Now shift-click on the three clips and drag them into the Timeline (Xpress). MC users press the Option key and drag them into the Record Monitor .

The problem with this technique is that the entire clip is now in your Timeline. You will need to edit each clip. Frankly, it's much easier to mark sections of the clip in the Source Monitor and then splice or overwrite what you've selected into the Timeline. So, it looks cool and shows off the Avid's drag-and-drop power, but it isn't that useful.

Lasso and drag.

Figure 3.4

THE BIN FAST MENU

At the bottom of the bin you see a button that looks a bit like a hamburger. It's the bin Fast menu. Clicking on this Fast menu brings up the same commands found in the Bin menu. It's just a handy way of putting the features of the Bin menu close at hand.

SUBCLIPS

You may have clips that are overly long. Perhaps when you digitized a tape, you kept several different shots together in one long master clip. For example, you might have a single clip that includes a wide shot of a man climbing a ladder, a closeup of his face, and a shot of a crowd of people watching him. You realize that it would make editing easier if each shot were separated from the others. You can do this by making subclips. It's easy.

To create a subclip in Xpress in either Frame or Text View:

1. Double-click on the clip to get the Pop-up Monitor.
2. Play the clip and mark the IN point and then mark an OUT point.
3. Press and hold the Option key, then click and drag the picture from the Pop-up Monitor to the bin in which you want to store the subclip.
4. Drop it in the bin.

You'll see that the subclip has the same name as the clip with the addition of *sub n*. *N* is the number of times that the master has been subdivided.

To create a subclip in Media Composer:

1. Load the clip into the Source Monitor.
2. Play the clip and mark the IN point and then mark an OUT point.

3. Press and hold the Option key, then click and drag the picture from the Source Monitor to the bin in which you want to store the subclip.

4. Drop it in the bin.

In our example of the man climbing the ladder, we would create three subclips. We'd create the first by marking the IN and OUT points of the man climbing the ladder. The second one would be created by marking the IN and OUT points on the closeup of his face. The last subclip would come from the footage of the crowd. Now rename each subclip so that you can easily find those shots.

During editing, subclips behave exactly like clips.

DELETING SEQUENCES AND CLIPS

You can delete just about anything you've created. You do this by working in the bin. Say you wanted to delete a sequence. Just click on the sequence icon and press the Delete button on the keyboard. Because you don't want to accidentally delete something important, the Avid will immediately bring up a dialog box—kind of an "Are you sure?" prompt just like the one in Figure 3.5. The dialog box provides a list of things you can delete. If you've selected a sequence, the sequence choice is black. Click in the box, and then click OK.

You'll probably delete a lot of sequences in the course of your work. Let's face it, not everything is worth saving. But think twice before you delete a master clip. Remember a master clip is "the shot." It's your footage or sound. It has

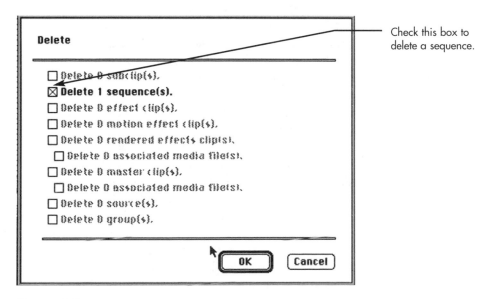

Figure 3.5   Deleting a Sequence

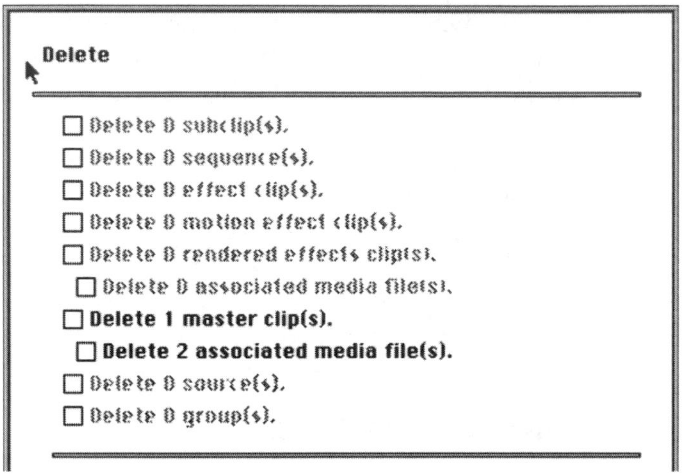

```
┌──────────────────────────────────────────────────┐
│ ┌──────────────────────────────────────────────┐ │
│ │                                                │ │
│ │   **Delete**                                   │ │
│ │ ▶                                              │ │
│ │ ─────────────────────────────────────────────  │ │
│ │                                                │ │
│ │     ☐ Delete 0 subclip(s).                     │ │
│ │     ☐ Delete 0 sequence(s).                    │ │
│ │     ☐ Delete 0 effect clip(s).                 │ │
│ │     ☐ Delete 0 motion effect clip(s).          │ │
│ │     ☐ Delete 0 rendered effects clip(s).       │ │
│ │      ☐ Delete 0 associated media file(s).      │ │
│ │     ☐ **Delete 1 master clip(s).**             │ │
│ │      ☐ **Delete 2 associated media file(s).**  │ │
│ │     ☐ Delete 0 source(s).                      │ │
│ │     ☐ Delete 0 group(s).                       │ │
│ │                                                │ │
│ │ ─────────────────────────────────────────────  │ │
│ └──────────────────────────────────────────────┘ │
└──────────────────────────────────────────────────┘
```

Figure 3.6   Deleting a Master Clip

two parts: the master clip itself, which contains all the timecode information, and the media file, which is the digitized material on the hard drive.

If you have selected a master clip for deleting, you can either delete the media file or the master clip, or both. This is an important decision! Let's look at why we might want to delete any part of a master clip.

Let's say you select a clip in one of your bins and press the Delete key. Figure 3.6 shows the dialog box that appears.

Here are your choices:

1. If you want to get rid of the shot because it's worthless, you'll never use it, and you want to permanently remove it, then check *both* boxes: *Delete master clip(s)*, and *Delete associated media file(s)*. The clip and its media file are deleted. Yes, the footage still exists on your source tape, but the Avid doesn't know anything about it. Check both boxes if you want to get rid of a shot.

2. If you are running out of storage space, and you need to make room for other material, delete the associated media file, but not the master clip itself. In this case *only* click the box *Delete associated media file(s)*. The actual footage gets erased from the hard drives but all the information about the clip, including editing choices about the shot, remain with the Avid. If you used the shot in a sequence, all that information is still there. Whenever you look for that clip you'll find it in the bin, but an "Media Offline" tag will appear in Frame View. To get your clip back, you'll need to redigitize it, which is fairly simple. The neat thing about the Avid is that once you redigitize that clip, not only is it restored in the bin, but it will also reappear everywhere that it has been cut into a sequence.

3. The third choice isn't a choice at all. You'd *never* want to check the *Delete the master clip* by itself. If you did, you'd be using up space on your hard drive with material you couldn't use because the Avid couldn't find it.

We've examined the Bin and the Bin menu in considerable detail because it's at the heart of nearly everything you do with your clips. The other important part of the Project window has to do with Settings.

SETTINGS: HAVE IT YOUR WAY

The folks from Tewksbury, Massachusetts (Avid's Headquarters) have created, in the Media Composer, an editing system that you can configure and rearrange in so many different ways that it's mind-boggling. Some critics say there are too many choices and too many ways of doing the same thing, and all those choices have turned what was supposed to be intuitive and fun-to-use editing machine into anything but. I can understand where the critics are coming from. The Media Composer is a mature system, in computer life cycles, and it has gone through many changes. We're already at version 9.x and counting. While the Avid has gained lots of features along the way, it hasn't lost many, and, as any kid knows, if you keep adding blocks to your tower, it can grow out of control.

Since this book is primarily for beginning users, I'm only showing you what I think you need to know in order to create outstanding films or videos. If I included every trick or feature, you'd be overwhelmed. The Settings window is one area where you can easily feel swamped.

Let's explore just a few of the ways the Avid can be set up.

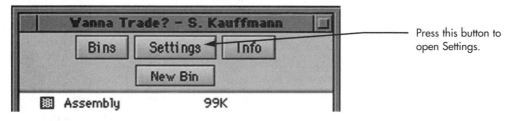

Press this button to open Settings.

Figure 3.7

KINDS OF SETTINGS

There are three different kinds of settings: User settings, Project settings, and Site settings. User settings are ones that you control and that reflect your editing preferences. Project settings are specific to a project, and if a change is made, the change affects all the editors using the project. Site settings establish the default settings for a specific Avid at a specific site.

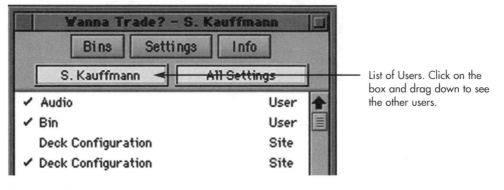

List of Users. Click on the
box and drag down to see
the other users.

Figure 3.8

If you go to the top of the Project window and click on the Settings button (Figure 3.7), the Settings window appears. On the top-left of the Project window is a pull-down menu listing all the different users. You'll see your name at the top of the list. The Users menu is interesting. Up until now, you've been using the default settings. As you begin to select settings, under your name, those settings will stay with you every time you open the project under your name. Tanaja Martin might select different settings, and her choices will be brought up each time she launches the project. You can even create several different user names. You might, for example, want the Avid to have a certain look for client screenings that's different from the look it has when you're engaged in heavy-duty editing. Close the project, and when the New User/New Project window opens, click on New User and type "Client Screenings." Any changes to the way the Avid is set up will be saved under Client Screenings.

The right-hand menu lists the setting options: All Settings, Base Settings, Title Styles, and Video Tool Settings. We'll leave it on All Settings.

Beneath the Settings window you'll see the main scroll list. If you want to see more of the list, drag the size box or scroll down the long list of settings.

Almost every feature on the Avid can be altered to suit your preference. The scroll list shows you the Avid features you can change. To make changes, double-click on the setting whose parameters you want to change and a dialog box, with a number of choices or options, will open. Simply type in the changes, or check a box, and click OK.

There are more items on the Media Composer scroll list than on the Xpress scroll list because you can configure the MC in so many more ways.

We're not going to go through each item on this scroll window, because we don't need them all yet. We'll get to some items later in the book. As you become more familiar with your Avid, I recommend that you go through all the items. By then you'll be able to make informed choices. For now, let's open up some of the items that are the most useful at this stage in the learning process.

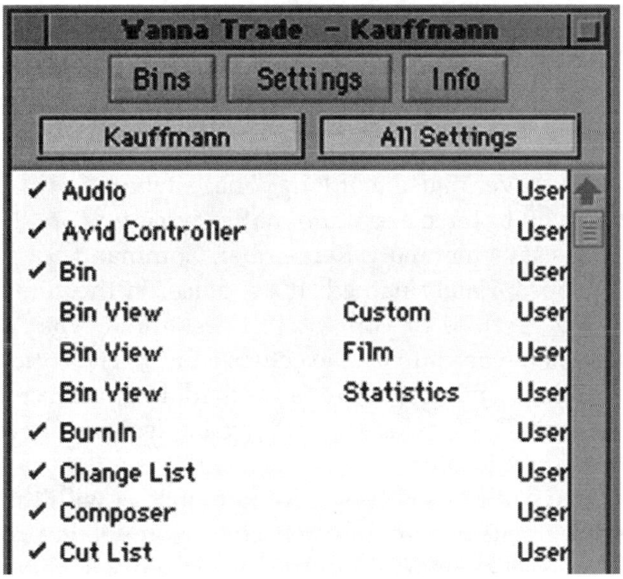

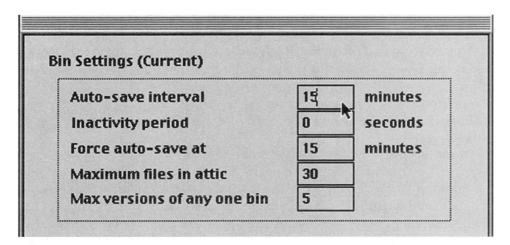

Figure 3.9

Bin Settings

This dialog box provides options for backing up and saving your work (Figure 3.10).

Your work is important, and any bugs or glitches that suddenly crash the system and wipe away your morning's work could be upsetting. To avoid such a calamity, the Avid has an auto-save feature. You determine at what time interval the auto-save kicks in. Depending on your system and the complexity of the

Bin Settings (Current)		
Auto-save interval	15	minutes
Inactivity period	0	seconds
Force auto-save at	15	minutes
Maximum files in attic	30	
Max versions of any one bin	5	

Figure 3.10

work you're doing, auto-save can take a few seconds and seem like a real interruption. So 15 minutes seems about right. There is also a feature called Inactivity Period so that the Avid will wait before it saves if you are really editing like crazy. Genius should not be interrupted. Change it to 10 seconds, and it will wait until you've paused in your work for 10 seconds before beginning the auto-save. But what happens if you never pause that long. That's where force auto-save comes in. It will interrupt you to force a save no matter what you are doing.

You can always save manually. Remember, Command-S.

The *Attic* is appropriately named. It's a place on the computer's internal drive where the old versions of your project are stored. The Avid sends your work to the Attic whenever you, or it, executes a Save. The Attic stores a certain number of files, and when that number is reached, begins discarding the oldest in favor of the newest. That's what the last two choices are about. We'll go into more detail about the Attic later.

On the MC you can have Pop-up Monitors just as with the Xpress. If you select "Double-click opens new monitor for clip," you will get Pop-up Monitors whenever you double-click on a clip in the bin. When you choose "Loads clips into source or record monitor," you don't get Pop-up Monitors. The clips go right into the Source Monitor.

Keyboard Settings

The commands on the Xpress keyboard cannot be changed. The ones you get are the ones you're stuck with. To many people, it's not a big problem. They get used to the command keys offered and learn to work efficiently with them. Others find the Xpress's lack of mapability a serious drawback.

In Xpress, when you go to the Keyboard settings in the Settings scroll list and double-click on Keyboard, it shows you the keyboard you're stuck with. When you select the keyboard setting on a Media Composer, you see the standard keyboard, which is similar to the one found on the Xpress. But, you can change every single key.

Not only can you place any of a hundred different commands on any key, but you can place items found in any of the pull-down menus onto keyboard keys.

Let's make some changes. If you're on an Xpress, you can't make these changes, but you can learn how it's done so you're ready whenever you get on a Media Composer.

In the Project window with the settings scroll list open, double-click on Keyboard. A picture of the keyboard opens. Then go to the Tools Menu and select the Command Palette (Figure 3.11). You'll see that all the command buttons have been organized according to their function and are accessible by clicking on a tab. Make sure the box next to "Button to Button" Reassignment is checked. Now simply drag the button you would like to have on the keyboard to the key of your choice. Let's place the Find Bin button onto F9.

Find Bin ⟍

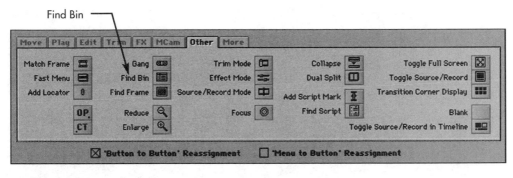

Figure 3.11

You get the idea. I don't want you to change the standard keys because it will make instruction a bit more difficult. Wait until you reach the end of the book before you do that. By the way, the Command Palette works like a giant Fast menu. You can open it from the Tools menu and click on any button to execute that command.

Composer Settings

The Avid Media Composer let's you change the look of the Composer Window, which contains both the Source and Record Monitors. Double-click on the Composer settings and a dialog box will open.

For now, we're interested in just two items. The first is called "Second Row of Info," and the second item is called "Second Row of Buttons." Click in the

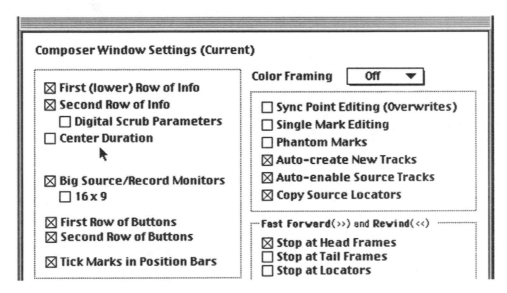

Figure 3.12

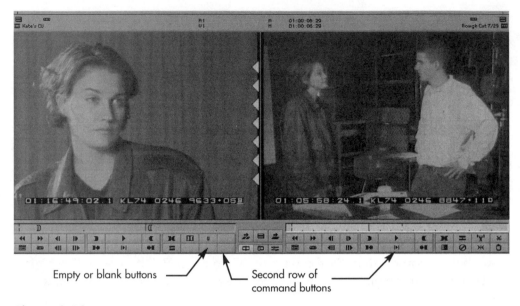

Empty or blank buttons ———/   \——— Second row of
                                          command buttons

Figure 3.13

empty boxes to select them. Now click OK. Return to the Bin window (press Bins at the top of the Project Window) rather than the Settings window, and examine the changes to the Composer window. Notice that you now have a second row of information at the top of the window and a second row of command buttons at the bottom of the Source/Record Monitors.

Now you've got some handy command buttons available to you that you didn't have on the screen before. The button just below the Play button is one I particularly like. It plays from your IN to your OUT. Try it.

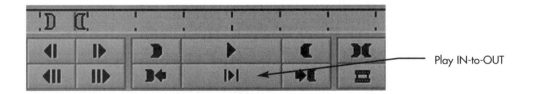

Play IN-to-OUT

You'll notice that a number of the buttons are empty, or blank. You can map command buttons from the Command Palette to these keys (or to any key for that matter). Lets try it. Open the Command Palette from the Tools menu. Click the Edit tab. Drag the red Segment Mode button to a blank button on the second row. Now drag the yellow Segment Mode button, as I have in Figure 3.14. We'll use these two buttons in Chapter 8.

Figure 3.14

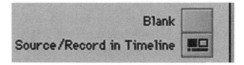

Figure 3.15

To get rid of these buttons, or any buttons or keys, you can drag the Blank button from the Command Palette (Figure 3.15) and place it on top of any button or key.

Wait until you're further along in this book before you map any more buttons. By then you'll have a better idea of which commands you like on the keyboard and which ones you'd rather click with the mouse.

Trim Settings

In the next chapter we're going to learn all about trimming. To get ready for our trim work, let's set up the Avid to perform in Trim Mode the way I think will work best at this stage of your instruction. Double-click on Trim in the Settings window. The dialog box gives you a number of choices—more if you're working on a MC. The Transition Play Loop box is found on both the MC and Xpress. Here you can determine what happens when you press the Review Transition button to look at your trim.

Set the Pre-roll, Post-roll and Intermission.

- The *Pre-roll* and *Post-roll* should both be set at 1:00 (one-second).
- The Intermission, which is like a pause at the end of a loop, should be 0:00, meaning no pause.

We'll discuss other settings and make more changes as we get further along. For now, we've explored the main parts of the Project window. To return to your bins, click on the Bins button at the top of the Project window.

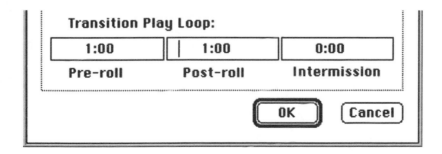

SUGGESTED ASSIGNMENTS:

1. Register as an editor by becoming a New User.
2. Create a new bin. Name it.
3. Duplicate your sequence. Change the name of the duplicate version to today's date.
4. Place this version of your sequence in the new bin.
5. Examine your clips in Frame View, Text View, and Script View.
6. Delete the duplicated version of the sequence you just made.
7. Open the Headings list and change your headings.
8. Move the columns around.
9. Sort the columns using various headings.
10. Reverse the selections.
11. Open a clip and make a subclip of a portion of it.
12. Open the Settings window.
13. Scroll through the list and examine various settings.
14. Set Trim Settings so that the Transition Play Loop is set up as described in the chapter.
15. MC users, add a first and second row of buttons in the Composer Setting.

4

Trimming

Whenever I'm teaching a class on editing, one of the questions students often ask me is, "How do you know how long to hold a shot?" The first time I was asked that question I gave the worst possible answer. I said, "I don't know. (beat) You just know."

I've given the question a bit more thought since then. Sometimes it's obvious how long to hold a shot. If the shot is of a specific action, you've got to hold the shot until the action is finished. For example, if someone is putting a cake into an oven, you don't want to cut before the cake is safely on the cooking rack. But everyone knows that. The ones that are tricky involve the length of a cutaway, or the how long to hold on a person who is talking, or how long to hold a static shot, or a reaction shot. My students know there is no one answer, just as they know there are no rules. What they are really asking is, how do you learn timing?

The answer to that goes back to watching. You make the cut the way you think it should be, and then you watch it. And you watch it again, and you pay attention to the timing. Is the cut too fast? Too slow? Confusing? Does it increase the energy of the scene or drag it down? You try adding and shortening the shot, until it's just right.

This is where digital editing machines, and especially the Avid, are light-years ahead of analog systems. The Avid has a special feature called *Trim Mode*. In trim mode you can quickly and easily lengthen or shorten the shots in your sequence. This is the tool that has made Avid famous, and it's the main reason an Avid will make you a better editor. Not only is it easier to shorten or lengthen shots, but you can also make those changes while you are watching! Remember, the key to being a good editor is having the ability to really watch. In Trim Mode, you can cut and watch at the same time. Sounds incredible, and it is.

TRIMMING THE OLD WAY

Let's think for a second about a film editor, working on a KEM or Steenbeck. She decides she wants to shorten a reaction shot. She plays the scene several times and then stops the machine on the frame where she thinks she would like to make the cut. Taking her grease pencil, she reaches for the picture head and marks the frame with an X. She then takes her Sharpie and marks the magnetic sound track with an X. Then she rolls the sound and picture to her left, takes her splicer and cuts the film and sound track on the frame marked by the X. She then removes the splicing tape at the original cut point and pulls out the excess film and sound. She counts the frames she's removed and sees she's trimmed the shot by 16 frames (two-thirds of a second). She hangs the strip of film and sound on a hook on her trim bin. Now she splices the picture back together by placing the two strips of film in her splicer and applying clear tape across the strips. She does the same for the sound. Now that the picture and sound tracks are rejoined, she can play the scene and see how it looks with the reaction shot shortened. She watches it. Hmmm. She watches it again. Not quite what she was hoping for. She took out too many frames. The reaction shot is now too short. What to do? She could go to the trim bin and take the 16 frames of the reaction shot and put, oh, maybe five frames back in. Or she could go to lunch and hope the cut looks better after a good meal.

What took three to five minutes on the KEM or Steenbeck would take 15 seconds on the Avid. And after 15 seconds, our editor would not only have made the 16-frame trim, but would have tried four other possibilities, until she arrived at the perfect length. How? By using Trim Mode.

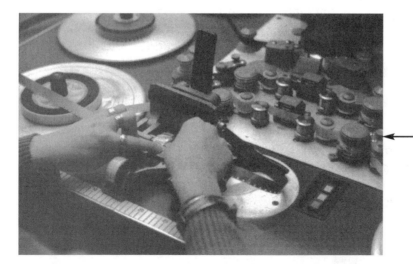

Traditional film editing. The editor, working on a Steenbeck, is tape-splicing the sound track.

Figure 4.1

TRIM MODE

Most of your editing with the Avid takes place in the Timeline, and that's particularly true of Trim Mode. Trim Mode takes place at the cut points. Some call them transitions. On the Timeline, these are the lines that show where one shot ends and the next shot begins.

GETTING INTO TRIM MODE

To enter Trim Mode, drag the blue position indicator to the cut point, or transition, you want to work on and click the Trim Mode button.

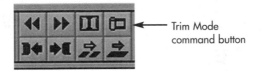

Trim Mode command button

Because it is so useful, the Trim Mode button is located on the keyboard as well as on the Composer Monitor tool palette. In the Media Composer, it's also on the bar at the bottom of the Timeline.

Edit Mode button ———   ———— Trim Mode button

To help explain what happens when trimming, people talk about the A-side and B-side of the transition. The A-side is the outgoing shot, and B-side is the incoming shot. Because we have a sequence involving two actors, we'll place Kate's CU on the A-side and Tim's CU on the B-side, so you'll be sure of what you're looking at in Figures 4.2 and 4.3.

AVID XPRESS TRIM MODE

When you press the button, two things happen. First the Composer monitor changes to a split screen, and you see the last frame of the A-side (Kate's CU) and the first frame of the B-side (Tim's CU). Second, you will see colored rollers appear on either side of the cut point in the Timeline. You are seeing the Trim Mode display.

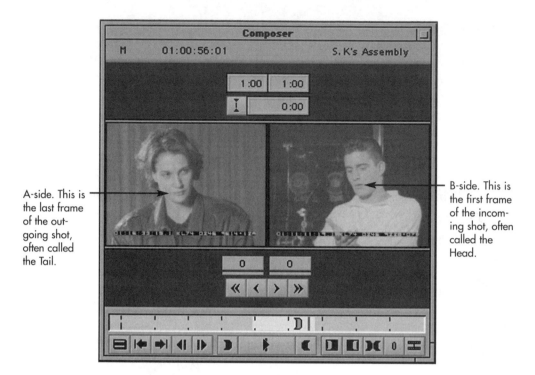

A-side. This is the last frame of the outgoing shot, often called the Tail.

B-side. This is the first frame of the incoming shot, often called the Head.

Figure 4.2 Trim Mode Display

Figure 4.3 Rollers appear on either side of the transition point for all selected tracks.

MEDIA COMPOSER TRIM MODE

There are actually two trim modes in the MC: Big Trim Mode and Small Trim Mode. Small Trim looks and behaves a lot like the Xpress Trim Mode. The Record Monitor splits in two, giving you incoming and outgoing frames. In Big Trim, the Source Monitor becomes the outgoing frame and the Record Monitor becomes the incoming frame (Figure 4.4). To go from Big to Small Trim, toggle the Trim button.

Because it will simplify instruction, I suggest that MC users start with Small Trim. You can go to the Setting window and open Trim Settings. In the dialog box choose "Always Use Small Trim Mode" as shown in Figure 4.5.

Figure 4.4   Big Trim Mode

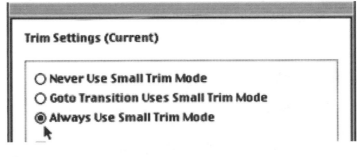

Figure 4.5

LASSOING THE TRANSITION

There's a faster way to enter Trim Mode.

Click the mouse pointer in the gray area above the tracks and to the left of the transition you want to work on. Drag down, left to right, encircling the transition including all the tracks, and let go (see top of page 66). You are instantly in Trim Mode. Lassoing the transition is the fastest method, because you don't need to select the tracks. It's the method you should practice most often. Remember, be sure to place the mouse above and to the left of the transition point.

Be careful that you don't lasso an entire clip. If you do, you'll enter Segment Mode (see Chapter 8). The Avid behaves quite differently in Segment Mode. If you inadvertently enter Segment Mode, click on the Segment button, which is highlighted at the bottom of the Timeline. You'll be back in Edit Mode. Now, try lassoing just the transition.

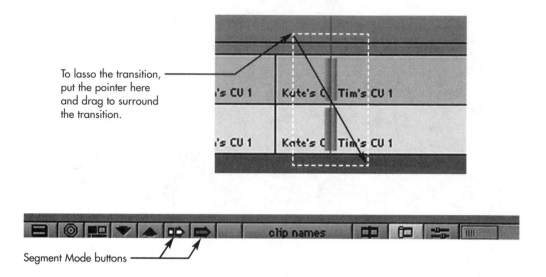

To lasso the transition, put the pointer here and drag to surround the transition.

Segment Mode buttons

Now that you know how to get into Trim mode, you need to be able to get out of Trim mode.

LEAVING TRIM MODE

Any one of these methods will take you out of Trim mode:

- Press the Trim Mode button again (Xpress).
- Press the Edit Mode button (MC).

- Press either one of the Step one-frame buttons.
- Click the mouse in the Timecode track (TC1) at the bottom of the Timeline.

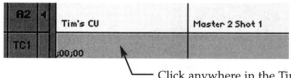

Click anywhere in the Timecode track, and you will leave Trim Mode. The position indicator will jump to the spot you clicked.

I prefer to click on the Timecode track to get out of Trim Mode. I usually click to the left of the transition I just trimmed. That way the position indicator jumps to the spot where I clicked, and I'm ready to watch the transition I just trimmed.

There are two kinds of Trims: Dual-Roller Trim and Single-Roller Trim.

DUAL-ROLLER TRIM

This is the default Trim Mode. When you press the Trim button, or lasso a transition, you go into this mode.

In Dual-Roller Trim Mode:

- The overall length of your sequence remains the same.
- You lengthen the A-side while shortening the B-side.
  or
- You shorten the A-side while lengthening the B-side.

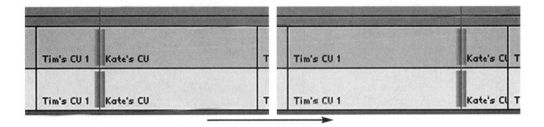

As you can see from the two screen captures, Tim's CU has been lengthened, while Kate's CU has been trimmed. If Tim was lengthened by 40 frames, Kate's would be shortened by 40 frames.

TRIM FRAME KEYS

If you look at the Trim Mode monitor, Figure 4.6, you'll see a number of Trim Frame keys. The < > keys are single-frame trim keys. They will trim the shot by one frame. The <<, >> keys will trim the shot by 10 frames. In Dual-Roller Trim Mode the direction of the arrow tells you which side will have the frames added and which side will have the frames removed.

Let's look at a specific cut and see what happens as we dual-roller Trim. Here Kate is finishing her dialog, and Tim is beginning to say his dialog.

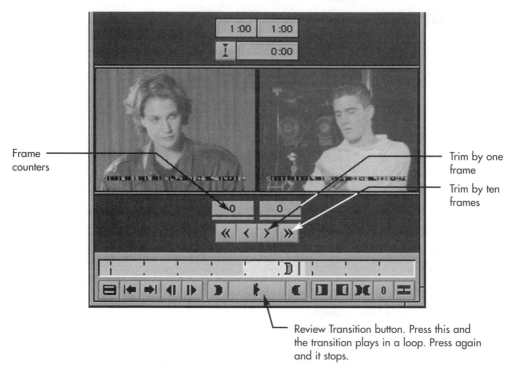

Frame counters

Trim by one frame

Trim by ten frames

Review Transition button. Press this and the transition plays in a loop. Press again and it stops.

Figure 4.6   Trim Mode Display

- If you press the > key you are adding one frame to the tail of Kate's CU, while taking one frame off the head of Tim's CU.
- Press the > key *five times*, you will add five frames to the tail of Kate's CU, while taking five frames off the head of Tim's CU.
- Click the < key. Now you are trimming Kate's CU by one frame, while lengthening Tim's CU by one frame.
- The <<, >> keys add or trim by increments of 10 frames.
- The boxes above the trim keys keep track of the frames you have moved.

REVIEW TRANSITION BUTTON

After you have trimmed in either direction, press the Review Transition button, and you'll see how the scene looks with the new transition points. This button will review the scene as you just cut it, in a continuous playback loop. Press the button again, and you'll stop the loop and return to the Trim Mode display.

FRAME COUNTERS

The frame counters show you how many frames you have trimmed. If you press the trim keys that point left (<<, <), the numbers will be minus. If you press the trim keys pointing right (>, >>), they will be positive numbers.

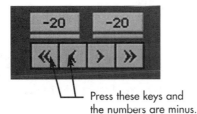

Press these keys and the numbers are minus.

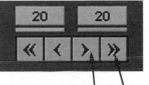

Press these keys and the numbers are positive.

In the screen capture on the left, the << key was pressed twice. In the screen capture on the right, the >> key was pressed twice.

Let's say you're working on the part of the scene where Kate asks Tim for her letters.

KATE
Where are they?
TIM
I guess they're not here.

Imagine that when you spliced it in, you cut Kate too soon—she barely gets her last words out before you cut to Tim. And imagine that when you cut to Tim, you cut it too long, so we're waiting and waiting for Tim to answer. What you want to do is add frames to the tail of Kate—lengthen her shot—and shorten the head of Tim's shot.

In dual-roller Trim Mode, it's easy.

To get into Trim Mode:

1. Go to the transition.
2. Lasso the transition point, including all of the audio track *or* press the Trim Mode key.

Let's say the cut's off by 20 frames.

1. Click *twice* on the trim by ten-frames key >>, and you'll be adding 20 frames to the end of Kate's shot while taking away 20 frames from Tim's shot.
2. Press the Review Transition button

Now, watching the cut, you see that Kate finishes her line, and Tim isn't waiting so long to speak.

To get out of Trim Mode do one of the following:

- Press the Trim Mode button again (Xpress).
- Press the Edit Mode button (MC).
- Press either one of the Step one-frame buttons.
- Click the mouse in the Timecode track (TC1) at the bottom of the Timeline.

Dual-roller trim has the advantage of keeping all your tracks in sync. Why? Because whenever frames are taken from a shot, the exact number of frames are added to the neighboring shot.

UNDO IN TRIM MODE

Undo and Redo work in Trim Mode. For instance, if you click the > key and you want to get back to zero, just press Command-Z. If you made several trims, keep pressing Command-Z until you're back where you started (0 in the frame counters).

TRIM BY DRAGGING

You don't need to click on the Trim keys at all. Once you are in Trim Mode, you can simply click on the rollers at the transition point and drag the rollers to the left or right!

Try it. It's not as precise as clicking the Trim keys, but it really gives you a sense of how the rollers work. Notice that the frame counter boxes keep track of how many frames you've dragged left or right.

If you drag the rollers so far that you reach the end of the shot, you'll hear a beep and see a small red marker in the frame to indicate that you can't roll any further because there are no more frames to extend.

SINGLE-ROLLER TRIM MODE

This is the Trim Mode that you will use most often to trim your shots. To sum it up and compare it to Dual-Roller Trim Mode.

With Single-Roller Trim Mode:

- The overall length of your sequence *will* change.
- You lengthen or shorten the A-side.
- You lengthen or shorten the B-side.

Let's work with Single-Roller Trim Mode.

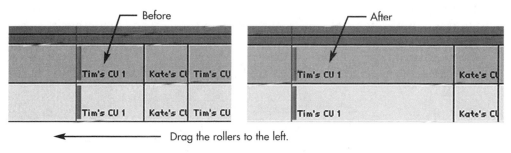

As you can see in the diagram, when you enter Single-Roller Trim Mode, there is only one roller, and it falls on one side of the transition point. Here we are working on the B-side, the head of Tim's CU.

Getting into Single-Roller Trim Mode

You enter Single-Roller Trim Mode the same way you enter Dual-Roller Trim Mode.

- Click the Trim button or lasso the transition. You're now in Dual-Roller Trim Mode.
- Place your mouse in the Trim Mode display and click on the A-side picture (left). The rollers move to the A-side in the Timeline.
- Place your mouse in the Trim Mode display and click on the B-side picture (right). The rollers move to the B-side in the Timeline.

In the example below, we have clicked on Tim's picture in the Trim Mode display, and the roller's have jumped to his side of the transition. Now, if we drag the roller to the left, we will be making Tim's shot longer. If we drag the roller to the right, we will be making Tim's shot shorter.

In Figure 4.7 and 4.8 you can see we have lengthened Tim's shot by moving the rollers left. We move Tim's rollers simply by clicking on one of his rollers and dragging it to the left, or, we could click on the trim frame keys: <<, <.

Figure 4.7   **Figure 4.8**

Let's examine these Trim Frame keys, while looking at Figure 4.8.

The << and < keys will make Tim's shot longer.

The > and >> keys will make Tim's shot shorter.

It took me a while to figure out how the Trim Frame keys worked with single-roller trims. Remember, when you're in Single-Roller Trim Mode, all the Trim keys affect just one side, in this case the B-side—Tim's.

If we now click on Kate's picture in the Trim Mode display, the rollers will jump to the A-side. All the Trim Frame keys now affect Kate's shot.

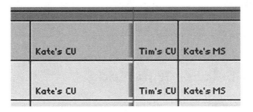

Look at these Trim Frame keys as you look at the screen capture.

The << and < keys will make Kate's shot shorter.

The > and >> keys will make Kate's shot longer.

Examine these two diagrams and the explanations that go with them. You must understand the relationship between the direction the rollers travel and the effect that has on a shot's length before you go any further.

TRIM PRACTICE

Before you learned how to use Trim Mode, you used splice and overwrite to lay down the shots, leaving them long to begin with. If you wanted to shorten a shot you marked an IN and an OUT in the Timeline and used Extract to shorten the shot. If you wanted to lengthen the shot, you spliced in more. Now that you have Trim Mode at your disposal, the way you edit changes significantly. If you see that a shot in the Timeline is too short or too long, it's so easy to cut it to just the right length.

Let's say you are playing your sequence, and you see that the tail of Kate's shot is much too short. When you spliced it in, you marked it at the wrong point, and you've clipped part of her last word of dialog. You need to lengthen the shot.

Action	Result
Go to the transition and lasso it.	You're in Trim Mode.
Click on Kate's picture in the Trim Display.	You're in Single-Roller Trim Mode.
Click the >> Trim key.	You've lengthened Kate by 10 frames.
Click on the Review Transition button.	The new cut point plays in a loop.

As you watch it, you see that adding 10 frames wasn't quite enough.

Action	Result
Click on the Review Transition button.	The looping stops.
Click on the > button three times.	You've added three more frames (13 total).
Click on the Review Transition button.	The new cut point plays in a loop.

When you watch it you see the new transition point works. Now you want to get out of Trim Mode.

Action	Result
Click on the Review Transition button.	The looping stops.
Click in the timecode track	You're out of Trim mode.

CHANGING FROM SINGLE-ROLLER TO DUAL-ROLLER TRIM MODE

If you're in Single-Roller Trim Mode and you want to be in Dual-Roller Trim Mode, simply move the mouse to the Trim Mode display and click on the line *between* the outgoing and incoming frames.

The Media Composer has three keyboard keys not found on the Xpress. These three keys, the P, [, and], will change the Trim Mode from Single-Roller Trim A-side, Dual-Roller Trim, and Single-Roller Trim B-side, respectively.

ADDING TRACKS FOR TRIMMING

If you get into Trim Mode and notice that one or more of your tracks doesn't have rollers, it's probably because the Track Selector box wasn't selected. To add rollers to that track, simply click on the track selector.

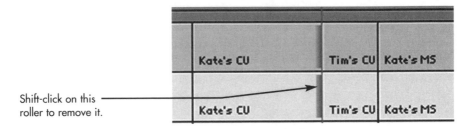

Shift-click on this
roller to remove it.

Figure 4.9

ADDING AND REMOVING ROLLERS

Once in Trim Mode, you sometimes want to add a roller or remove a roller so that you're working with some tracks and not others. A quick way to add or delete rollers is to hold down the Shift key while clicking on the transition point you want to change.

- Shift-click on a roller to remove it.
- Shift-click on a transition to add a roller.

ADVANCED TRIM MODE TECHNIQUES

Assuming that you're comfortable with trimming as explained in this chapter, and you want to work even faster and with more precision, let's look at a couple of advanced techniques.

Trimming while Watching

We talked about the important role that watching plays in every phase of editing. There's a very simple technique that involves trimming a cut while watching it.

1. Get into Trim Mode.
2. Choose a side that you want to work on, either the A-side or the B-side.
3. Press the Review Transition button.
4. While the transition is looping, hit the trim frame key(s) <<, <, >, or >>.

When you're just starting this exercise, you'll want to hit the trim by ten frames >> or << keys so you can see a big change. What happens is that the Avid makes the trim and then shows you what the new transition point looks like. You can keep hitting the trim keys until the cut looks right. You can go in either direction, depending what works. Go ahead and try this.

For example, let's say you're trying to fix the head of Tim's shot to give him just the right amount of pause before he speaks.

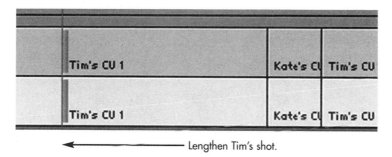

 Lengthen Tim's shot.

Figure 4.10

Say you click the << key, lengthening his shot by 10 frames. As the loop plays, you see it needs even more, so you press the << key again. Now you've added 20 frames and realize it's close, but it still needs to be lengthened a bit more. Now press the < key five times. Now, you like the length of the shot. When you press the Review Transition button to stop the loop, you'll still be in Trim Mode.

Look at the frame counter under Tim's frame in the Trim Mode display. It will display 25. You added a total of 25 frames to the head of Tim's shot. But notice it is -25 (minus 25). Why? Whenever you go left the numbers are negative, even though you added to Tim's shot.

How many frames you add and remove doesn't really matter. What matters is that the shot is now working. And it's working because you trimmed and watched, trimmed and watched, trimmed and watched—until you got it right!

Trim One Side, Then the Other

It often happens that after you've finished cutting one side, it becomes apparent that the other side needs to be trimmed. Without leaving Trim Mode, simply click on the other frame in the Trim display and the rollers will jump to the other side. Now press the Review Transition button and use the Trim Frame buttons to trim the other side.

If you want to shorten the tail of Kate's CU, you would press the << or < button. Let's say the transition point was way too long to begin with. Kate finishes her line, and then she just stands there. Click the << key three times, and you've trimmed 30 frames (a second) off Kate. You see that's too much. Click the

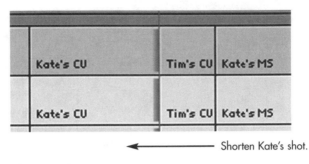

Shorten Kate's shot.

Figure 4.11

>> once, and now you've put 10 frames back on. You've now shortened her shot by 20 frames. As you continue to watch it in playback, you can fine-tune the cut by using the trim by one-frame buttons (< and >) until the cut looks right. Say you decide to add two more frames (press > twice) for a total of 18. You have shortened Kate's shot by 18 frames.

Now, without ever having left Trim Mode, you've worked on both sides of the transition, and the frame counters will show you what you've done. They would look like this:

Why? Because you trimmed Kate's side by 18 frames and you added to Tim's side by 25. They both are negative numbers because in both cases we dragged to the *left*—left to shorten Kate, and left to extend Tim. I don't like the way the Avid does this. I think that if you add to a shot it should be a positive number. If you shorten a shot, it should be a negative number. Someday. In the meantime, review this section until you understand what we did.

Using the Keyboard Not the Mouse

You can use the trim keys in the Trim Mode display, by clicking on them with the mouse. However, it's faster to use the trim keys that are on the keyboard, which do the same thing. As the transition point loops around, you press the trim keys with your fingers, while keeping your eyes on the screen. Watch and trim, watch and trim, until the shot works.

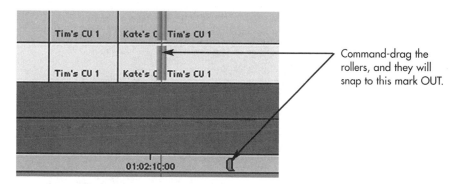

Command-drag the rollers, and they will snap to this mark OUT.

Figure 4.12

Dragging to a Mark

Earlier we discussed dragging the rollers to extend or shorten a shot. By simply clicking on the rollers, you can drag them left or right. It's less precise than using the Trim Frame keys. However, if you combine dragging with a mark IN or a mark OUT, then dragging can be very efficient. Use this technique when you know where you want to go with the trim.

Before you go into Trim Mode, play your sequence. If you find a shot that needs trimming (or extending), you can place a mark IN, if it's to the left of the transition, or a mark OUT, if it's to the right of a transition. Then, enter Trim Mode. Now hold down the Command key, click on the roller and drag it to the mark. The Avid stops precisely on the mark.

This works with either Single-Roller or Dual-Roller Trim Mode.

Picture and Sound Overlaps

Just about everyone knows what a straight cut looks like. When the picture and sound end at the same point, you have a straight cut. When you splice in the next shot, it too is a straight cut. So far, we've worked with straight cuts. But it often happens that the best place to cut the picture isn't necessarily the best place to cut the sound. When a picture and its sound are cut at different points, you have an overlap. Some editors call these overlaps "L-cuts."

Let's say you have spliced two shots together, and you love the way the dialog flows from one person to the next. But you're not really happy with the picture cut point. If there were a law that said you had to have straight cuts, you'd be stuck. But there isn't and you're not. You decide to create an overlap. This is where Dual-Roller Trim Mode excels.

Let's say we have Kate finishing her line and Tim about to say his line. What you decide to do is to remove 30 frames of Kate's picture and replace it with 30 frames of Tim's picture. The sound stays where it is.

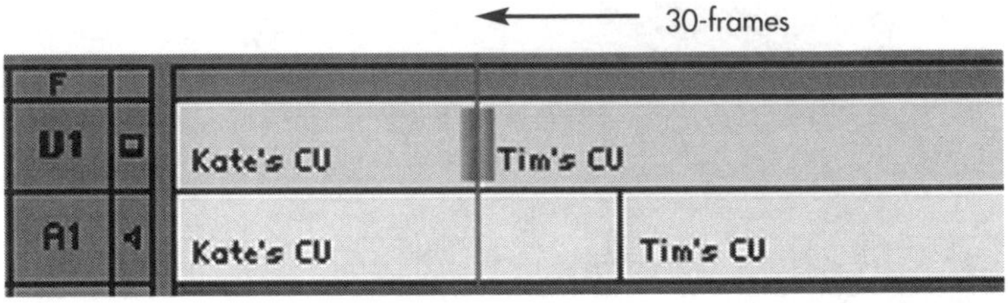

Figure 4.13

1. Enter Trim Mode by lassoing just the video track at the cut point. You are now in Trim Mode with the dual rollers on V1 but not on the sound track.

    If you do get rollers on the sound track(s), remove them by clicking on the track selector box (not the speaker icon). They're removed.
2. Drag the rollers 30 frames to the left or press the trim ten frames key << three times.
3. Press the Review Transition button to see how it works.

When the overlap is made, you have Kate talking, then before she finishes talking we see Tim listening over her words, and then Tim talks. Tim's picture has overlapped Kate's sound.

Here's another example:

Say you have a three-shot sequence. First you have a shot of a woman sitting at her desk, telling a man she must leave to catch a plane. Then you have a medium shot of the woman putting papers in her briefcase. Then you cut to a shot of the woman walking through a busy airport. When you spliced them together, you used straight cuts. The pictures are cut perfectly, but you realize that the sequence of shots would have more power if we heard the sound of the airport come in over the shot of her packing up her briefcase.

How? Simple. What you'll want to do is to get into Dual-Roller Trim Mode, deselect the video track so that the rollers are only on the sound track(s). Then drag the dual rollers on the sound track to the left. You'll be replacing some of her office sounds with the sound of the busy airport.

When the audience first hears the airport noises breaking into the shot of her in her quiet office, they may be momentarily confused, but that confusion creates a bit of suspense, which is quickly resolved when the picture of her walking through the airport comes onto the screen. Sound overlaps like this are used quite often to set up the next scene. How much should you overlap the sound? Try about two seconds of overlap, and then trim from there.

Removing an Overlap

After working on a transition and creating an overlap, you might decide that in fact a straight cut would work better. A quick way to turn an overlap back into a straight cut is to Command-drag.

1. Get into Trim Mode.
2. Select the track that has been overlapped and deselect the track that is already a straight cut.
3. Hold down the Command-key while you drag toward the straight cut. The trim will snap to the transition point.

A word of caution. You always want to create overlaps using the Dual-Roller Trim Mode. Because you are working with one track and not the other(s), Dual-Roller Trim Mode keeps everything in sync. If you use Single-Roller Trim Mode and trim one track and not the other track(s), you will immediately go out of sync.

SYNC PROBLEMS IN SINGLE-ROLLER TRIM MODE

This is a good time to examine what happens when you use Single-Roller Trim Mode on one track and not on the other(s).

In Figure 4.14, I went into Single-Roller Trim Mode, but only the video track was selected. The trim action affected only the picture. Without thinking, I trimmed anyway and dragged the roller to the left. Thus I lengthened Kate's picture by nine frames. Since the audio was not trimmed, the clip went out of sync! Kate's audio is now nine frames shorter than her video and thus out of sync by nine frames. As you can see, anything downstream of this transition point will also be out of sync by nine frames. Tim's CU wasn't trimmed, but because Kate's is out of sync, his clip is thrown out as well. Remember, in order to keep picture and sound in sync, you must cut the picture *and* sound at the same time. When you add picture, you must add sound.

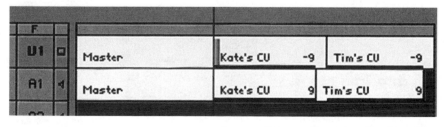

←——— Picture track was lengthened by nine frames. Audio track was not lengthened.

Figure 4.14

Fortunately, the Avid tells us whenever we are out of sync. Here it tells us that we are off by nine frames. To get back in sync, we must either trim nine frames of Kate's picture, or add nine frames to Kate's audio. Let's add nine frames to Kate's audio.

When you're out of sync, you need to go into Single-Roller Trim Mode to fix the problem. Now, we need to click on the A1 track and deselect the V1 track. The single-roller will jump to trim Kate's audio. Remember, we want to lengthen her audio by nine frames. We can use one of several methods:

- We can hit the < frame key nine times.
- We can hit the << frame key once (10) and then the > key once for a total of nine frames.
- We can drag the roller to the left and watch the frame counter until negative 9 appears.

THE TILDE KEY

There's a special key at the top left of the keyboard (next to the 1) called the Tilde key. It acts like a superplay button. When you press it, your clip or sequence will play. But it also works as a Review Transition key in Trim Mode. I use it instead of pressing the Review Transition button on the Trim Mode display.

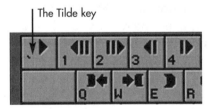

The Tilde key

TRIM MODE REVIEW

We've spent a lot of time discussing Trim Mode, devoting an entire chapter to its many advantages and features. Let's review some of the how and whys of Trim Mode.

Getting into Trim Mode:

- Lasso the transition.
- Drag the position indicator to the transition and press the Trim mode key.

Getting out of Trim Mode:

- Press the Trim Mode button again (Xpress).
- Press the Edit Mode button (MC).
- Press either one of the Step one-frame buttons.
- Click the mouse in the Timecode track (TC1) at the bottom of the Timeline.

Switching Trim Modes:

- To go from Dual-Roller Trim Mode to Single-Roller Trim Mode, click either the A-side or the B-side frames in the Trim Mode display.
- To go from Single-Roller Trim Mode to Dual-Roller Trim Mode, click the frame line between the A-side and B-side frames.

Add Rollers and Delete Rollers:

- In trim mode, shift-click on the transition side where you want to add a roller.
  If there is a roller you want to remove, shift-click on it and it will be removed.

Drag the Rollers:

- Click and drag the rollers left or right.
- Command-drag to IN or OUT marks.
- Command-drag to transition points.

Trim While Watching:

1. In trim mode, press the Review Transition key to have the transition go into a loop.
2. Use the Trim Frame keys <<, <, >, and >> to trim as you watch.

SUGGESTED ASSIGNMENTS:

Although Trim Mode is a fantastic feature, it isn't always intuitive. Study this chapter and then practice, using all of the many techniques discussed.

1. Make a duplicate of your sequence and give it today's date.
2. Practice getting in and out of Trim Mode.
3. Practice dual-roller and single-roller trims, trimming and lengthening the A-side and the B-side, and creating picture and sound overlaps.
4. Practice dragging the rollers.
5. Practice trimming while you watch, using the trim keys.
6. Practice adding and deleting rollers.
7. Using Trim Mode, create a fine cut, with sound overlaps where appropriate, of "Wanna Trade," or whatever assignment you have been editing to date.

5

Menus

In this chapter we're going to take a look at the various menus and menu commands the Avid provides, including those at the top of the computer screen and those found on the monitor screens. We'll discuss each command, point out the ones you'll use most often, and explain when you will find them most useful. But before we begin, let's talk about screening the sequence you've been editing of the scene "Wanna Trade." If you edited a different scene for your first project, it doesn't matter, since we'll be exploring the whole process of screening your work. Your last assignment involved using Trim Mode to fine-cut the scene. Now it's time to get some feedback.

SCREENING A WORK IN PROGRESS

Most editors place a high value on screening their work while still editing it. Call it a rough cut or a fine cut screening, but whatever name you give to it, it's a screening of your work in progress. You've spent a lot of time and energy cutting the material; you've given it your very best, but usually you've been working in a vacuum. What you're looking for now are fresh eyes and ears. You want an audience (it can be one or two people, or a classroom full of fellow students) to give you feedback. Nothing teaches you more about your work than screening it in front of an audience. Sometimes screenings are painful, sometimes they are exhilarating, and always they are useful.

Whenever possible, I like to start off small, with an audience of just a few people. I like to split my attention between the audience and the screen. Usually if something isn't working, I know it by feeling the attention (or lack of attention) the audience is giving to a particular section. After you've screened the footage, start your inquiry as wide as possible, and then work toward the specific. Take notes! If the audience members aren't all that forthcoming, ask them questions. How did it work? Were you confused about what was going on? What emotion did it evoke? If it's a narrative piece, you might ask about the actors' perform-ances. Which actor did they like best? Because you're working on a digital machine, you can quickly go to any section to review it. If your project is over ten minutes long, there's probably a lot to talk about in terms of structure, pacing, character development, and dramatic tension. With a scene as short as "Wanna Trade," you can probably move on to an analysis of specific editing problems. At this stage you're trying to find places where your audience tripped over things that didn't work.

If you're lucky, the audience will give you feedback that's right on the money:

Audience member: When Tim searches the desk, pretending to look for the letters, I didn't like the cut from the mas-ter shot to Tim's close-up.

You: Why not?

Audience member: I couldn't see what he was doing.

That's specific. Or someone might say that she thought a cut seemed awk-ward, or an actor remained on the screen for too long before you cut to the next shot. More times than not, especially if your audience knows nothing about video or filmmaking, they won't tell you what tripped them because they hon-estly don't know. In those instances, you have to play detective and figure out what's going wrong. It's not easy, but it can be rewarding. I've often found that when people who don't know much about editing say something doesn't work, the problem isn't where they think it is; it's usually before that.

If they can't tell you what is bothering them, but they feel a bit confused, I suggest you slow down the beginning. Make sure the audience is grounded at the start. Once they know who's doing what, then you can speed things up.

Whatever you do, don't argue with your audience. You might be the expert on the project you're cutting, but they're the experts on their feelings about it. If they criticize your work, and point out shortcomings, it's human nature to be defensive. I've never met anyone who *liked* being criticized. But if you argue with them, you're missing the point of the screening, which is to learn what is work-ing and what isn't. You don't have to take any of their suggestions. If you think they're way off base, so be it. Toss out your notes and find another audience.

Sometimes you leave a screening embarrassed. The suggestions were so good you feel embarrassed that you didn't see the problems yourself. Other times you feel grateful because you identified a problem, know how to fix it, and can't wait to get back to work. Then there are the times when you realize there are lots of problems and it's depressing to think how far you have to go. Those are the days when, if possible, you take the afternoon off and go for a long walk. Once in a while, people will pat you on the back, shake your hand, and tell you it's brilliant. (I've never had this experience myself, but I've heard about it.)

Unless you get raves from everyone, you'll probably head back to work, fix the problems, and try to schedule another screening with another group with fresh eyes and ears.

MENUS

Pull-down menus are at the heart of the Macintosh and Windows interface. On the Avid a lot of choices and commands are located on the menus. Many operations can only be carried out by menu commands, while others have keyboard equivalents. Sometimes an item is grayed out, meaning it isn't available. You'll need to select something or do something for it to come into play.

File   Edit   Bin   Clip   Output   Special   Tools   Windows   Script

Different Avid systems have different pull-down menus. Menus change as Avid software is upgraded. Xpress Avids have fewer menu functions than Media Composers. Given all the different Avid systems and software upgrades, there's really no way to keep up with all the changes in a guidebook like this one.

Even so, I believe it's useful to examine the many menu commands in some detail. All Avids share about 90 percent of the same commands. And they tell us a great deal about how the Avid functions. By going over each command, you can learn a lot about the work you'll soon be able to do. Some commands are geared for advanced users, and we won't go much beyond the brief description provided here. Others are so important to our daily use of the Avid that we'll review them often and in great detail in later chapters.

Since the book you're reading is probably yours—you paid for it and own it—I suggest you use a highlighter pen and highlight a command the first time you use it. That way, the ones you use will be highlighted, and the ones you don't use won't get in your way. When you want to look up a command, you'll quickly look at the ones you use, and your eyes can skip over those you don't. Over time you'll use most of them, but it might be interesting to see how many you never use.

I've included menus from the Media Composer and the Xpress. The Media Composer comes from a Mac, and the Xpress is from a Windows NT. The only difference, besides their appearance, is that shortcut commands on a Macintosh use the Command key, ⌘, and Windows machines use the Control key, Ctrl.

FILE MENU

If you've used just about any software on a Windows or Macintosh computer, you're already familiar with most of these File commands. Open, Close, Save,

File	Edit	Bin	Clip	Ou

New Bin   ⌘N
Open Bin...   ⌘O
New Script...

Close   ⌘W
Save All Bins   ⌘S
Save a Copy as...

Page Setup...
Print Timeline...   ⌘P

Get Position Info   ⌘I
Reveal File

Export...
Import...

Load Media Database
Mount All
Eject...

Quit   ⌘Q

File	Edit	Bin	Clip	Tools	Windows

New Bin   Ctrl+N
Open Bin...   Ctrl+O
New Script...

Close   Ctrl+W
Save All Bins   Ctrl+S
Save a Copy as...

Page Setup...
Print Frame...   Ctrl+P

Get Clip Info...   Ctrl+I
Reveal File

Export...
Import...

Refresh Media Directories
Load Media Database
Mount All
Eject...

Exit   Ctrl+Q

Figure 5.1   Media Composer File Menu 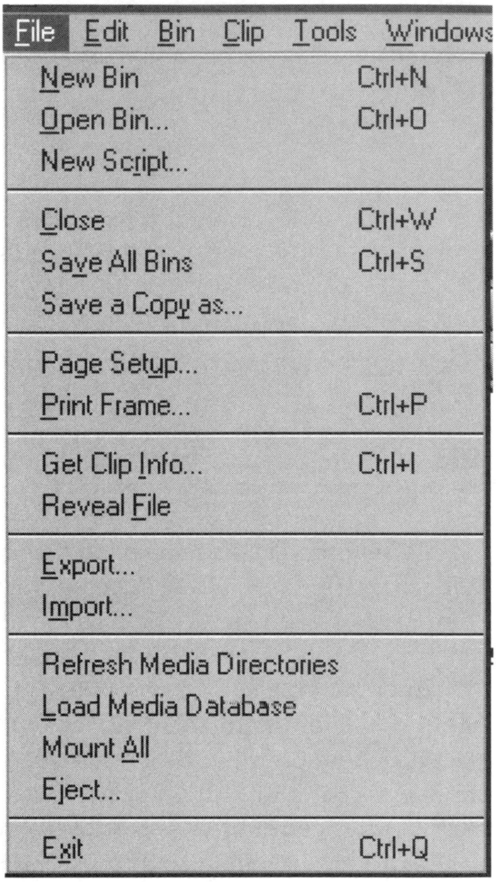   **Figure 5.2**   Xpress File Menu

Print—they're all standard. Although the File menu on Media Composer and Xpress machines are pretty much the same, your commands may be slightly different.

As you can see, some of the commands have keyboard equivalents. Either drag down the menu and select an item, or memorize the keyboard equivalent and type it instead.

New Bin: Creates a new bin. In the past, we clicked on the New Bin button on the Project window. Avid gives you many ways to do the same thing.

Open Bin: In fact this is more than it seems. If a bin is selected, and you choose this, the bin opens. But you'll probably just double-click on the bin to open it. This command does more than just open a bin, however. When you select this menu command, you're presented with a dialog box. That dialog box taps into all the bins on all the projects on the Avid. Let's say you want to take a clip of music from another project and use it in this project. Hit Command-O and then navigate through the computer's hierarchical menus until you find the bin you want. Open it and you can open a music clip from another project and put it into your current project.

New Script: This command works with the Script Integration feature offered on Media Composer and Xpress 3.0.

Close Bin: This command closes the active bin. We usually click on the close box in the corner of the bin itself.

Save Bin: This saves any bin that is selected. The Avid has an autosave function that automatically saves your work. But if you want to make sure you save what you just did, then type Command-S, or select this menu item.

Save a Copy As: This saves a copy of the open bin.

Page Setup: If you have a printer hooked up to your computer, you can print out a lot of different items and information. This command opens a dialog box so you can determine the page setup.

Print Bin/Frame: This opens a dialog box that lets you choose what you would like to print on your printer: an active bin, a frame of a clip, or the Timeline.

Get Bin/Clip Info: This tells you the name and the start timecode for the clip you have selected and information about the number and length of clips in your bin. To tell you the truth, I rarely use this because it also places items in the Console, and I avoid the Console, which is designed for Avid programmers. Mess with the Console, and you could screw up the software.

Reveal File: This is a rather advanced command and one you won't often use. If you select a master clip, you can use this command to go to the computer's Finder level to locate the media file associated with that master clip.

Export: Because Avid deals with digital information (1's and 0's), almost anything that can be digitized can be brought in or sent out as a file. The Avid allows you to bring in and send out many kinds of files: picture files, animation files, and audio files. When you export, you send out digital information you have created in the Avid. Perhaps you have sound that needs cleaning up; you've got camera noise or an irritating hum. You could export the sound clip as an audio file and give it to a sound engineer who could filter out the offending hum or camera noise.

Import: Import is the flip side of export. You use Export to send files you created in the Avid to other computers. You use Import to bring all sorts of files into your Avid. You could import digital photographs, digital audio, animation you created in After Effects™, or titles you created in Photoshop™. The list of importable files is quite extensive. We'll spend some time learning how to export and import later in the book.

Load Media Database: The media database is like a card catalog that keeps track of what's being put on and taken off the external drives. After certain actions, some of your sequences might be offline—the images or sounds don't play, and you'll see that the media is listed as "Media Offline." When you load the Media Database, the Avid may find the missing offline material.

Mount All: This command mounts, or makes active and available, all the media drives attached to your Avid.

Eject: This opens a dialog box that allows you to select drives or disks for ejection.

Quit/Exit: This command closes everything currently opened, including bins and monitors, and quits the Avid application software. You are returned to the computer desktop.

EDIT MENU

The Edit Menu contains some commands that are quite similar to those found on other common software types, so again, much of this will be familiar to you. Cut, Copy, Paste, Undo, Redo, and Duplicate are commands I'm sure you've used before. They behave a bit differently here, but probably as you would expect.

Undo: You are no doubt already a devoted user of this command. The Avid gives you 32 levels of Undo. You can go back and change actions that you took up to 32 actions ago.

Redo: Redo replaces the action that you undid. Just as handy as Undo.

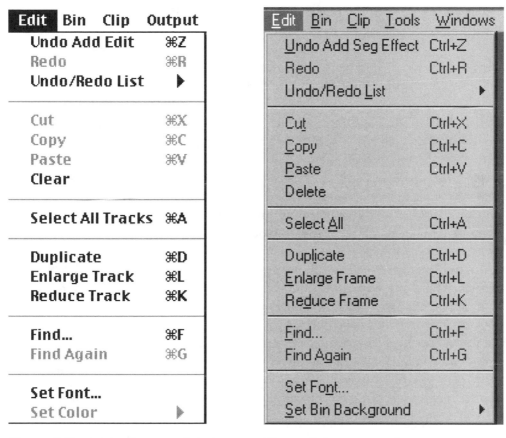

Figure 5.3   Media Composer Edit Menu   **Figure 5.4**   Xpress Edit Menu

Undo/Redo List: Xpress users don't get this command until 3.0. It provides a list of the last 32 actions (either Undo or Redo). Instead of working through all of them, one at a time, to reach the one you want, with this list you can search the list and then select the action you want to change. Remember that all previous actions—those actions above it on the list—will also be changed.

Cut: If you select material in the Timeline by using a Mark IN and a Mark OUT and then choose Cut, the selected material is removed and immediately goes into the Clipboard. Cut works just like Extract.

Copy: If you select something by using a Mark IN and a Mark OUT and then choose Copy, the selected material is copied to the Clipboard, where it is stored until you Paste it in somewhere. This is a great way to get audio from one area of the sequence, copy it to the Clipboard Monitor, and then put it somewhere else.

Paste: This command places whatever is in the Clipboard at the blue position indicator, or at a Mark IN in the Timeline.

Clear/Delete: This works just like the Delete key. It opens a dialog box for deleting clips from a bin or tracks from the Timeline.

Select All: This is a terrific way to quickly select all of the things you're working on. You can select all the clips in a Bin or select all the tracks in the Timeline.

Duplicate: We already practiced this in Chapter 2. There will be many times that you want to duplicate sequences. Just select the sequence you want to copy, and hit Command-D. Rename the copy and you can make changes to the new version, while holding on to the previous version.

Enlarge Track/Frame: This enlarges tracks in the Timeline. It also enlarges frames, when you're working in the bin in Frame View. You'll use this frequently. Remember, enLarge for Command-L (Ctrl-L).

Reduce Track: This reduces frames in Frame View, or reduces tracks in the Timeline. You'll use this frequently.

Find: This is just like Find in most word-processing programs, but it is used to find clips in the Timeline.

Find Again: This command repeats the previous Find command.

Set Font: You can customize the way things look on the screen, including the font used in bins and certain windows. Not very useful, unless you have nothing to do with your free time.

Set Color: Like Set Font, this command is for those who want to make their bins and Composer window look "different." Waste of time, if you ask me.

BIN MENU

Now we arrive at the pull-down menus that are not like those found on most word-processing programs. Not all of the Media Composer items are found on the Xpress, and there are a few Xpress items not found on the Media Composer. We'll begin by examining all the commands on the Media Composer, explaining which ones are found on both systems and which ones are only on the MC. Then

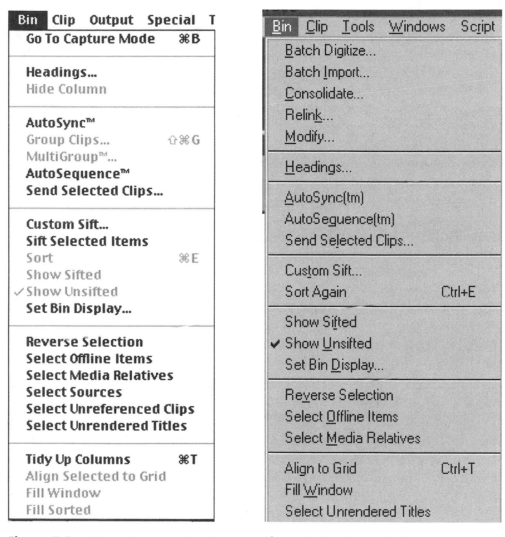

| **Bin** | Clip | Output | Special | T |

Go To Capture Mode ⌘B

Headings...
Hide Column

AutoSync™
Group Clips...   ⇧⌘G
MultiGroup™...
AutoSequence™
Send Selected Clips...

Custom Sift...
Sift Selected Items
Sort   ⌘E
Show Sifted
✓ Show Unsifted
Set Bin Display...

Reverse Selection
Select Offline Items
Select Media Relatives
Select Sources
Select Unreferenced Clips
Select Unrendered Titles

Tidy Up Columns   ⌘T
Align Selected to Grid
Fill Window
Fill Sorted

| **Bin** | Clip | Tools | Windows | Script |

Batch Digitize...
Batch Import...
Consolidate...
Relink...
Modify...

Headings...

AutoSync(tm)
AutoSequence(tm)
Send Selected Clips...

Custom Sift...
Sort Again   Ctrl+E

Show Sifted
✓ Show Unsifted
Set Bin Display...

Reverse Selection
Select Offline Items
Select Media Relatives

Align to Grid   Ctrl+T
Fill Window
Select Unrendered Titles

Figure 5.5 Media Composer Bin Menu   **Figure 5.6** Xpress Bin Menu

we'll discuss those commands on the Xpress that you won't find in the MC's Bin menu.

The main difference between the Media Composer and the Xpress is one of scope. The Xpress does nearly everything the MC does, but presents you with fewer options to accomplish the same task. You can usually get there with the Xpress, but perhaps not as quickly or easily.

Keep in mind that the Bin menu is made up of commands that act on things you'll find in a bin. It seems obvious, but sometimes we overlook the obvious. Often you need to have a bin open and selected in order for these commands to be available.

Go To Capture Mode: (MC ONLY) This initializes the capture tools you'll use for digitizing material. It opens the Digitize Tool, the Compression Tool, and the selected, or active, bin.

Headings: We've already discussed this in Chapter 2. It opens a dialog box that lists all the possible columns, listed by headings, that are available to you. You select the ones you want and deselect the ones you want hidden from view.

Hide Column: (MC ONLY) This is a fast way to remove selected columns from view in the bin. In Xpress you must go back into Headings to do this. Here it's a menu item.

AutoSync: This is especially handy when you're working on film projects. Remember, film is recorded double-system, meaning the sound is recorded on a tape recorder and not by the film camera. When the film is transferred to video, the sound is not generally added to the videotape (although it can be, at an additional expense). You digitize the picture, then the sound. The sound and picture are then placed in sync in the Avid. Once synced, they can be locked together so that sync breaks appear whenever sync is broken.

Group Clips: (MC ONLY) This is an advanced feature. You can take clips that were shot with different cameras, or on different days, and group them together into one clip. Once they are grouped, you can use Avid's MultiCamera editing features. Let's say you grouped four clips into one group. In Quad Split mode, for instance, the Source Monitor shows all four clips. You can see all the choices and then cut into your sequence whichever one works best. It's a quick way to build a montage of different shots, or to edit together various shots of the same action.

MultiGroup: (MC ONLY) This is also an advanced feature used primarily for editing big budget situation comedies. It's similar to Group Clips, except that all the different camera shots covering the scene must have identical timecode. Shots from the different cameras are grouped together so they act as one clip, staying in sync and playing together. In essence this feature is designed so an Avid editor can "switch" between camera angles as she edits the show, just as a television director would use a switcher when producing a live show.

AutoSequence: If the original videotape had no audio, as with a film-to-tape transfer, you could bring in the sound, sync it up, and then use this command to put the synced audio back onto that videotape.

Send Selected Clips: Avid created a file transfer protocol named AvidNet™, which enables you to send and receive material from one Avid to another Avid. This command helps you do that. Avid has now gone beyond AvidNet and created a more sophisticated system called Avid Unity MediaNet™, with which five or more editors, using Macintosh, NT, or even SG machines can share material stored on a large central storage device.

Custom Sift: This command opens a dialog box in which you set various options and parameters for sifting through a bin to find clips you want to locate. You can sift by name, creation date, tape, duration, and so on.

Sift Selected Items: (MC ONLY) This command sifts selected items according to your sift parameters.

Sort/Sort Again: We spent some time in Chapter 3 discussing this command. It enables you to choose a column in a bin and sort all the clips alphanumerically by that chosen column. After you have sorted, it will change to Sort Again.

Show Sifted: During sifting, this command displays only those items in a bin that met the sift criteria. All others are hidden from view.

Show Unsifted: This command restores the unsifted items for viewing.

Set Bin Display: This command presents a dialog box that lets you determine which items you want displayed in the bin. There are many choices. You're familiar with only a few. The choices are as follows:

> Master clips (you know all about these)
> Subclips (you know about these)
> Sequences (you know all about these)
> Sources (lists the tapes the material comes from)
> Effects (dissolves, wipes, etc.—we'll learn about these)
> Motion effects (freeze frames, slow motion—we'll learn about these)
> Rendered effects (we'll learn about these)

If you checked off all the choices, your bin would be packed with too much information, making it hard to find the sequences, clips, and subclips you need. When we learn about effects, titles, and motion effects, and start creating them, we'll sometimes want to see them displayed in the bin.

Reverse Selection: This is a handy command. Let's say you select a clip in a bin. It becomes highlighted. If you click on this command, your selection is reversed. What that means is that the clip you selected is deselected, and all the other clips in the bin are selected. Let's say you want to select all those clips that are close-ups. And let's say that of the 40 clips in the bin, two are wide shots and the other 38 are close-ups. Shift-click on the two that are wide shots, and then on Reverse Selection—all 38 close-ups are selected. The two that are wide shots are deselected. You reversed your selection.

Select Offline Items: Later on we'll learn about logging and digitizing clips. Often when you're digitizing, you're looking for clips that are offline—meaning they have no media files because they haven't been digitized, just logged. It makes your life easier to be able to go to a bin, select this command, and have all the offline clips selected.

Select Media Relatives: This enables you to select a sequence or a clip and then have the Avid highlight all the objects related to it. Let's say you've finished the final sequence and you want to make sure you used all the shots available to you. Click on the sequence and then on Select Media Relatives; the Avid will highlight every clip that was used in the Sequence.

Select Sources: (MC ONLY) This command selects (highlights) all the source clips that make up a selected object.

Select Unreferenced Clips: (MC ONLY) This command works like the flip side of Select Media Relatives. Select a sequence and then choose this command. It shows you all the clips in the bin that have *not* been used in the sequence.

Select Unrendered Titles: Titles often need to be rendered (created) by the computer before they play in real time. This command shows you all the titles that have not been rendered.

Tidy Up Columns: When you are in Text View, this command puts the columns in nice neat rows. When you are in Frame View, this command changes to Align to Grid.

Align Selected to Grid: (MC ONLY) When you are in Frame View, this command aligns to a grid all those frames you have selected.

Fill Window: When you are in Frame View, this command distributes all the frames evenly inside the window.

Fill Sorted: (MC ONLY) When you are in Frame View, this command sorts the frames while distributing all the frames evenly inside the window.

ITEMS FOUND IN XPRESS BIN MENU AND NOT IN MC BIN MENU

Batch Digitize: This opens a dialog box that leads you through the process of digitizing selected clips. Normally you use this command after you have logged a good number of clips. You've set the In and Out timecode for the clips, but you haven't digitized them. By invoking Batch Digitize, you can go to lunch while the Avid digitizes each of the selected clips. (In the Media Composer this is in the Clip menu.)

Batch Import: (Xpress 3.x) Some projects contain a great many imported files, such as graphic and animation files. Until now, the process of moving from a low-resolution sequence to a high-resolution sequence has meant that graphic intensive projects were at a severe disadvantage because each file would have to be re-imported at a higher resolution and then manipulated individually. Batch Import makes it much easier to bring in files at a higher resolution (Included in the Media Composer version 8.x).

Consolidate: Consolidate has two functions. It allows you to send media files to the drive of your choice, which means you can better organize your media files. More importantly, it helps you get rid of material that you digitized but no longer need, enabling you to reclaim a large amount of space on your hard drives. When you consolidate a sequence, you are telling the Avid to keep all the media from the clips that went into the sequence and to throw out all the media from the clips that didn't get edited into the sequence. You don't want to consolidate until you've made a very fine cut. You might fine-cut the first half of your project and consolidate that half to free up a lot of drive space to enable you to digitize all the footage you need for cutting the second half. (In the Media Composer this is in the Clip menu.)

Relink: It sometimes happens that the connection (link) between the master clip and the media file is broken. The clip appears offline, even though you know the media file is on the drive somewhere. In this case you need to relink the clip to the media file. (In the Media Composer this is in the Clip menu.)

Modify: This command allows you to change important data about a clip. For instance, you might need to change the timecode information about a clip in order to get it to digitize properly. (In the Media Composer this is in the Clip menu.)

Menu Madness

As we continue to work our way across the menus on top of the computer screen, from left to right, the menu items found on the Media Composer and the Xpress begin to vary more significantly. The Clip menu is next, but many items found on the Xpress are not found on the Clip menu of the MC. And after the Clip menu, the Xpress has the Tools menu, whereas the MC has the Output menu and the Special menu. So now we'll examine them separately, looking first at the menu on the Xpress and then at the menu on the Media Composer. Because there are similarities, there will be some duplication of commands. Again, I think it is important to learn both the MC and Xpress menu items, because you never know which one you'll work on next.

CLIP MENU - AVID XPRESS

In my opinion, Clip menu is a bit of a misnomer, since many of the commands here don't really have much to do with actual clips. I think these commands have a lot more to do with the Timeline. But here we go. Since we're discussing the Xpress only, I've included both the Clip menu for Mac and the Clip menu for NT.

Clip Tools Windows	Clip Tools Windows Script Send
New Sequence ⇧⌘N	New Sequence Shift+Ctrl+N
New Video Track ⌘Y	New Video Track Ctrl+Y
New Audio Track ⌘U	New Audio Track Ctrl+U
New Title...	New Title...
Freeze Frame ▶	Freeze Frame ▶
Load Filler	Load Filler
Audio Mixdown...	Audio Mixdown...
Video Mixdown...	Video Mixdown...
Render In/Out...	Render In/Out...
✓Render On-The-Fly	✓Render On-The-Fly
Recreate Title Media	Re-create Title Media
	16:9 Monitors
	VTR Emulation
Digital Cut	Digital Cut

Figure 5.7   Xpress Clip Menu—Mac   **Figure 5.8**   Xpress Clip Menu—NT

New Sequence: Whenever you want to create a new sequence, use this command. Often you'll begin a new sequence by simply splicing a marked clip to the Timeline. Whenever you do, you'll automatically begin a new sequence. Using the menu command is a more formal way of doing it.

New Video Track: This command creates a new video track on the Timeline. Later, when we create effects and titles, we'll want to put them on a new video track, such as V2, so there can be a superimposition of picture images—for example, a title superimposed over a visual.

New Audio Track: The Avid can play between 8 and 24 tracks of audio simultaneously. If you add music in stereo, a narration track, and several sound effect tracks to your dialog tracks, you can easily need six or seven audio tracks. This command instantly creates a new track on the Timeline.

New Title: This command opens the Title Tool, which we'll use to create titles.

Freeze Frame: This command opens up a list of freeze frame lengths: 1 second, 5 seconds, 10 seconds, etc., and creates the freeze frame of your choice.

Load Filler: This opens up a Pop-up Monitor that contains black fill. For filmmakers, it's like grabbing a roll of fill that you then splice onto your tracks to create a pause, or to replace picture or audio. Let's say you want to put 30 frames (a second) of black between the end of one scene and the beginning of the next. Choose Load Filler. In the pop-up window, mark an IN, go 29 frames, and mark an OUT. Then mark an IN on the Timeline where you want the fill to go. Select all your tracks and hit Splice. It acts just like any clip, except that this one has only black. (The Media Composer places this command in the Monitor menus. We'll examine these Monitor menus at the end of the chapter.)

Audio Mixdown: Currently, the Xpress can only monitor eight of your audio tracks. But what if you have ten tracks? Before outputting to tape, you could "mix down" (combine) three of the ten tracks onto one track. Now you have eight tracks.

Video Mixdown: The same explanation and rationale given for audio mixdown applies here.

Render In to Out or Render at Position: Most effects, such as wipes, freeze frames, conceal effects, and motion effects, need the computer to create a combination of media in order to create something new—the effect. The creation of the digital effect inside the computer is called *rendering*. If you have one effect to render, you place the position indicator on that effect and choose Render at Position. If you have a number of effects that need to be rendered, you'll mark an IN before the first, and an OUT after the last, and then you'll choose Render In to Out.

Render On-the-Fly: This turns on or off Render On-the-Fly. You will often be editing your sequence with effects that have not been rendered (created by the computer). Since they haven't been created, you won't see them when you play the sequence. However, with Render on-the-Fly selected, you can see the effect by dragging the position indicator through the Timeline. With this turned off, you don't see the effect when you drag through it.

Recreate Title Media: It often happens that you edit your project at a low resolution, because it saves hard drive space, and then you redigitize the final sequence at a much higher resolution, for output to tape. You'll create titles in that low resolution and then, when you go to the higher resolution, those titles won't play. To get them to play at the new resolution, you'll need to select Recreate Title Media. Now you have your titles in the higher resolution.

16:9 Monitors: (Xpress 3.0) This configures the Pop-up and Composer Monitor for the wide-screen aspect ratio.

VTR Emulation: (Xpress 3.0) If you have the right cable, you can have an external videotape editing system play your sequence. An external edit controller takes control of the Avid, and plays the sequence as if it were just another source video in a videotape deck. That way you could have multiple source tapes, including the Avid sequence, edited together onto a master videotape.

Digital Cut: The Avid can be connected to sophisticated analog and digital video decks for recording the final, completed sequence onto tape. When you use the Digital Cut Tool, the Avid controls the videotape deck and records your digital cut to tape using timecode.

CLIP MENU - MEDIA COMPOSER

Some of the items found on the Xpress Clip Menu are found here as well, but there are differences.

New Sequence: Whenever you want to create a new sequence, choose this command.

Figure 5.9   Media Composer Clip Menu

New Picture Track: This command creates a new picture (video) track on the Timeline. Later, when we create effects and titles, we'll want to put them on a new video track, such as V2, so there can be a superimposition of picture images—for example, a title superimposed over a visual.

New Sound Track: The Avid can play between 8 and 24 tracks of audio simultaneously. If you add music in stereo, a narration track, and several sound effect tracks to your dialog tracks, you can easily need six or seven audio tracks. This command instantly creates them on the Timeline.

New Title: This command opens the Title Tool, which we'll use to create titles.

Freeze Frame: This command opens up a list of freeze frame lengths: 1 second, 5 seconds, 10 seconds, etc., and then creates the one of your choosing.

Center Pan: When we get to the chapter that discusses audio, we'll spend time on panning, but basically sound is said to come from the left speaker, to be centered on both speakers, or to come from the right speaker (and anywhere in between). This command centers the sound on all the clips you select.

Batch Digitize: This opens a dialog box that leads you through the process of digitizing selected clips. Normally you use this command after you have logged a good number of clips. You have set the In and Out timecode for the clips, but you haven't digitized them. By invoking Batch Digitize, you can go to lunch while the Avid does the digitizing.

Consolidate: Consolidate has two functions. It allows you to send media files to the drive of your choice, which means you can better organize your media files. More importantly, it helps you get rid of material that you digitized but no longer need, enabling you to reclaim a large amount of space on your hard drives. When you consolidate a sequence, you are telling the Avid to keep all the media from the clips that went into the sequence and to throw out all the media from the clips that didn't get edited into the sequence. You don't want to consolidate until you've made a very fine cut. You might fine-cut the first half of your project and consolidate that half to free up a lot of drive space to enable you to digitize all the footage you need for cutting the second half.

Decompose: A bit gruesome sounding, but this is a power feature not found on the Xpress. When you edit your project, you'll no doubt be editing at a low resolution to save space on the hard drive. When you go to redigitize the final sequence, you are redigitizing the clips in the final sequence to a much higher resolution. On the Xpress, this redigitizing process takes place in one way. With Decompose, you're free to set up the process in any of a hundred ways. For instance, you can determine the order in which source tapes will be redigitized. You can't do that on the Xpress.

Render at Position or Render In to Out: Most effects, such as wipes, freeze frames, conceal effects, and motion effects, need the computer to create a combination of media in order to create something new—the effect. The creation of the digital effect inside the computer is called *rendering*. If you have one effect to render, you place the position indicator on that effect and choose Render at Position. If you have a number of effects that need to be rendered, you'll mark an IN before the first, and an OUT after the last, and then you'll choose Render In to Out.

Recreate Title Media: It often happens that you edit your project at a low resolution, because it saves hard drive space, and then you redigitize the final sequence at a much higher resolution, for output to tape. You'll create titles in that low resolution and then, when you go to the higher resolution, those titles won't play. To get them to play at the new resolution, you'll need to select Recreate Title Media.

Relink: It sometimes happens that the connection (link) between the master clip and the media file is broken. The clip appears offline, even though you know its media file is on the drive somewhere. In this case you need to relink the clip to the media file.

Modify: This command allows you to change important data about a clip. For instance, you might need to change the timecode information about a clip in order to have it digitize properly.

Add Filler at Start: This command adds a second of filler at the start of a new sequence. Handy.

Remove Match Frame Edits: We'll get to what are more often called *add edits* later in the book. With this command you can mark an IN and then an OUT and remove add edits from your sequence.

Lock Bin Selection: You can prevent clips, subclips, or sequences from being deleted accidentally, by locking them. Just click on the bin item and choose this command from the Clip menu.

Unlock Bin Selection: To unlock, simply select the bin items and choose this command.

Lock Tracks: When working in the Timeline with tracks, the Clip menu changes so you can lock and unlock tracks. This command enables you to lock one or more tracks. It's especially handy as you get to the end of your editing phase and don't want a lot of work dislodged inadvertently. A padlock symbol appears in the track selector box in the Timeline.

Unlock Track: This command unlocks the tracks.

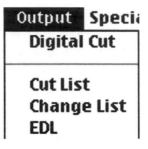

Figure 5.10   Media Composer Output Menu

OUTPUT MENU - MEDIA COMPOSER ONLY

The Xpress doesn't have an Output menu, but it has all the same capabilities.

Digital Cut: The Avid can be connected to sophisticated analog and digital video tape recorders (VTR) for recording the final, completed sequence onto tape. When you use the Digital Cut Tool, the Avid controls the VTR and records your digital cut to tape, using timecode.

Cut List: When you do a film project on an Avid, the film negative is transferred to videotape and then digitized for editing on the Avid. You cut the sequence, and then you get a cut list so that a negative cutter can use the Avid's sequence, with all its timecode decisions, to cut the original film to match the Avid sequence. Not all Media Composers have this command; only those models with the 24-frame option or the matchback option have it. (Xpress models with matchback option have this command as well.)

Change List: A change list is a list that shows all the changes made to a sequence since the last cut list was generated.

EDL: This opens a tool that organizes the generation of an Edit Decision List. Many projects that originated on high-end videotape are not "finished" on an Avid. The Avid is instead used to make all the editing decisions. Then the final master copy of the project is made by taking the original videotapes to an online video-editing suite and making a finished tape using the EDL the Avid generates.
    You can create an EDL on the Xpress by finding the application software called the EDL Manager that resides in an Avid folder on the internal drive. It's actually easy to access, but it's not as simple as selecting the EDL from the Output menu.

Figure 5.11   Media Composer Special Menu

SPECIAL MENU - MEDIA COMPOSER ONLY

The Xpress doesn't have a Special menu, and many of the items found here aren't found on any of the other Xpress menus, which has mostly been the case up to this point. Many of these commands are, well, special. And I guess if you apply the logic at work here, then if the Xpress had them, they wouldn't be special.

The Xpress is an incredibly powerful machine, especially given how much less it costs when compared to a Media Composer. That being the case, Avid has to make sure the Xpress doesn't have all the bells and whistles that are included on the Media Composer, because if it did . . . . You get the picture.

Site Settings: The Avid can be set up in a variety of ways, depending on user preferences and the project demands. Most of the choices are made in the Settings window, where items are listed as user or site settings. This opens the Site Settings window.

Bin/Composer Settings: This command opens up the Settings window for whichever window is active.

Restore to Default: This command restores whatever setting you have selected to the default settings. Open the Settings window. Click a setting to highlight it, and choose this command.

Audio Mixdown: Depending on the model, most Media Composers can monitor 24 audio tracks. But there may be instances when you want to combine or "mix down" two or more audio tracks.

Video Mixdown: Certain projects demand sophisticated graphics involving many video tracks. It's often helpful to combine several tracks into one track, using this command.

Read Audio Timecode: The Avid can read the longitudinal timecode recorded on any audio track and display that information in the bin. Select the clips and then choose this command. A dialog box opens, giving you choices as to how this will be accomplished.

Restore Default Patch: In the Timeline, patching involves routing source audio to the record track of your choice, rather than to the default track. For instance, you might want music that is coming in on source track A1, to go onto record track A5. To do this, you patch the tracks. This menu command ignores your patching and restores the default patching setup.

Sync Point Editing: This command activates a special type of overwrite editing based on sync points. You can line up a point in the source material (one sync point) and have it overwrite at an exact point in the sequence (the second sync point). This is often used when editing rock videos.

Show Phantom Marks: We spent a lot of time going over the rule that says, "It takes three marks to make an edit." In fact, whenever an edit is made, there are really four marks, IN and OUT on the source and IN and OUT on the record. You don't set the fourth mark—it's just there. The fourth mark is called a Phantom Mark and when you choose this command, the MC will display all four marks in the source or record window.

Render On-the-Fly: This turns on or off Render On-the-Fly. Much of the time you will be editing your sequence with effects that have not been rendered (created by the computer). Since they haven't been created, you won't see them when you play the sequence. However, with this selected, you can see the effect by dragging the position indicator through the Timeline. With this turned off, you don't see the effect when you drag through it.

MultiCamera Mode: When clips have been grouped together and created into a grouped clip, they can be cut by switching between the different camera angles or shots. This is called MultiCamera editing. There are three displays available when using MultiCamera editing. This command calls up one of the choices.

VTR Emulation: If you have the right cable, you can have an external video-tape editing system play your sequence. An external edit controller takes control of the Avid, and plays the sequence as if it were just another source video in a videotape deck. That way you could have multiple source tapes, including the Avid sequence, edited together onto a master video tape.

TOOLS MENU - XPRESS AND MEDIA COMPOSER

The Xpress and Media Composer share many of the same tools, and so the Tool menus for each are quite similar. I have placed the two menus side by side (Figure 5.12 and Figure 5.13) for purposes of comparison. As we go through each command, I'll state whether it is found on both, or on one or the other.

New Deck Controller: (MC ONLY) This command opens up a tool for controlling a videotape deck. You can screen footage from your source tapes without having to open the digitize tool.

Audio Mix: This is an important tool. When it opens, you see what looks like a mixing board, with all your tracks lined up with volume and pan sliders. You can adjust volume and pan by dragging the sliders. The change happens not to the entire track but to audio clips in the Timeline.

Audio EQ: This opens a tool that enables you to adjust the equalization of individual audio clips in the Timeline. By changing the low, middle, and high frequencies, you can alter or improve your sound.

Automation Gain: This tool looks a lot like the Audio Mix tool, but it allows you to actually mix your tracks on the fly. As you play the sequence, you can change volume levels, and the ramps you create as you raise and lower the volume sliders are marked by key frames. When you look at the Timeline you'll see a visual representation of your level changes.

AudioSuite: This command opens a tool that gives you access to audio processing plug-ins, such as pitch processing and reversing of audio.

Audio Tool: This command brings up a tool that is like a digital VU meter. It measures the strength of the incoming or outgoing audio signal(s). For instance,

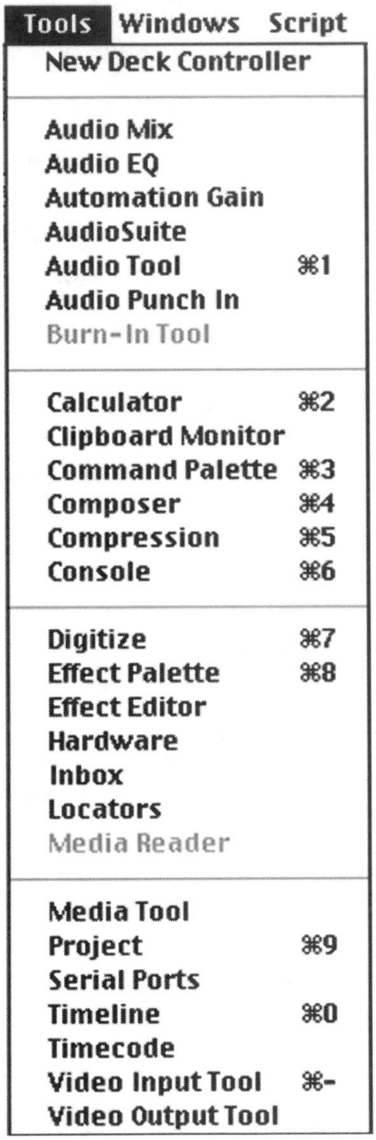

Tools	Windows	Script
New Deck Controller		
Audio Mix		
Audio EQ		
Automation Gain		
AudioSuite		
Audio Tool		⌘1
Audio Punch In		
Burn-In Tool		
Calculator		⌘2
Clipboard Monitor		
Command Palette		⌘3
Composer		⌘4
Compression		⌘5
Console		⌘6
Digitize		⌘7
Effect Palette		⌘8
Effect Editor		
Hardware		
Inbox		
Locators		
Media Reader		
Media Tool		
Project		⌘9
Serial Ports		
Timeline		⌘0
Timecode		
Video Input Tool		⌘–
Video Output Tool		

Tools	Windows	Script	Send
Audio Mix			
Audio EQ			
Automation Gain			
AudioSuite			
Audio Tool		Ctrl+1	
Audio Punch In			
Calculator		Ctrl+2	
Clipboard Monitor			
Composer		Ctrl+4	
Console		Ctrl+6	
Configuration			
FilmScribe			
Digitize		Ctrl+7	
Effect Editor			
Effect Palette		Ctrl+8	
Hardware			
Media Tool			
Project		Ctrl+9	
Serial (COM) Ports			
Timecode Window			
Timeline		Ctrl+0	
Title Tool			
Video Input Tool		Ctrl+-	
Video Output Tool			

Figure 5.12   Media Composer Tools Menu 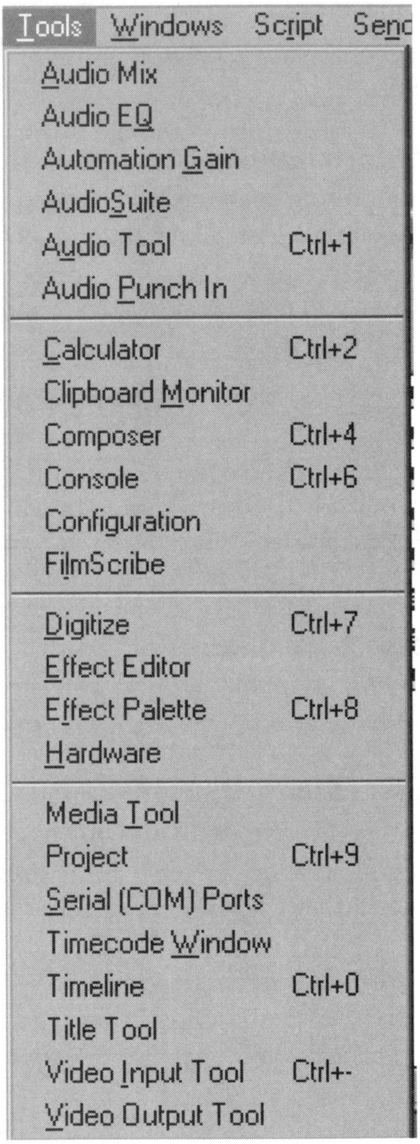   **Figure 5.13**   Xpress Tools Menu

when you digitize a tape with an audio signal, you get this tool so you can check to make sure the levels are correct.

Audio Punch In: (MC and Xpress 3.0) This command opens a tool that allows you to record audio directly in the Timeline. Used primarily to quickly add voice-over narration.

Burn-in Tool: (MC ONLY) If you have a Media Reader attached to your Avid, you can "burn in" the tape's timecode.

Calculator: This opens up a special calculator that helps you figure out different film and video durations. For instance, you could enter a duration in timecode numbers and then calculate the number of feet and frames it would equal in the 35 mm film format.

Clipboard Monitor: A number of actions, such as Lift, Extract, and Paste, as well as clicking the Clipboard button, will send whatever has been marked in the Timeline to the Clipboard Monitor for temporary storage. This command opens the Clipboard Monitor, which acts just like a Pop-up Monitor. You can then Splice or Overwrite any or all of the Clipboard's contents into the Timeline.

Command Palette: (MC ONLY) The Media Composer puts all its command buttons on a palette; there are over a hundred to choose from. You can map any of them to the keyboard and create a custom keyboard, and you can map them to the Source and Record row of command buttons. The palette looks like a file cabinet with tabs for categories of commands: Move, Play, Edit, Trim, FX, 3D, Mcam, Other, More. Click on the tab for the category you want, and you'll see all the command buttons. This is not available in the Xpress because you can't customize the commands. You only have the ones Avid gives you, and they stay where they are.

Composer: This activates the Composer Monitor window.

Console: This opens the Console window which gives you detailed information about your system, including your ID number and model. It provides information about bin objects and the sequence in the Timeline. It also provides a log of error messages, which you might read to an Avid technician who is trying to help you solve a problem over the phone.

Configuration: (XPRESS ONLY) This opens up the system's Configuration Check Report window. If you need to call Avid Support for help, you may be asked to open this.

FilmScribe/Cut List: When you do a film project on an Avid, the original camera negative (the film) is transferred to videotape and then digitized for editing on the Avid. You edit the sequence, and then you get a cut list so that a negative cutter can use the Avid's sequence, with all its timecode decisions, to cut the original camera negative (film) to match the Avid sequence.

Digitize: This opens up a tool used to control the digitizing process. When opened, it looks a lot like the working face of a video deck, with buttons for playing, fast-forwarding, and rewinding tapes. We'll devote a lot of time to this tool in the chapter on digitizing.

Effect Palette: This tool opens up a palette from which you can select all the various visual effects available to you.

Effect Editor: This tool opens the Effect Editor, which you use to adjust an effect's parameters. We'll examine it in detail in the chapter on effects.

Hardware: This tool gives you information about the computer hardware that makes up your Avid. This tool also shows you how much space is available on your various disk drives. Open it and you'll see all your drives, with a bar graph next to each one that shows the amount of the drive that is filled and the amount that is currently available.

Inbox: (MC ONLY) This works with AvidNet, which permits different Avids to be networked together so they can share media with other Avids on the network.

Locators: (MC ONLY) Locators are like little colored labels that you can place on any track in the Timeline. They help you flag important points. You can even write yourself notes. This tool opens a window that shows you where all the locators are on your sequence.

Media Reader: (MC ONLY) This is a separate standalone device that reads and encodes several lines of LTC and VITC timecode while you digitize. It places the timecode information in the bin. Most Avids don't come with this device. You purchase it as an option.

Media Tool: This is a tool that looks a lot like a bin in Text View. It lists all the project's media files.

Project: This command makes the Project window the active window.

Serial Ports: This command opens a tool through which you can designate the use of the CPU's serial ports (the modem port and printer port). You could use the tool to assign an Avid Media Reader to a printer port, while a video tape deck is assigned to the modem port.

Timeline: If you inadvertently close the Timeline, or find you don't have a Timeline, select this command and a Timeline will appear.

Timecode: This opens a window that can display up to eight lines of time-code information. If you click on the window, a pop-up menu appears, giving you options, such as IN to OUT, sequence duration, remaining time. These choices also exist in the timecode displays on the Monitors, but this gives you a window that you can resize, allowing a much easier-to-read display.

Video Input Tool: When you are digitizing video, you open this tool to mon-itor and change the incoming video signal. We'll discuss this tool at length in the chapter on digitizing.

Video Output Tool: This opens a tool for measuring and calibrating the video output signal. This is important whenever you are recording your sequence onto videotape.

SCRIPT MENU

This feature is found on Media Composers and Xpress models that have what Avid calls "script integration." Script integration is based on the style of editing commonly used on feature films. During production, information about the way each scene was shot, or covered with different camera angles and different takes, is written onto the script by the script supervisor. For instance, a scene like "Wanna Trade" might be shot first with a master shot, showing both actors, and then shot again with a closeup of one actor, and then a third time with a closeup of the other actor. Each of those three shots might be repeated several times, as Take 1, Take 2, and so on. The script supervisor draws lines through the script indicating the amount of the scene each camera angle and each take covered. At the end of production, the editor receives a copy of this "lined script." With the lined script in hand, the editor knows what footage is available for each and every line of action and dialog.

An Avid with script integration follows this lined script system, but adds its own powerful digital editing tools to it. You import the screenplay or shooting script right into the Avid. You then select the portion of the script that is covered by a particular clip (Scene 2A Take 1), and then drag the clip to that highlighted section of the script. Once all the clips are linked to the right sections of the script, you can click on a line of dialog and have the different takes play automatically so you can compare them. Once you're ready to start editing a scene, you can quickly go through the script, double-click on the preferred takes, and create a rough cut in a matter of minutes. This is a rich and powerful feature that would take more space to describe and explain than is available here.

HELP MENU

The Avid offers an online reference tool, in the form of a directory listing hundreds of items. If you're stuck and can't figure out how to do something, scroll though the entries until you find Avid's explanation.

MONITOR AND TRACKING MENUS

Above the Source/Pop-up Monitor and Record Monitor, there is a bar that displays information about your project. It also contains pull-down menus. Try selecting and dragging the different menus to see what information they display and the options you have for displaying the information.

Tracking Menu

The Tracking Menu provides information, in timecode format, about your clip or sequence. It is updated continuously as you play either the source material or the sequence. When you drag and select one of the choices on the menu, that choice will be displayed in the tracking information display. In Figure 5.14, the I/O has been selected, and the check mark confirms the choice. Let's look at all the choices.

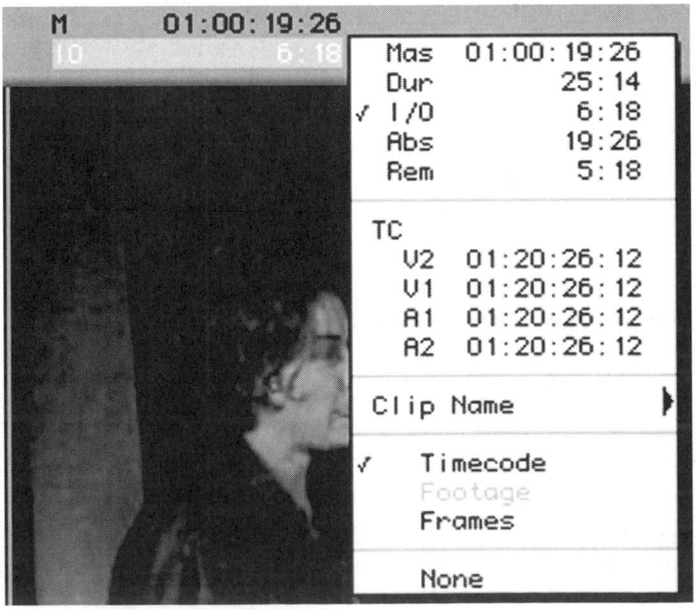

Figure 5.14   Tracking Menu on Media Composer

Mas - This displays what is called the master timecode at the point where the position indicator is currently located. Usually a sequence's starting timecode is set at one hour, so the very first frame would read: 01:00:00:00. As you can see in Figure 5.14, we are stopped at 1 hour, 0 minutes, 19 seconds and 26 frames. The Media Composers that are designed to cut film can display film footage and film frames instead of timecode.

Dur - This displays the total duration of the clip or sequence.

I/O - This displays the duration between your IN and OUT marks. Very handy.

Abs - This number displays the running time of the sequence, from the first frame to the position indicator. Notice that it is identical to Mas, but with the 1 hour subtracted.

Rem - This displays the time remaining from the position indicator to the end of the sequence.

TC - These are the timecode numbers for the various tracks in the Timeline at the point where the position indicator is located.

Clip Name - This provides a submenu of the clip names for each track in the Timeline at the point where the position indicator is located.

None - With this chosen, no tracking information will be displayed.

Monitor Menu

On the MC, both the Source and Record Monitors have a Monitor menu. Just click on the name of the clip in the Source Monitor, or the name of the sequence in the Record Monitor to open the Monitor menu. On the Xpress, only the Composer Monitor has this menu, and not all of the choices listed below are included.

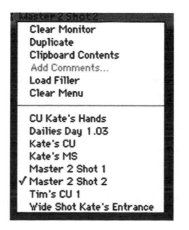

Figure 5.15   Media Composer's Monitor Menu—on the Source Monitor

Clear Monitor - This clears the clips or sequences from the monitor. The monitor screen goes black, and the Timeline is empty. However all the clips or sequences are still loaded.

Duplicate - This duplicates the clip or marked segment.

Clipboard Contents - (MC ONLY) When you save something to the Clipboard, it appears as a Pop-up Monitor when you select Clipboard from the Tools menu. The Media Composer also places it here. It is available as a source clip.

Load Filler - (MC ONLY) This loads filler into the Source Monitor. On the Xpress, this feature is located on the Clip menu.

Clear Menu - This deletes all but the current sequence or clip from the Monitor menu.

Clip/Sequence List - Below the Clear menu is a list of all the shots in the Source Monitor, or all the sequences loaded into the Record Monitor.

Whew! We have spent considerable time and energy trying to digest the scores of commands located in the pull-down menus that are at the heart of Avid editing. We now have a much better sense of the Avid's rich working environment, and we've had a preview of the work we'll be doing from here on in. We also know where we can find the commands we'll need to do different sorts of tasks. You may never use some of these commands, while others will be in your repertory continually. Whenever there are keyboard equivalents listed in the menu, try learning them, since they will speed up your work considerably.

MAPPING MENU ITEMS ON THE MEDIA COMPOSER

Media Composer users can place any command located in a pull-down menu onto any key on the keyboard or onto any of the command palettes.

1. Open the Keyboard in the Settings window, or open the monitor or fast menu of your choice.
2. Select the Menu to Button Reassignment box on the Command Palette (get it from the Tools menu).
3. Click on a target button on the fast menu, monitor button bar, or keyboard. The button or key will turn white.
4. Choose the menu command from the pull-down menu that you'd like to map to that button or key.
5. The initials of the menu command will appear on the key or button.

I think it best that you don't map any menu commands until you've finished reading the entire book. Having the standard keyboard and palettes will make instruction a lot easier.

SUGGESTED ASSIGNMENTS

1. Hold a screening of your edited scene, taking notes of the various suggestions.
2. Duplicate the sequence.
3. Make changes to the new version of the sequence.
4. Compare your old version to the one that is based on the feedback you received.

6

Digitizing

Now that we've finished cutting "Wanna Trade," it's time to move on to new material. It is my suggestion that you now work on documentary footage, or a public service announcement (PSA). Avid used to supply footage for a PSA about saving the rain forest, and if that's available, this is a good time to work with it. If it's not available, any documentary footage with voice-over narration and music will work. Many of the techniques we will introduce in the next few chapters work nicely with visual footage and narration. A script-based, dramatic scene with sync dialog, like "Wanna Trade," is great for introducing you to the Avid basics, but as we move on to more complex tools, documentary material is best for showing off these features.

GETTING YOUR PROJECT INTO THE COMPUTER

In the beginning of this book, we were working under the assumption that someone (your instructor or you) loaded material into the Avid system for you to edit. We delayed the whole subject of digitizing because we wanted you to dive right into editing. Now, we need to go back to the beginning and look at what is usually the first step in the Avid editing process.

In order to take advantage of all the Avid's digital editing capabilities, you must first get your material into the Avid. You must digitize the sounds and pictures on your source tapes so they are stored inside the computer, not as analog signals, but as a series of 1's and 0's. Once your material is digitized, your computer can recognize it, and the Avid software can manipulate it. How this digitizing process is accomplished depends on two factors: the tape format you've used and your Avid's video capture board.

TAPE FORMATS - DIGITIAL AND ANALOG

The videotape world can be divided in two parts: digital videotape and analog videotape. There are several professional digital videotape formats. I won't list them all, just several of the more popular ones:

> Digital Betacam
> D-1
> D-2
> D-5
> Digital-S

There are also a number of low-cost, "prosumer" digital formats, which are becoming increasingly popular in the documentary world because their image quality rivals that of professional analog tape, while the cameras that use them cost less than $10,000. In the case of the Digital Video (DV) format, excellent cameras cost less than $5000. Three popular DV formats are:

> DV
> DVCAM
> DVCPRO

In the analog world, Betacam SP has long been an industry standard for professional video. During the 1990s and much of the 1980s, the vast majority of television news and documentaries were shot on Beta SP.

There are two popular "consumer" analog formats: Hi-8 and S-VHS. Before the advent of the DV format, many independent documentaries were shot on these formats because, although the picture quality had limitations, they could meet broadcast television standards if enough money was spent to cover up their limitations.

VIDEO CAPTURE BOARDS

The kind of *video capture board* inside your Avid determines whether you can digitize analog tapes, digital tapes, or both. There are currently three kinds of Avid video capture boards. The older type, called *NuVista+ video board*, no longer ships inside Avids, but there are a number of them still in use. The *Avid Broadcast Video Board*™ (ABVB), was the most popular board through 1999. It is now being supplanted by the *Meridien board*™. The NuVista+ can only digitize analog tapes. The ABVB can digitize either an analog tape or a digital tape. What makes the Meridien board so special is that it can easily digitize analog *and* digital signals.

An Avid with the standard ABVB board is capable of digitizing analog tapes, such as Betacam SP. It can digitize digital tapes, but only after they are first converted to an analog signal. However, if you purchase a special serial digital ABVB (often called SDI), you can bring the digital signal directly into the Avid, without having to first convert it to an analog signal. Avoiding the digital-to-analog conversion means higher-quality images. Unfortunately, you can't use the serial digital ABVB to bring in an analog tape without buying a special converter. You get one or the other, but not both.

One clear advantage of the Meridien system is that it allows you to digitize from any analog tape or any digital tape without any conversion.

CONNECTING YOUR EQUIPMENT

In order to digitize the picture and sound, you need to run cables from your tape deck to your Avid video and audio capture boards. Most likely the cables have been connected for you and all you need to do is turn on the power to the deck, boot the Avid, and insert your tape. But let's take a minute to examine the cables going from your deck to your computer's CPU.

Let's say you have a standard analog videotape deck, such as a Beta SP deck or VHS deck. Let's start with the audio. On the back of the tape deck there are connections for Input and for Output. Since we are sending the signal from the tape deck to the Avid, you would connect the audio cables to the deck's Output. These audio cables could either go into a mixing board, and from there to the Avid's audio card for digitizing, or directly to the Avid's audio card.

The video signal from the tape deck could come in one of two forms. The video signal's luminance (brightness) and chrominance (color) could be combined as one signal, called a *composite* signal. Or the video signal could be split, so that one channel holds the luminance (Y), and chrominance is separated into red (R-Y) and blue (B-Y) signals. This system is called *component*. Component video is a professional signal, whereas composite video is associated with consumer products such as Hi-8, S-VHS, and VHS. If you were using a Betacam SP deck, you would take the cable marked Video In (because the video signal is going "in" to the Avid's video capture board) and plug its three BNC connectors into the tape deck's three Video Output connectors.

If you have a Meridien board, there is an external I/O box which makes the connections much easier. On the back of the box there are connections for component and composite, as well as for S-video and serial digital video.

Now there is one other important cable that needs to be connected; it's called the Serial Deck Control cable, often called the serial control. This cable enables the Avid to control the video deck. When this is connected, you can play, fast-forward, rewind, even eject tapes using the Digitize Tool on the Avid. You connect this cable to the videotape deck's 9-pin D connector, usually labeled

Remote or Remote In/Out. The other end is usually connected to the CPU's modem (8-pin DIN) connector.

Now your deck and the Avid are connected.

IMAGE RESOLUTION

Before you begin the digitizing process, you need to decide whether you are going to bring the video signal in at the highest resolution (most beautiful image quality) or at some resolution that sacrifices image quality. One key factor in making this decision is storage space on the hard drives. If you have a lot of source material—hours and hours of tapes—and you want to have all of the footage available to you, then you will be willing to sacrifice image quality. Usually you do this knowing that after you finish editing, you can redigitize the finished sequence at the highest image quality.

If you have a lot of storage space on the hard drives, and only several minutes of material, then you may decide to digitize the material at the highest resolution. Perhaps you are under a tight deadline, and there isn't enough time to digitize at a low resolution and then, after editing, redigitize at a higher resolution. Or perhaps you have a client who can't stand to look at his or her footage at low resolution.

When the Avid digitizes video, it usually *compresses* the signal. Compressing your video is a bit like packing a suitcase; you can't get it all to fit, so you start tossing things out. If you have a big suitcase (hard drive) you don't have to toss much out. But if you have a small suitcase, those wild paisley shirts might not make the trip. When you compress a video signal, you keep a certain percentage of the signal and throw away the rest. Obviously the more signal you throw away, the worse the image looks, but the greater the savings in storage space. Since each frame of video is made up of two fields, one way to save storage space is to digitize only one field. Avid offers single-field resolution (one of the two video fields is tossed out) and two-field resolution (both fields are digitized).

Avid describes image resolution in two different ways, depending on the

Figure 6.1   Resolution choices offered on an Avid with a Meridien board

sort of capture board you have. The Meridien board describes resolution as a ratio. A ratio of 1:1 is a full, noncompressed video. A ratio of 20:1 indicates a lot of compression. Choosing a ratio of 15:1s would mean you could store the most footage possible on the drives because not only is there a lot of compression, but one of the two video fields is missing.

With the ABVB board, Avid describes resolution in terms of AVR (Avid Video Resolution). AVR 2s (single field) is the lowest resolution, and AVR 77 (two fields) is the highest resolution.

Let's look at the chart below to see how resolution affects storage space on the hard drive. Let's assume we're working on an Avid with 18 gigabytes of storage. The numbers in the table come from an Avid spec sheet for the ABVB board system. A range is provided because so much depends on the complexity of the images on your video. A static head shot uses up less space than a panning wide shot of a crowded street.

Range of Minutes per Gigabyte at

AVR 2s	AVR 3s	AVR 12	AVR 70	AVR 75	AVR 77
21–28 min.	19–25 min.	13–19 min.	5–9 min.	3–6 min.	2–5-min.

If you digitized your material at AVR 2s, and you had an 18-GB storage system, you could digitize between 378 and 504 minutes of material. That's between 6 and 8 hours! However, if you brought your footage in at AVR 77, you could only digitize between 36 and 90 minutes of material. Obviously, you must decide at which resolution you will digitize your videotapes.

AUDIO SAMPLING

When analog audio is digitized, the signal is sampled and then converted to digital information. *Sampling* means that not all the sound is converted, but a representative sample of it is. The more samples that are taken, the better the fidelity, or faithfulness to the original analog signal. Most Avids give you a choice as to which sampling rate you would like to use. The choices are 44.1 kHz or 48 kHz. Compact discs use 44.1 as their sample rate, so you can see that 48 kHz is high quality indeed. Older Avids only offer 44.1 kHz, but I think only a few people in the world can hear the difference. In the Settings window, you can select the sample rate for your project. I suggest you use 44.1 kHz for now, since it's easier to import CDs into the Avid if your project is already at 44.1. To set the sample rate, double-click on Audio in the Settings window.

Sound takes up a fraction of the storage space needed by video—really it's almost insignificant—so you don't have to worry about running out of hard drive space whenever you digitize sound.

GETTING ORGANIZED

After you have gathered together your source tapes and decided upon an appropriate resolution, you should come up with a system for naming the tapes. In a way, you might want to consider your system of naming tapes even before you start shooting, so the name you give the tape in the field is the same name you give it when digitizing. One of the worst mistakes you can make when digitizing is to give two tapes the same name.

Your naming system need not be complicated. My suggestion is that whenever you begin a new project you simply call the first tape 001. The second tape is 002. Because the Avid knows which project you are working on, you don't have to include the project name with the tape. So you need not type Wanna Trade Tape 001. Just 001. Keep it simple.

Starting a New Project

Now you're ready to begin at the beginning. If you're about to digitize your material, that probably means you're about to start a *new* project. You are no longer working on the project "Wanna Trade," and you don't want to confuse things by digitizing material into that project. Get to the desktop, and click on the Media Composer or Xpress icon. The New Project window will come up, and now you click the New Project button. Type a name and click OK. Now, whenever you want to go into this project, select it from the list of projects.

Organizing Your Bins

Before you begin the actual digitizing process, you must decide into which bin your newly digitized material will go. On film projects, many editors prefer to organize their bins according to what was shot on a given day. All the tapes from the first day of shooting would go into a bin called Dailies - Day 1. On a video project, it might make sense to have a bin for each tape. So tape 001 goes into a bin called Tape 001. Begin by creating a bin into which clips from the first tape will go. Just click the New Bin button at the top of the Project window and a new bin will be created (or select New Bin from the Bin menu). Click on the name the Avid gave it (the name you gave the project) and type 001 or Dailies - Day 1.

Remember, before you open the Digitize Tool, open the bin you want the material to go to and close any other bins that may be open. Make sure the deck you are using is set to *remote* and not local. Remote gives control of the deck to the Avid.

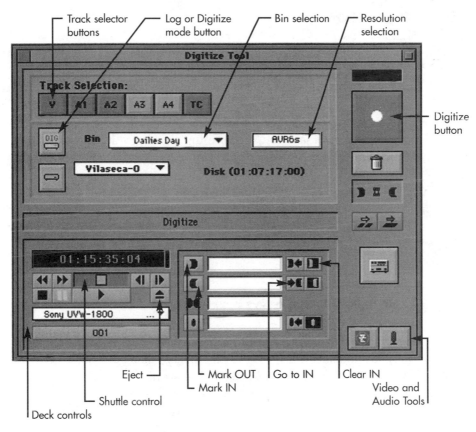

Figure 6.2   Digitize Tool

OPENING THE DIGITIZE TOOL

Now open the Digitize Tool, either by selecting it from the Tools menu or pressing the keys Command+7. The Media Composer's Digitize Tool has more audio track buttons, and a couple of special features not found on the Xpress, but the ones we'll examine now are found on both the Xpress and MC.

Examine the tool's user interface. Parts of it look exactly like a video deck. Other parts are logical renditions of the actions they perform.

The buttons on the deck control are self-explanatory. You have buttons for fast rewind, fast forward, stop, pause, play, step one frame backwards, and step one frame forwards, and a slider that acts like a shuttle control. There's even an eject button.

LOG OR DIGITIZE

The Digitize Tool has two modes of operation, one for logging the shots and one for digitizing them. When you *log* your tape, you are choosing the shots you want to digitize, Marking IN and OUT points, but not digitizing them. Many editors log each tape first and then digitizing those clips they selected. Why? Basically it's better to divide your tasks. Concentrate first on selecting the shots to be digitized, and then later on, performing the digitizing task. In some cases you may find it's better not to log, but to digitize each shot on the tape as you come to it. For instance, you may find that the field audio is uneven and one level won't work for the entire tape. In that case you may need to change your audio levels as you digitize each clip, one at a time.

Lets go through the options on the Digitize Tool and set it up to digitize material coming from a Beta SP tape, containing pictures and two tracks of audio.

CONFIGURING THE DIGITIZE TOOL

1. Select the tracks. As you can see in Figure 6.2, the video track is selected (V), and the audio tracks A1 and A2 have also been selected. Make sure the TC (timecode) track is selected as well.
2. Select the target bin. If there are several bins open, the Avid might select the wrong bin. Go to the Bin menu, drag the pointer, and select the bin you want.
3. Select the AVR or ratio. In this case we have chosen AVR6s, because there is a lot of material to digitize and we want to be able to fit it all onto the hard drives. Drag on the menu, and you'll see the other choices. If you have a lot of tapes, you might consider AVR3s.
4. Select a target drive. Your instructor may have assigned you a drive. If not, you'll want to use the drive that has the most space. Go to the drive menu (Figure 6.3) and drag down to select the assigned drive or the drive with the most space. That drive is always the darkest drive.

Figure 6.3   Drive Window

Figure 6.4 Digitize Mode

5. Select Log Mode or Digitize Mode. Press the Log/Digitize selector button to switch from Digitize Mode to the Log Mode, and vice versa. When you press the button the tool will switch to Log Mode. Notice that the pencil icon shows that you are in Log Mode.

6. Select the type of video signal. Click on the Video Tool button.

You'll see a window called Input. It's a pull-down menu that lists the types of video signals your system can import. A Meridien system would list Component, Composite, S-video and Serial Digital (see the figure below). Whatever your system, you want to choose the correct one for the signal you are going to digitize.

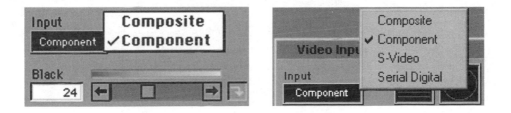

The Beta SP tape we are going to insert is component video, so we'll select Component from the Input window. If Component is selected, you can leave the window as it is. But if Composite is selected, you need to select Component. (If you are using a VHS tape, the signal would be Composite.) Once you have selected Component, you may close the Video Tool window by clicking in the tiny Close box.

What's the mistake most new Avid editors make when digitizing? They forget to check this setting. If you aren't getting anywhere, make sure you've picked the right signal for the kind of tape you're digitizing.

7. Insert your first tape. A prompt will appear, asking you either to select the tape's name, if a name has already been entered, or to give the tape a new name. Since we haven't named any tapes, you will click on the New button and then type the name 001. Once you have typed the name, click OK. (After typing, you have to click on the tape's icon to highlight the tape before you can click OK.)

Now, you should have control of the tape through the deck controls on the Digitize Tool. Hit the play button on the Digitize Tool, and the tape plays. Hit the rewind button and it rewinds. Notice how the tape's timecode appears in the Timecode window, just above the deck controls.

Figure 6.5

SETTING VIDEO AND AUDIO LEVELS

When you digitize video or audio, you want to bring in the signal at its optimum level. You don't want to digitize the audio at a level that is too low, so it's barely audible, or too high, so it overmodulates and breaks up. And you don't want to bring in the video signal so the picture is too dark or the colors look terrible. To help you bring in the signals at the right levels, the Avid provides you with two tools: the Video Tool and the Audio Tool. You can get these tools from the Tools menu, but they are also on the Digitize Tool deck. Since the Audio Tool is easiest to use, let's start with it. Mac users, simply press the microphone icon at the bottom of the Digitize Tool, and the Audio Tool appears. Windows NT users, press the speaker icon at the top of the tool.

Audio Tool - NT

The tracks should be set to I for input as shown in Figure 6.6. If they are set to O for output, just click on the Input/Output toggle, and they will change to I.

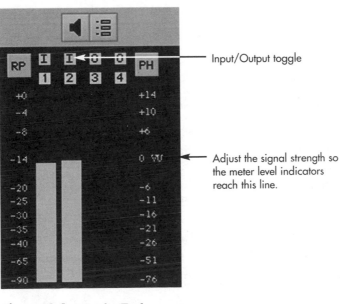

Input/Output toggle

Adjust the signal strength so the meter level indicators reach this line.

Figure 6.6   Audio Tool

Audio Levels

Play your tape. If the tape has *color bars* and a *tone* (1000 hertz) at the head of the tape, you should use that tone to set your levels. If there is no tone, play the tape until you come to a sound that best represents what was recorded in the field, and use that as a reference.

Setting audio levels on the Avid is similar to setting levels on a tape recorder. The Avid has a Peak Level Meter which uses green bars instead of a needle to show signal strength, and includes both a digital scale (left) and an analog VU scale, measuring in decibels. As the tape plays, watch the levels. If you have a 1000-hertz tone, the top of the green bars should just touch the –14 and 0 VU meter line. If you don't have a tone and are using the sound recorded in the field, have the loudest section of the audio just touch the –14 and 0 VU meter line. I would bring normal conversation, dialog, or narration in at around –22 on the digital scale. That way, louder sounds have room to go to –14.

Your tape deck may be connected to a mixing board, and that's how you adjust the levels. Or you may have some sort of sound panel with knobs to adjust your levels. Depending on your system, you now raise or lower the strength of the signal so that the audio will be digitized at the correct levels.

Don't worry if some loud sounds go a bit over the –14 (0 VU) line, or if quieter sounds barely register. The Avid can faithfully capture a wide range of audio levels. If you are going to make a mistake, err on the side of lower levels rather than higher levels, because you can boost low levels, but overmodulated sounds in the digital realm can sound simply awful.

Once you have set your audio levels, you can move the Audio Tool to the side so that you have room for the Video Tool, or close it altogether.

Video Settings

Setting video levels is more complicated than setting audio levels. With video levels you are concerned about the *luminance*, or brightness, of the signal, and the *chrominance*, or color, of the signal. I'm not going to go into too much detail on this topic because it is beyond the scope of this book. Basically, if the picture looks good, then leave the settings as is. However, if the color is off, or the image appears too light or dark, you can change the levels by adjusting the sliders on the Video Tool.

Let's examine the Video Tool. Click on the Video Tool button at the bottom of the Digitize Tool, or select it from the Tools menu.

By clicking on the Waveform Monitor and the Vectorscope icons, you can bring up the Avid's version of these two important tools used to measure your signal. The Waveform Monitor measures the luminance, or brightness, of your signal, and the Vectorscope measures the chrominance, or the color, of your signal.

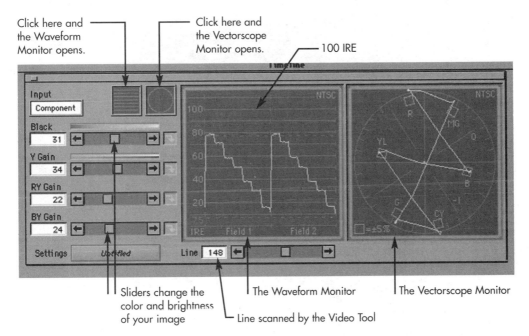

Click here and the Waveform Monitor opens.

Click here and the Vectorscope Monitor opens.

100 IRE

Sliders change the color and brightness of your image

The Waveform Monitor

The Vectorscope Monitor

Line scanned by the Video Tool

Figure 6.7   The Video Tool

The standard way to set proper video levels is to play your tape's color bars with the Video Tool open and then adjust the sliders until the Waveform Monitor and Vectorscope display the "correct" pattern of lines. As you move the sliders, you'll see the pattern of white lines move and change. There are different types of color bars, but the most common bars in the NTSC world are SMPTE Bars.

The setting of the Line number (the scan line on the color bars the Avid is reading), depends on whether you are using the color bars to check luminance or chroma. Line 148 is used to examine the chroma (color) signal. If the Video Tool is changed to scan Line 247 on the SMPTE Bars, it will examine the luminance, or brightness, of your signal. Reading at Line 247, the Waveform displays twin peaks reaching all the way to the 100 IRE line—or peak white (Figure 6.8).

We could fill chapters about the correct use of Vectorscopes and Waveform Monitors. For now, if your tape has bars, try moving the sliders while playing the color bars and observe the changes that take place. I wouldn't suggest this if the Avid didn't give you a nice feature. See the downward-pointing green arrows (Figure 6.9) next to the slider bars? As you move the sliders from the factory pre-set level, the arrow turns gray, showing that the preset levels have been changed. To return to the factory preset levels, simply click on the arrow and the Avid returns the slider to the factory preset level, indicated by the green color. You're back where you started.

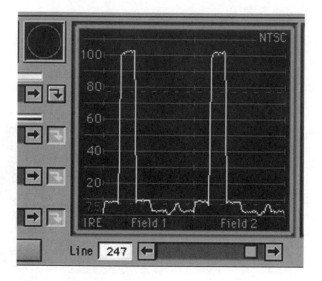

Figure 6.8

Figure 6.9

DIGITIZE TOOL ON WINDOWS NT

The Digitize Tool looks a bit different on the NT Avids (Figure 6.10), but if you take a moment to examine the features, you'll figure out where everything is located. One difference is the inverted arrows that reveal or hide sections of the tool. There's also a place where you can type the clip's name, even while the clip is being digitized. Since this is a Meridien machine, resolution is given in ratios, not AVRs.

THE DIGITIZING PROCESS - VIDEO OR AUDIO OR BOTH

There are three ways to capture your material. We'll examine all three.

Digitize button   Digitize/Log Mode   Video & Audio Tools

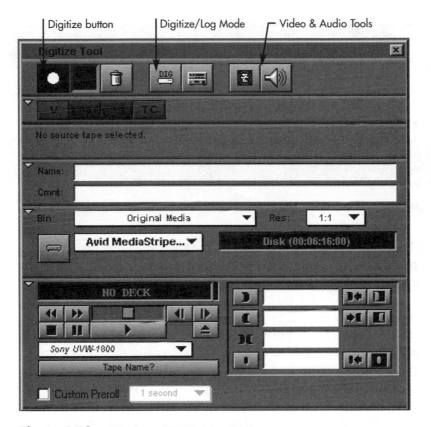

Figure 6.10   Windows NT Digitize Tool

Logging

In this method, you log the clips first and then digitize them after they have been logged. With this method, you first go through your tape and select the shots you want to digitize, marking IN and OUT points.

To get into Log Mode, click the Log/Digitize Mode button. You know you're in Log Mode when the pencil icon appears in place of the red Digitize button.

Play the tape using the deck controls. When you come to the first clip you want, go to the beginning and Mark an IN. Notice that the timecode of the exact spot you chose is displayed in the window next to the IN marker (Figure 6.11).

Now play the tape until you come to the end of the clip you want. Mark an OUT. The timecode for that spot is displayed, as well as the duration of the clip, listed in the IN to OUT window. Once you have your IN and OUT points, click on the large pencil button.

The Avid enters the clip into your bin. The Avid automatically gives it a name based on the name of the bin, and that name is highlighted. If, before you touch another button on the Digitize Tool, you type the name you want, the

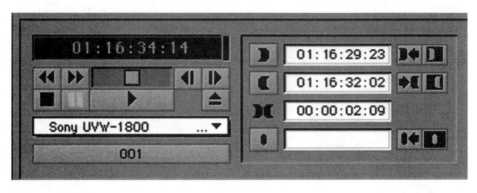

Figure 6.11

clip will be renamed to match your typing. Use names that best describe the shot. If the shot is of a man on a ladder, name the clip: Man on Ladder.

Repeat the steps above to log in all your shots.

Logging Tips

You can click on the Mark buttons while the tape is playing. In fact that's often how I do it. I might find the IN point by playing the tape and then locating the exact spot by hitting pause and shuttling slowly. When I see I'm at the head of the shot I want, I mark an IN. Then I hit play. As I approach the end of the shot, I keep clicking on the OUT button—many times. The OUT point will keep changing as the shot plays and I keep clicking. When I see I've gone past the shot, there's no need to rewind and mark an exact OUT, because my last click was close enough. Click on the Go to OUT button if you want to check. The Avid will shuttle the tape back to the spot you marked.

Batch Digitizing Your Logged Clips

Once you have logged all the clips on the tape, you're ready to *batch digitize*.

1. Select all the clips in the bin. Hit Command-A to select all the clips, or lasso the clips, or Shift-click all the clips, or go to the Edit menu and choose Select All.
2. If you're on an MC, go to the Clip menu and select Batch Digitize. If you're on an Xpress, go to the Bin menu and select Batch Digitize.

A dialog box will appear. Since you have no media, it doesn't matter whether or not you checkmark the box "Digitize only those items for which media is currently unavailable." But later on you'll want this box selected, so get in the habit of checking the box. Then click OK.

The Avid will rewind the tape to the first clip, find the IN point, roll back a few seconds for preroll, and then begin digitizing. It will stop when it reaches your OUT point. After digitizing the first clip, it will go to the IN of the second clip on the tape and digitize it. You can watch the bin and see the progress the Avid is making as it digitizes each clip.

Digitizing Each Clip As You Mark It

If you have to change audio levels or video levels because different sections of the tape need different correction, then this method will work best for you. With this method, you mark the clip and then digitize it before going to the next clip.

To get into the Digitize Mode, click the Log/Digitize Mode button. You'll know you're in Digitize Mode when the big, red Digitize button replaces the pencil icon.

Now:

1. Play the tape using the deck control, and Mark an IN.
2. Play the tape using the deck control, and Mark an OUT.
3. Hit the large Digitize Button, and it will flash red as it digitizes the clip.
4. Name the clip in the bin.
5. Repeat the steps above to digitize all shots.

You can abort the digitizing process while it is in progress by clicking on the Trash icon.

On some Avids, once the digitizing has started, you can actually type the clip's name without waiting for the digitizing to end. Just start typing. When the clip has been digitized, the name you typed will appear in the bin. Try it.

Digitizing "On-the-Fly"

When you use this method, you don't bother using the Mark IN or Mark OUT controls. You simply digitize various portions of the tape as you play it.

To get into the Digitize Mode, click the Log/Digitize Mode button. You'll know you're in Digitize Mode when the big, red Digitize button replaces the pencil icon.

1. Play the tape using the deck control, and hit the large Digitize button as you approach the material you want (the IN). The red button will flash to show you that it is digitizing material.
2. When you reach the end of the segment of the tape you want (the OUT), press the large Digitize button again, or hit the Esc (Escape) key.
3. Repeat the steps above to digitize all the material on the tape.

You can abort the digitizing process while it is in progress by hitting the Trash icon.

Often with this method, you'll end up digitizing longer clips than you might if you were marking your clips. You might have five shots included on one master clip. Remember, if this happens and you want to divide the long master clips, subclip them.

If you use this digitizing "on-the-fly" method with material that has timecode, the Avid will provide IN and OUT points determined by the point on the tape where you pressed the Digitize button to start or stop the digitize process.

DIGITIZING MATERIAL WITHOUT TIMECODE

Without timecode the Avid can't control the deck, and it obviously can't remember IN and OUT marks if no timecode exists. That doesn't mean the Avid can't digitize the tape, it just means that the material will not have timecode associated with it. For instance the Avid can't control a Nagra 4.2 tape recorder or a VHS or 8 mm deck, and it can't control cameras hooked directly to it. But you can bring that material into the Avid. The problem is that if the media file is lost or erased, there's no way to batch digitize the clip and retrieve it.

Let's say you shot footage on a Hi-8 camera. You can connect the camera to the Avid by connecting the Avid's yellow CV In cable (Composite Video) to the camera. If you need an adapter, such as a BNC connector on one end, and your camera's Video Out connector on the other, go to Radio Shack™ and they'll probably have it. While you're there, you may need to pick up audio connectors so you can send the camera's audio into your mixing board or Audio In. If you have an Avid with a Meridien video capture board, practically every type of connection is provided right on the Meridien I/O box.

Now, bring up the Digitize Tool. Because the Avid can't control the camera or deck, you need to configure the tool a bit differently.

Press the Deck Control button and you'll notice that a "you can't do that" line, like in *Ghostbusters*, appears across the picture of the deck. Once in this mode, the Digitize Tool changes appearance. Your deck controls disappear. To name the tape, press the Source Tape Name display, and the Tape Name dialog box appears.

Since you are not bringing in timecode, the TC track is missing from the Digitize Tool. But make sure the correct video and audio tracks are selected.

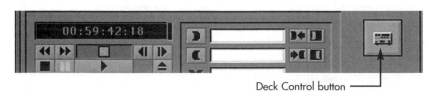

Deck Control button

Figure 6.12

Since the Avid can't redigitize this footage at a higher resolution after editing (because there's no timecode), you'll probably want to bring the footage in at a high resolution, such as AVR77 or 2:1 or 1:1.

If you're capturing a videotape, bring up the Video tool and switch to Composite Video.

Your only choice is to digitize "on the fly." You can't mark IN or OUT points. Instead, play the tape, using the camera's (or deck's) controls. When you reach a section you want, hit the Digitize button and begin the digitizing process. When you reach the end, hit the button again. Now, go in the bin and name the clip. Keep doing this until you've captured all the material you want.

Once the material is digitized, it behaves just like any other digitized material. In fact, the Avid will provide fake timecode as it digitizes the material. Don't be fooled. The numbers have no relation to your video or audio.

DECK SETTINGS

In Chapter 3 we discussed settings, and one of the settings choices is Deck settings. In the Project window, click the Settings button and then double-click on Deck. Here you can select options such as preroll and fast cue, which affect the way the deck works.

LOGGING WITHOUT AN AVID

You may work on a large project involving over 100 field tapes. If you do, you'll realize what a huge job it is to log all those tapes. You're tying up an expensive Avid machine for a time-consuming but uncreative task.

It's possible to actually log your footage using a videotape deck, a computer, and MediaLog software. You don't need an Avid to log the IN and OUT points or name the clips. A deck control cable runs from the computer's serial port to the videotape deck, giving you control of it. Once you've logged all the tapes and saved information to a floppy, you can copy the bins right into the Avid's Composer Projects file. Then, simply select and then batch digitize the clips in each bin.

If the Digitize Tool and the whole digitizing process seem complicated to you, you're not alone. It seemed daunting to me at first. Like anything, it gets easier with practice, so take every opportunity to get practice. There are a lot of jobs out there for assistant editors on Avids. One of the Avid assistant's primary responsibilities is digitizing.

SUGGESTED ASSIGNMENTS

1. Create a new project, create a new bin, and then open the Digitize tool.
2. Name your source tape.
3. Set the video levels using the Video tool and the audio levels using the Audio tool.
4. Digitize five clips from the tape by marking IN and OUT points and then digitizing. Name the clips in the bin.
5. Log five clips into the bin. Now, batch digitize the clips into the bin.
6. Digitize five clips on the fly. Name the clips in the bin.

7

Sound

THE IMPORTANCE OF SOUND

Many videomakers and filmmakers don't realize just how important sound is to the success of a project. "It's a visual medium," is the common wisdom handed down as gospel. Well, half-right is better than all wrong.

I've organized a number of film festivals, and served as a judge at others, and while I've often been amazed by the stunning cinematography on display in student projects, just as often I've been dismayed by the poor quality of the sound. I think what separates a student project from a professional project is the lack of care that students give to their sound tracks.

On most films and videos, the only sound you care about during shooting is the sync sound—the dialog or words spoken by the subject(s). A good sound recordist works really hard *not* to record the ambient sounds—the traffic, people in the background, footsteps, and so on. Yes, ambient sounds are vitally important, but you add them during editing.

If, for example, you record the hum of an air conditioner on your dialog track, it's very difficult to remove. However, if you turn the air conditioner off just before shooting, you have much clearer dialog. If the air conditioner's hum is important to the story, you can always tape the hum separately, and add it to your scene during editing. That way you can adjust the relative levels of the dialog and air conditioner.

Most sounds are added to films and videos after the picture and dialog have been edited. This stage is often called *picture lock*. Once picture lock is reached, sound editors begin finding and creating the sound effects that were kept out during shooting. Often sound editors must invent sounds. What does a dinosaur sound like? What sound does Darth Vadar's laser sword make? Sound designers and sound editors like Walter Murch (*The Conversation*, *Apocalypse*

135

Now), Cecelia Hall (*Witness*, *Top Gun*, *Wayne's World*), and Gary Rydstrom (*Terminator 2*, *Jurassic Park*) deserve as much credit for the success of the films they've worked on as the cinematographers who shot the films, because so much of the emotional impact comes from the sound track. Film is shot. Sound is built a layer at a time during editing.

Although the Avid is known for its ability to cut pictures, you'll soon realize that's only half the story. The Avid gives you tremendous control over your sound tracks. Take advantage of that capability. It'll make a huge difference in the success of your work.

TRACK MONITORS

The tiny speaker-shaped buttons next to the track selector boxes show you that a track is being monitored. These are called *track monitors*. If you click on a track monitor, it disappears, indicating that you won't hear any sound from that track. To turn the monitor on, simply click in the track monitor box, and the speaker reappears. Examine Figure 7.1.

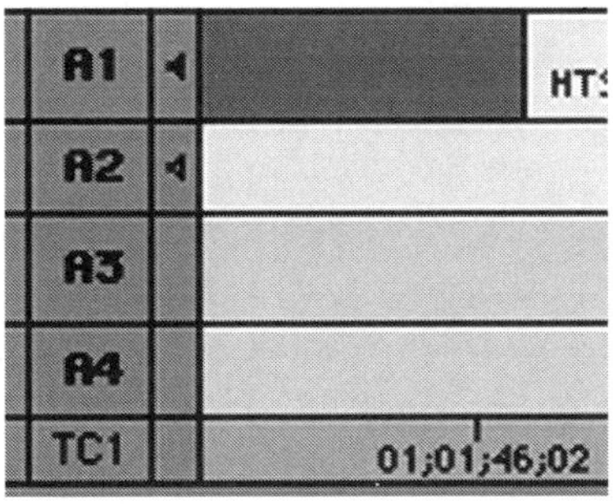

Figure 7.1   Track monitors for A1 and A2 are on, while A3 and A4 are turned off.

Monitoring Only One Track

Let's say you are monitoring eight tracks, and you hear a sound glitch, but you aren't sure which track it's on. You think the problem is on the narration track A1, but you aren't sure. One way to monitor just A1 is to deselect all the other record track monitors. However, if there are eight of them, that's a pain. There's a fast way of monitoring one track.

- Hold down the Command key and click on that track's monitor indicator. The indicator box turns *green* to show that this is the only track "on." All the other tracks are off. Refer to Figure 7.2.

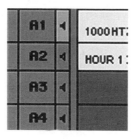

Figure 7.2

This is helpful when you're trying to find which track contains a certain sound. Command-click the monitor indicator again to return to monitoring the other tracks as well.

The Hollow/Green Speaker Icon

If you look at Figure 7.3 below, the speaker icon for track A1 is hollow.

Windows NT users will see that one of their speaker icons is green. The track with the hollow or green speaker icon is special. That's the track you are listening to when you play the sequence at a speed other than normal (30 fps) or when you "scrub" your audio.

AUDIO SCRUB

"Scrubbing" the audio is a technique used to concentrate on a particular piece of audio. You scrub it. There are two types of audio scrub: smooth audio scrub and digital audio scrub. Smooth audio scrub is quite simple:

- Hold down the K key (pause) while pressing the L key (forward). You hear what's on the hollow icon track in slow motion. It works backwards as well. Use the J key.

Digital audio scrub involves sampling a frame of audio. Because it's sampled, the pitch and speed don't change.

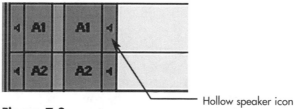

Hollow speaker icon

Figure 7.3

1. Select the track you want to scrub.
2. Press the Caps Lock key or hold down the Shift key.
3. Step forward or backward by clicking the step-one-frame forward or step-one-frame backward button, or drag the position indicator forward or backward.

This is great for locating a specific sound that will become your cut point. Say you're searching in the Timeline for the first frame of a hammer striking a nail. Click on the Caps Lock and press the step-one-frame forward button. (Pretend it's five frames away). Step, step, step, step, step-*CRUNCH*. Ah, there it is.

Selecting the Track for Scrubbing

Now, let's say the hollow/green icon is on track A1, and the sound you want to scrub is on track A3. To move the hollow/green speaker icon to track A3, simply hold the Option (Alt) key and then click on the A3 speaker icon. There. A3 is now the track with the hollow/green icon. Remember: Option-click (or Alt-click) on the speaker icon you want to scrub.

ADDING AUDIO TRACKS

In the later stages of editing, you will want to add sound effects and music to your sequence. Those sounds need their own sound tracks; you don't want them messing up your sync dialog tracks. To create additional tracks:

*   Go to the Clip menu and select New Audio Track, or
*   Press Command-U.

PATCHING AUDIO TRACKS

When you want to splice or overwrite a shot of video, it usually goes onto the V1 track. Your sync sound—the sounds that come with that video—usually goes onto A1, or, if you have stereo sync sound, onto A1 and A2. If you're bringing in music or sound effects, you don't want them to go onto A1 or A2 because they'll replace your sync sound. Music, sound effects, and narration are additional sound elements, and they need to go onto additional audio tracks.

Let's pretend you have a stereo music cue that you want to add to the scene. You want it to play "underneath" the dialog. You need to create two additional

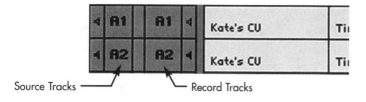

Source Tracks ────── Record Tracks

tracks, A3 and A4, and *patch* the audio onto A3 and A4. When you put a music clip into the Source Monitor (MC) or open a Pop-up Monitor (Xpress) that contains your music clip, you'll see the source track A1 and A2 appear in the Timeline, parallel to record tracks A1 and A2.

If you splice the music into A1 and A2, you throw your dialog out of sync. If you overwrite it, you erase your dialog. Instead, you create two additional tracks, A3 and A4, and patch the tracks so that your music will get spliced onto them.

To patch: Click the mouse on the first source track that you want to patch. In the example provided here, it's source track A2. Click the mouse on A2 and drag it to the record track A4. As you hold down the mouse, a white pointer arrow appears, and when you release it, the source track (A2) moves down to line up with your record track on A4. Try it.

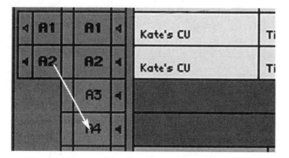

Drag the mouse from A2 to A4. The white pointer appears, and when you let go, the source track A2 slides down to A4.

Do the same thing with A1. Move it to line up with A3. Now when you splice or overwrite, that's where your music will go—onto A3 and A4, and not onto A1 and A2.

		A1	◄	Kate's CU	Tim's CU
		A2	◄	Kate's CU	Tim's CU
◄ A1		A3	◄	4M1 -Opening	
◄ A2		A4	◄	4M1 -Opening	

DELETING TRACKS

It sometimes happens that you need to get rid of one or more tracks. Perhaps you've created more tracks than you need, and the extra tracks just take up space on the computer screen. To delete a track, deselect all the other tracks and select the one you want to delete. Press the Delete key on the keyboard. A dialog box will ask if you are sure you want to do that, and you click OK. If you make a mistake, and inadvertently delete an important audio track, don't worry. Just press Command-Z to undo the action. Deleting tracks works with video tracks just as well as with audio tracks.

CHANGING AUDIO LEVELS

When you digitize your audio, the sound levels aren't always perfect. Often you need to raise or lower the levels once you start editing. Changing levels becomes especially important when you begin to add audio tracks and mix a number of sounds together. For example, you wouldn't want your music to drown out the actor's voices, or to have unintelligible narration because the sound effect track is too loud. The Avid provides several tools to help you control the sound levels of your tracks so they work well together. Just imagine what it would sound like if you had 12 audio tracks, and you couldn't change any of the levels.

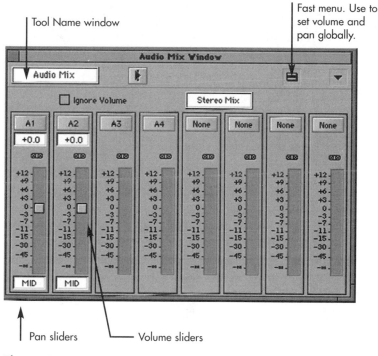

Figure 7.4 Audio Mix Tool

AUDIO MIX TOOL

The first tool we'll look at is the Audio Mix Tool. Open it by going to the Tools menu.

The Audio Mix Tool looks like a standard mixing board, with volume sliders for each track of audio. In the picture provided here, you see we only have two tracks. If you are monitoring eight tracks, eight sliders will appear. The window at the bottom of each track is for *panning* the audio. "Panning" is a technique used whenever you have more than one channel of sound coming from more than one speaker. When you set the pan you are determining how much of the sound will come from the left speaker, how much from the middle (both speakers equally), and how much from the right speaker. To set the pan, click on the window and a horizontal slider will appear. Drag it left or right.

To change the volume, simply click on the slider and raise or lower it to a different level, which is indicated in the windows, as shown in Figure 7.5.

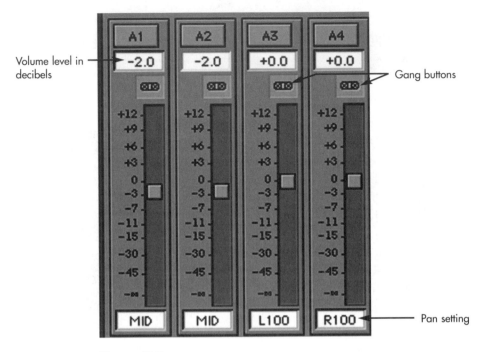

Volume level in decibels

Gang buttons

Pan setting

Figure 7.5

You'll notice as you practice changing levels that you are only affecting the level for the clip on which the position indicator sits. The entire track is not affected by the changes. This makes sense, when you stop to think about it, because often you want to raise one actor's level, while keeping another actor at the same level you started with.

There are a couple of tricks that speed up the adjustment process. Let's say that A3 and A4 are stereo music tracks, and you want to lower both of them at the same time. Click on the gang buttons for A3 and A4, and as you click on one slider, the other moves up and down with it. See Figure 7.5.

Let's say you want to go back to 0 dB. Sure, you could drag the slider back to 0, but that's time-consuming. Simply hold down the Option key and click on the slider button. The level will jump back to 0 dB. Option-click on the Pan button, and it will jump to MID, the center pan position.

The Avid lets you see your levels in the Timeline, so you can tell at a glance where you've set a specific clip, without having to bring up the Audio Mix Tool.

Go to the Timeline Fast menu. MC users select Audio Data (Figure 7.6). A submenu will allow you to select "Volume." Xpress users go to the Fast menu and select "Show Audio Levels."

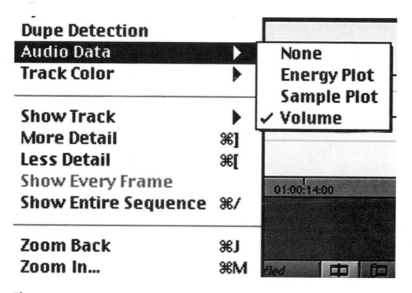

Figure 7.6 MC Timeline Fast Menu

Now, when you look at the Timeline, you'll be able to see every change you make to your audio levels by looking at the horizontal lines in each track. As you can see, I have lowered the volume on Tim's clip slightly. It registers a bit below the 0 dB line. If you look closely, you can see I dropped Kate's volume on her closeup even more—a bit below –7.0 dB. I have enlarged this audio track to twice its normal size. When the tracks are sized normally, you don't see the lines indicating decibels. But if you enlarge the tracks, the lines and numbers will appear.

Normally, you enlarge your tracks to this size only when you are making critical sound level adjustments, and you want to see the relationship between your setting and the 0 dB line.

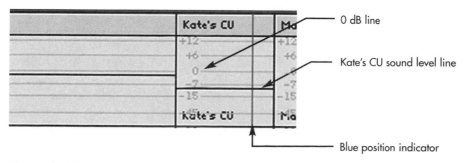

Figure 7.7

CHANGING VOLUME AND PANNNING ON MULTIPLE CLIPS

It often happens that you want to change the pan or volume throughout the sequence, or a large portion of the sequence, rather than making changes to individual clips. Open the Audio Mix Tool.

To affect pan or volume levels for a segment of a track(s) in your sequence:

1. Select the track.
2. Mark an IN inside the first clip; mark an OUT inside the last clip.
3. Click on the Gang button for that track(s).
4. Raise or lower the Volume slider or the Pan slider.
5. Go to the Audio Mix Tool Fast menu and drag down to Set Level In/Out or Set Pan In/Out.

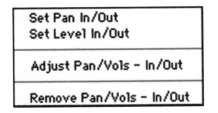

If you want to affect the entire track, rather than the area inside your marks, don't place any marks. Instead do the following:

1. Select the track.
2. Click on the Gang button for that track(s).
3. Raise or lower the Volume slider or the Pan slider.
4. Go to the Fast menu and drag down to Set Level (or Pan) Global.

```
Set Pan Global
Set Level Global

Adjust Pan/Vols – Global

Remove Pan/Vols – Global
```

There are a few things to remember when using the Audio Mix Tool:

1. When you choose the Show Audio Levels (Xpress) or Volume (MC) from the Timeline Fast menu, a straight line appears in the Timeline.
2. Whatever volume level you used when you digitized your audio, that is the "normal" or 0 dB setting.

3. Usually when you digitize, A1 is panned to the left speaker, and A2 is panned to the right speaker. This works great for music and sound effects, which often are panned. However, it is standard practice to have dialog and narration centered.

Since center pan is the standard for dialog and narration, the Avid allows you to set the pan before you bring the material in. In the Project window, select Settings. Audio is at the top of the list. Double-click it. Select "All Tracks Centered."

The Media Composer also provides a way to center pan using a Menu item. Set IN and OUT marks and then go to the Clip Menu and select Center Pan.

While the Audio Mix Tool is ideal for making changes to entire clips or large segments of your audio, Avid provides a second tool, called Audio Gain Automation so that you can really fine-tune your audio. With *Audio Gain Automation,* you can make many volume changes within a clip. If you have software version 2.0 or 7.0 and up, the software allows you to make real-time changes to the volume while *playing* the sequence. This imitates the way sound tracks are mixed in a professional mixing studio.

AUDIO GAIN AUTOMATION

This tool is also called volume rubber-banding. Instead of using a slider to change the level of an entire clip, this tool uses key frames in conjunction with the volume slider, to set and adjust levels *within* a clip.

There are several ways you can use this tool: (1) You can set the key frames manually, (2) You can play the sequence and let the Avid place key frames as you move the sliders, or (3) You can attach a fader. The Avid supports a fader manufactured by JL Cooper, called the FaderMaster Professional™. This is an external fader, and it allows you to use your fingers to move multiple sliders, rather than having to use the mouse to make volume changes on the Avid interface's sliders.

If you're going to attach an external fader, or have the Avid place key frames automatically, you'll need to open the Automation Gain Tool (Tools Menu). First let's learn how to set the key frames manually.

To set the key frames manually, you don't need to open the Automation Gain Tool. Just go to the Timeline Menu and select Show Audio Levels (Xpress) or Volume from the Audio Data submenu (MC). Now select the track(s) you want to work on.

A flat line will appear across selected tracks showing the audio volume level. Make the track larger by selecting the track and pressing Command-L or stretching the track with the mouse.

Key Frames

Place the blue position indicator in the Timeline where you want to make audio changes. Then hit the N key on the Xpress keyboard, the double quote key on the the MC keyboard, or the Key Frame command button.

Key Frame command button

A key frame appears in the Timeline. Because A1 and A2 are selected, key frames appear in both simultaneously. Move the blue position indicator in the Timeline further along the Timeline, and hit the Key Frame key again. Another key frame appears.

Using the mouse, move the pointer to the second key frame. Notice that the pointer changes into a "hand." Now drag the key frame down, vertically in the Timeline. You have created a volume ramp. Play the section in the Timeline and listen to the volume change. Add two more key frames further down the clip in the Timeline, and drag the fourth key frame—this time up. Now, you have created an audio dip, like the one shown here.

You may find that you have placed the key frame in the wrong place. You can easily move your key frames so that they affect the sound at a precise point.

Moving a key frame:

1. Hold the Option key.
2. Click the mouse on the key frame you want to move, and drag it to the new spot.

Deleting a key frame:

1. Bring the mouse pointer over the key frame(s) you want to remove. It turns into a "hand."
2. Press the Delete key on the keyboard. It's gone.

To remove multiple key frames, select IN and OUT points, and delete any key frame in the marked area.

Often, when working with stereo tracks, you want to create volume ramps on both tracks simultaneously. Simply select both tracks, and the key frames you place will appear in both tracks. All the actions you give to one track's key frame(s) will affect those on the other track.

AUDIO MIX TOOL VS. AUTOMATION GAIN TOOL

As soon as you place a key frame on a track, that track can no longer be changed by means of the Audio Mix Tool. In fact, if you open the Audio Mix Tool, the slider for that track is gone, and the word Auto appears in the decibel window to show you that the track is now controlled by the Automation Gain Tool. Conversely, if you have worked on a clip in that track using the Audio Mix Tool (and haven't set any key frames), the Automation Gain Tool will not show that track's slider, and the word "Clip" appears in the Automation Gain Tool decibel window. In other words, whichever tool you have used to work on a track, controls that track. How do you regain control if you want to use the other tool?

- If the clip is controlled by the Audio Mix Tool, it's simple. Just place a key frame anywhere on the track, and the Automation Gain Tool takes control.
- If the clip is controlled by Automation Gain Tool, you must get rid of all the clip's key frames in order for the Audio Mix Tool to take control.

There's a lesson here. Do your gross adjustments first, using the Audio Mix Tool. Then, fine-tune with the Automation Gain Tool. Don't set any key frames until you have set the volume and pan the way you want them in the Audio Mix Tool.

WAVEFORMS

The audio *waveform* is a visual representation of your audio's signal strength, or amplitude. The Avid's Timeline has the ability to show you the waveform of your audio. This feature provides a handy way of finding specific sounds, and "seeing" where to trim your sound.

If you're using an Xpress, first go to the Timeline Fast menu, deselect Show Audio Levels, and select Show Sample Plot (Figure 7.8).

If you're using a Media Composer, go into the Timeline Fast menu and select Audio Data. In the submenu deselect Volume and choose a waveform. There are two choices, Energy Plot and Sample Plot. I prefer Sample Plot, because it represents the entire amplitude of the waveform.

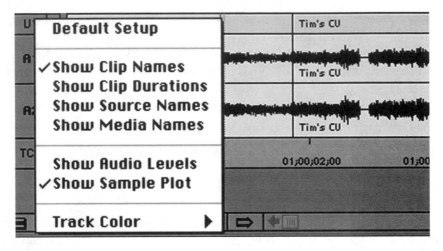

Figure 7.8

The Avid will draw the waveform. The speed with which the sample plot is drawn depends on your Timeline view and the number of tracks selected. Once the waveform is drawn, you can see where your sounds begin and end. This can be helpful when you're fine-tuning your audio. As you can see in Figure 7.9, the Timeline has been expanded so that we are looking at two frames of silence between audio cues.

There are a couple of commands that help you to better see the waveforms.

To make your tracks larger use enlarge track—Command-L.

To make the waveform itself larger, use Command-*Option*-L.

My main problem with waveforms is the length of time it takes to redraw them. In order to use them, you need to change the size of the Timeline. Every time you change the Timeline the Avid redraws the waveform. You wait and wait until the Timeline shows you a picture of the sound that you can work with. The newer versions of the software provide a setting that is supposed to alleviate this

Figure 7.9

problem. Click Settings in the Project window. Scroll down to Timeline and double-click. One of the options is "Show Marked Waveforms." Click in the box and then click OK. Now, when you set an IN and an OUT, the waveform is drawn within this marked region, not across the entire Timeline view. Does it help? No.

The problem is that you're using waveforms to help you edit the sound. Often you edit sound by using marks—IN and OUT. Well, as soon as you hit the mark IN button, the waveform shrinks and you're no longer looking at what you need to see. I don't use "Show Marked Waveforms" as a user setting. Instead, I get my Timeline view set up just right, and then, when it's all set, I get the waveform from the Timeline Fast menu.

Waveforms are quite helpful whenever you're trying to edit complex sounds, such as music. For example, let's say you wanted to lengthen a music cue because it ends a bit too soon. You can easily do this by copying a section of the music into the Clipboard, opening the Clipboard Monitor, marking the section, and then cutting it into the Timeline at the end of the music. Now the music is extended. The waveform shows you where the beats are in the music. Use those beats to make your marks and edit points. Try it.

USING TRIM MODE TO FINE-TUNE THE AUDIO

I do much of my audio work using Trim Mode. Let's say you have a lot of narration that you've cut into your sequence, and the narration track is a bit noisy. When the narrator speaks, you don't hear the hiss, but as soon as he/she stops talking, you can hear the hiss or hum on the track.

You want to clean the track up. The best way to do this is to enter Trim mode and cut the narration so that the only segments left in the Timeline are those that contain the voice, and not the "silent" bits, which are actually quite noisy.

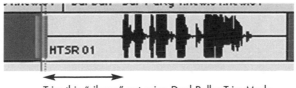

Trim this "silence" out using Dual-Roller Trim Mode.

Sometimes, when you're working on a cut in Dual-Roller Trim Mode, you'll hear a glitch in the audio, but it's so close to the transition point that you aren't sure which side of the transition has the sound glitch. As you play the transition, the sound loops around. Try this. Press the Go to Mark IN key (Q on the standard keyboard). The loop will play on the outgoing clip, but not the incoming one.

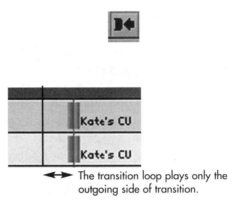

←→ The transition loop plays only the outgoing side of transition.

To hear just the incoming side of the transition, press the Go to Mark OUT key.

This technique enables you to locate spurious sound glitches. Once located, you can often get rid of them by using the Dual-Roller Trim to create a sound overlap. Let's say there was a glitch on the outgoing audio, five frames from the transition. The dialog is finished, but a table got bumped. You might be able to replace the glitch on the outgoing clip with five frames of "good" sound on the incoming clip. Create your overlap, and the "bump" is gone.

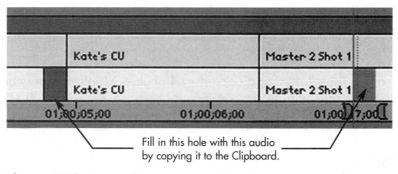

Fill in this hole with this audio
by copying it to the Clipboard.

Figure 7.10

USING THE CLIPBOARD TO FIX AUDIO

If we continue with the example of the sound glitch on the outgoing clip, what do we do if the sound on the incoming clip isn't a good match and the Dual-Roller Trim makes the sound even worse. Here's where the ability to copy and paste comes in handy. We can easily mark the area where the glitch is located and, using Lift, get rid of it. But you can't have *nothing* on your soundtrack. You need to replace what was cut out with some sort of roomtone, or ambient sound, in order to fill in the blank spot.

Measure the size of the gap by looking at the Composer Monitor menu's I/O. You see it's five frames. Now go find five frames of ambient sound that will

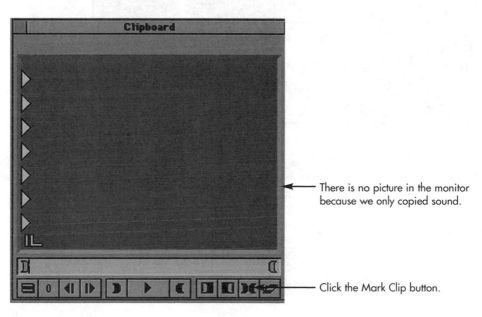

There is no picture in the monitor
because we only copied sound.

Click the Mark Clip button.

Figure 7.11

fit in. Here we locate five clean frames up ahead, in the Master Shot. Now we mark the frames of sound we want (select the audio track and deselect picture track), and hit the Clipboard icon (on the keyboard, it's the letter C). The sound is copied to the Clipboard.

Go to the Tools Menu and open the Clipboard Monitor. Now click on the Mark Clip button to set an IN and OUT, and overwrite the sound into the "hole" in your Timeline.

ADD EDITS

Sometimes you want to make an abrupt change in the audio level inside a clip. Let's say you have a scene where music is playing on a CD player in the living room, and you begin your scene in the kitchen. You hear the music, but because it's coming from another room, its level is low. Then you cut to the living room. The volume should change with the cut. The best way to do this is to split the music clip into two clips, so you can set different audio levels for each segment. To do this you use the *Add Edit* button.

An add edit is an artificial edit point made between continuous frames. To a filmmaker it would be like an unintentional splice. Yet this cut, or break between two frames in a clip, is quite intentional. Put the position indicator on the frame in the Timeline where you want the break to occur. Hit the Add Edit button. On the Xpress keyboard, it's P. MC users will find it on the Fast menu.

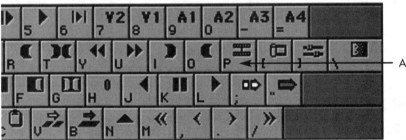

Add Edit key

In the Timeline, an Add Edit looks like an equal sign (=) that's been stamped at the transition point. Now you can go into the Audio Mix Tool and set different sound levels in the same clip.

SCR020	SCR020

As you can see, the same music clip, called SCR020, has been split in two, and the second half has the audio volume set above that of the first half. The audio will jump to the higher volume.

To Delete an Add Edit:

- Enter Trim Mode at the Add Edit and press the Delete key on the keyboard.

EQ - EQUALIZATION

On most sound mixing boards, there are dials that you can turn to boost or cut (decrease) various frequencies—low, midrange, high—to alter or improve the sound. Such alteration of frequencies is called equalization. For example, if a voice is too bass sounding, you can cut the low frequencies and boost the midrange frequencies.

The Avid has a tool that enables you to do the same thing. The EQ Tool is in the Tools menu. The EQ tool affects clips in the Timeline.

From the Tools menus choose Audio EQ. A window appears.

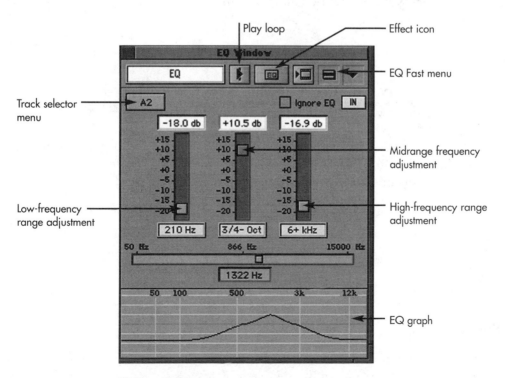

Figure 7.12

Setting the EQ

- The sliders enable you to emphasize (boost) or deemphasize (cut) the low, mid, and high frequencies.
- The horizontal slider allows you to change the shape and placement of the parametric curve. This adjustment allows you to locate the frequency that you most want to boost or cut.

Watch the EQ graph to see the changes.

There is a play loop button, which will play the sound in a continuous loop and allow you to hear the changes you make as you adjust the sliders. There is also an IN button, which gives you the opportunity to turn off the effect of the EQ so you can tell how your changes compare to the original sound. Are you making the sound better or worse? Click once and it turns gray, indicating that no EQ is taking place. Click again and it turns yellow, indicating that the effect is on.

Steps in applying EQ:

1. Select the track(s) you want to change.
2. Identify a portion of the track(s) with IN and OUT marks.
3. Click the play loop.
4. Drag the sliders to select values.
5. When you are satisfied, stop and then choose Set EQ In/Out from the EQ Fast menu.

You can also use the EQ Fast menu to remove the EQ. Or you can use the Remove Effect button located on a Fast menu command palette. Click on the effect in the Timeline and then press the Remove Effect button.

Remove Effect command

EQ Templates

Avid has a number of EQ templates that fix common audio problems. You can apply, but not change, any of these EQ templates.

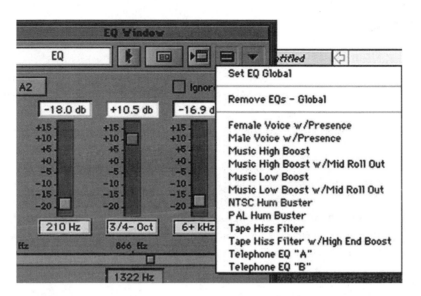

Figure 7.13

1. Put the position indicator on the audio clip in the Timeline that you want to change.
2. Choose the template from the EQ Fast menu. The EQ effect will be placed on the clip.

One way to learn how to equalize your sound is to examine the graphs that these different templates produce. Look at the frequencies that are boosted and cut. Examine the point where the center of the parametric curve is located. These EQ templates cover most of the problems you'll encounter. Use them as a jumping-off point for fixing your sound. It's true, you can't change them, but you can recreate them and then make adjustments to fit your own set of problems.

Saving Your EQ Effect

You can also save an EQ effect so you can use it later on in your project. Once you have the effect set up the way you want, simply click and drag the *Effect icon* (Figure 7.12) to whichever bin you would like it saved to. Try it. It's quite easy to do. Once it's in the bin, you can name it.

SETTING UP YOUR TRACKS

In the traditional analog film editing style, the editor would cut the entire film using, for the most part, only two tracks! That's because the KEM or Steenbeck is capable of playing only two or three tracks at a time. Most of the sound was added after the picture was cut. Once the film's editor reached picture lock, the sound editors would then take over and build whatever music, dialog, and sound effects tracks were needed to give the film its emotion and tone.

After the tracks were built, the film was mixed at a traditional mixing studio, using magnetic dubbers to play the magnetic film tracks in sync with the picture. A *cue sheet*, which is a paper diagram showing the location of the sounds on each track, would be prepared prior to the mix, and the mixer would use that as a sort of road map. Usually the tracks would be set up in a specific order, so that when the cue sheet was made it would read, from left to right on the page, like this:

Narration Tracks   Dialog Tracks   Effect Tracks   Music Tracks

A simple mix might involve seven tracks. You might have one track of voice-over narration, two tracks containing dialog, two sound effects tracks, and two music tracks. A complicated mix, involving lots of sound effects and music cues, layered on top of each other, might need 24 tracks.

With the Avid, it's easy to add tracks, but you should give some thought to how your tracks are laid out. Since analog filmmaking spans the entire twentieth century, the techniques which served it so well and for so long are often worth emulating, even in this digital age.

In the Avid's Timeline, the tracks go one on top of each other, flowing left to right. If you have narration, it should go onto the topmost audio track—A1. Reserve the next two tracks for dialog. The sound effects come next. Finally, your music tracks go at the bottom of your Timeline. If you have no narration, the topmost tracks will contain dialog.

We've examined many of the important techniques and tools at your disposal, all of which help you create clean, clear sound. Perhaps the most important advice I can give you is this: wait to add sound effects and music until as late in the editing process as possible. Often editors who are new to the Avid create complex sound tracks much too early in the editing process, making even the simplest change an onerous task. Tell the story first, by cutting the picture and sync sound. Then build your other tracks, laying down the sound effects and music cues that will give tone and emotional content to your project.

SUGGESTED ASSIGNMENTS

1. Move the hollow speaker icon to different tracks.
2. Enlarge all your sound tracks.
3. Make individual tracks smaller.
4. Add two additional audio tracks.
5. Splice sound into these new tracks by patching.
6. Adjust the volume of your tracks using the Audio Mix Tool.
7. Change the pan on three clips in one of your tracks.
8. Open the Automation Gain Tool. Get Audio Levels from the Timeline Fast menu, and place several key frames on a clip. Create volume ramps.
9. Move the key frames in the Timeline.
10. From the Timeline Fast menu, leave Audio Levels and go to Waveforms. Try cutting audio, using the waveforms as cutting guides.
11. Place an EQ template onto a clip in the Timeline.
12. Create an EQ effect for several clips in the Timeline and apply it using IN and OUT marks. (Remember, go to the EQ Fast menu and choose Set EQ IN to OUT.)

8

Advanced Editing

As we've noted on several occasions, the Avid is a complex editing system, loaded with features that give the editor tremendous flexibility. For the most part, we've stuck to the basics in order to limit the amount of material you must grapple with to get the job done. Now, we'll examine more advanced features, some of which are unique to nonlinear digital systems.

SEGMENT MODE EDITING

Segment Mode editing gets at the heart of nonlinear editing. For those of you with a background in film editing, this won't seem all that special, because you've been doing it on your Steenbeck or KEM all along. For those of you who are tape editors, this is the mode you've most often dreamed about. With Segment Mode editing, you can move clips around in the Timeline, changing the order of the shots in your sequence. The speed with which you can shift around whole segments of your project will astound you.

Let's say that you realize that the first shot in your sequence should actually be the third shot. Enter Segment Mode, click on the shot in the Timeline, and drag it to the new position. Presto!

Segment Mode editing isn't really all that advanced a feature, but I've held off introducing it because it's much more useful to an editor working on a visual montage or working with documentary footage than it is to an editor cutting a narrative scene. When we were editing "Wanna Trade," you didn't have many opportunities to change the order of your shots, but now that you're working on a documentary, or some other reality-based material, you'll find yourself wanting to move shots around.

When do you use Segment Mode editing, and when do you rely on splice and overwrite mode? Segment Mode is most often used once you have placed your shots in the Timeline, and you want to move them around.

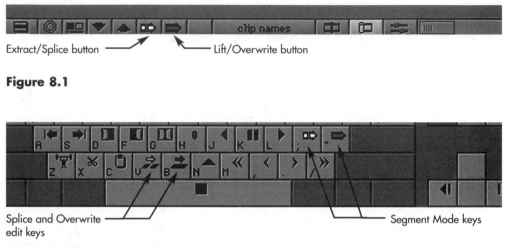

Extract/Splice button ——————— Lift/Overwrite button

Figure 8.1

Splice and Overwrite ——————— Segment Mode keys
edit keys

Figure 8.2

There are two Segment Mode buttons, and they appear on the Xpress keyboard and at the bottom of the Timeline (Figure 8.1). The yellow arrow that appears to be missing its midsection is called the Extract/Splice button, and the thick red arrow is called the Lift/Overwrite button.

MC users can also find the Segment Mode buttons on the second row of the Source Monitor command buttons. Remember, we placed them there in Chapter 3. Before we go any further, notice the similarities and differences between the Splice and Overwrite keys and the two Segment Mode keys. When I was first learning the Avid, I often clicked the wrong one, and it took me a while to figure out what I'd done.

Extract/Splice Segment Mode Button

When you click on the button, you'll enter Segment Mode.

To let you know you're in Segment Mode, the background color on the segment key at the bottom of the Timeline will lighten. If you then click on a clip (segment) in the Timeline, the clip is highlighted. If the clip has picture and sync sound, you normally want to move both of them together. To select the sound clip, hold down the Shift key and click on the sound. Now both are selected, as shown here.

Burning Hills		Woman gets water	Ext-Pool	Cooking in par
Burning Hills		Woman gets water	Ext-Pool	Cooking in par

Let's say we want the shot called "Ext-Pool," which is the third shot in this sequence, to become the second shot. We want to move it so that it comes after "Burning Hills." To move the clip, click on it and then drag it to the spot where you want it to go. As you drag, a white outline will appear around the clip to show you it is moving. Xpress users, when you drag your segment, it snaps to cut points or to the blue position indicator. MC users must press either Command or Option-Command to make the segments snap to cut points.

Burning Hills		Woman gets water	Ext-Pool	Cooking in pa
Burning Hills		Woman gets water	Ext-Pool	Cooking in pa

When you release the mouse, the clip moves to the new location.

Burning Hills		Ext-Pool	Woman gets water	Cooking in par
Burning Hills		Ext-Pool	Woman gets water	Cooking in par

As you can see here, "Ext-Pool" is now the second shot in the sequence. What was the second shot becomes the third shot. Because you're moving segments, the length of the sequence remains the same, and everything stays in sync. You can drag shots in either direction.

When you move a segment in Media Composer, the Source/Record Monitor changes from the normal display to a four-frame display, showing you the tail and head frames of the shot you are moving, and the head and tail frames of the shot in between. Avid calls this display "Segment Drag Quads." I call it confusing.

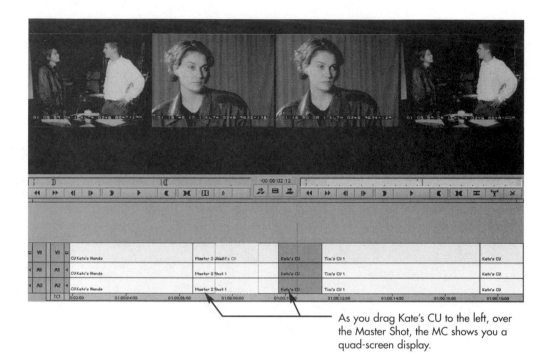

As you drag Kate's CU to the left, over the Master Shot, the MC shows you a quad-screen display.

Figure 8.3

You can suppress it by holding down the Shift key as you drag the segment. For a more permanent solution, go to Settings in the Project window and select Timeline Settings. Deselect "Show Segment Drag Quads."

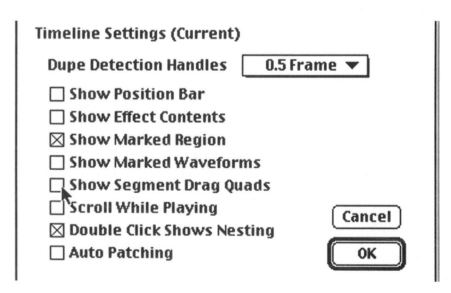

Figure 8.4

To leave segment mode:
* Click on the segment button.

Lift/Overwrite Segment Mode Button

This button is less helpful, and you'll use it less often when moving shots around. When you click on the Lift/Overwrite button (red button) and drag your segment, it moves the segment you've chosen (fine) and overwrites the segment it lands on (not good). That's not usually what you want to do.

Look at the example provided. Here we selected "Ext-Pool," using the Lift/Overwrite button.

Examine what happens when we use Lift/Overwrite to drag "Ext-Pool" to the same spot as we did using the Extract/Splice segment button. The shot is lifted from its old position, leaving blank fill in its place, and is moved to its new position. But instead of pushing "Woman Gets Water" to the third spot, it erases (overwrites) most of the clip.

However, the Lift/Overwrite Segment Mode button is important, particularly when you want to quickly move blocks of sound. Let's say we are working on a sequence involving a series of shots that are explained by voice-over narration. When you first cut in the narration, it doesn't flow as nicely as you might like. The narrator's sentences are too close together, so you decide to spread the narration out. Here's where the Lift/Overwrite Segment Mode button excels.

In the example given here, I want to move the narration on A1 toward the head of the visual on V1. I place the position indicator where I want the head of the narration to land.

Next I click the red segment button, click on the narration segment, and drag it to the position indicator.

When I release the mouse, the block of narration is right where I want it, and nothing has been thrown out of sync.

Another handy trick involves the use of the Lift/Overwrite segment button with the Trim keys. Press the red segment button, select the block of audio you want to move, and press the << or < Trim key to slide the segment of sound toward the head of the sequence, or the > or >> trim key to slide the sound toward the tail. Try it. It is quite precise.

Moving Sound to Different Tracks

You'll use the Lift/Overwrite segment button whenever you want to move a sound (or picture) clip that's on one track onto another track. In this example, the sound for "TeaTime" is on A3, and I want it to go onto A2, just below the narration track. It's easy.

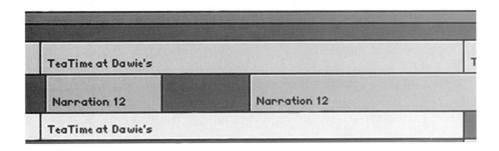

- Click the Lift/Overwrite segment button.
- Click on the sound segment you want to move.
- Drag it to the track where you want it to go to.

Again, a white outline will form around the box to show that it's moving and where it's moving to. The result is what you expected (and hoped). To keep the track from sliding horizontally, and going out of sync, hold down the Control key as you move the track vertically.

Lassoing to Get into Segment Mode

You've probably already done this by accident. As you know, you go into Trim Mode by lassoing a transition from left to right. If, instead of lassoing a transition, you lasso a segment, you'll go into Segment mode.

Burning Hills		Woman gets water	Ext-Pool	Cooking in park
Burning Hills		Woman gets water	Ext-Pool	Cooking in park

Which segment mode? The button that gets selected is the one you used last. If you want the other one, just click on the one you want. Lassoing is a great way to select a number of clips at once. Lasso all of the clips you want.

You can move more than one segment at a time. For instance you may want to take the fourth and fifth shots and move them to the beginning of your sequence. You could press a Segment Mode button, click on a segment, and then Shift-click to get all four segments selected (two picture and two sound), or you could lasso them all in one quick move. Although in the example here I'm only moving two shots, you can move 30 or 50 shots at once.

I	Cooking in park	Jewelry Sh	A
I	Cooking in park	Jewelry Sh	A

It sometimes happens that you'll be working on a larger project and realize that scene number 5 would work better at the beginning of the project. Scene 5 might encompass 20 shots. Just lasso the entire scene, click Extract/Splice, and drag all 20 shots to the head of the sequence.

To sum up the Segment Mode buttons:

- Use Extract/Splice to move shots around in the Timeline.

- Use Lift/Overwrite to move blocks of sound in the Timeline.

Delete Segments with Segment Mode

You can delete segments of your project without marking IN and OUT points. Go into Segment Mode and Shift-click or lasso the segments you want to delete. Then press the Delete key on the keyboard. The material is deleted.

- Extract/Splice will remove the material and close the gap. The Timeline shrinks.
- Lift/Overwrite will remove the material and leave a gap with black fill.

This is faster than marking IN and OUT points and using the Lift or Extract button, especially with multiple segments. Let's review this. Remember that in Chapter 2 we explored the Lift and Extract buttons. You marked an IN in the Timeline and then marked an OUT. The *Lift* button removed the marked material and filled in the gap, whereas *Extract* removed the material and left black fill. The Segment Mode buttons do the same thing. In fact, if you hit Command-X instead of the Delete key in Segment Mode, the material is removed and saved to the Clipboard.

Segment Mode Vs. the Extract and Lift buttons to Delete Material

In the Timeline, if you mark a clip or part of a clip with IN and OUT points so

that it is selected, and then extract it by hitting, , it will be removed and the gap will be closed.

Or if you lift it by hitting ![lift button], it will be removed and leave a gap with black fill.

If you use Segment buttons to select the clips, the function keys don't work. In Segment Mode:

- If you select clips with the Segment Mode buttons, you must use either the Delete key or Command-X:

![button] Will lift.

![button] Will extract.

In Segment Mode, if you press Command-X, it will lift or extract, and put the segments into the Clipboard.

TRIMMING IN TWO DIRECTIONS

Once you begin to add additional tracks to your sequence, using Trim Mode can get a little tricky. For instance, say we have a clip on V1 of people voting in the first free election in South Africa. Your narration describes the action on A1, and your sync track is on A2. You're happy with the way the narration works with the picture and sync track. But let's say you need to Trim the head of the clip because the sequence is running too long. I've placed locators on all three tracks to show what happens if you trim your voting clip without adjusting your narration track (Figure 8.5).

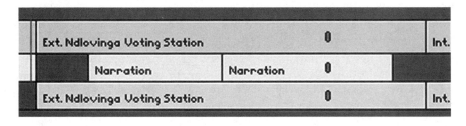

Figure 8.5   Before trimming

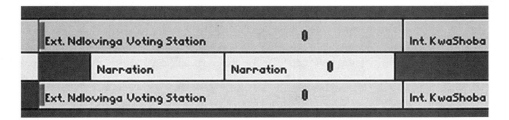

Figure 8.6   After trimming

In Figure 8.6 we have trimmed 30 frames off the head of the "Voting Station" picture and sync track. Track V1 and A2 have been shortened by 30 frames, while A1, containing the narration, has remained the same length. Everything is thrown off. You say, "Well trim 30 frames off the narration and everything will be in sync." But we can't, because if we trim the head of the narration, we'll be cutting off the narrator's words! The solution is *trimming in two directions*. The Avid realizes this is a common situation and allows you to Trim in the black, or fill area, to keep tracks aligned. Watch.

By placing a single-roller on the other side of the narration track, as shown in Figure 8.7, where there is fill and not voice, and then trimming, the Avid takes 30 frames of black fill off the narration track while it takes 30 frames off the 'Voting' clip. All the tracks are still aligned. As you can see, the arrows go in two different directions. We are trimming in two directions.

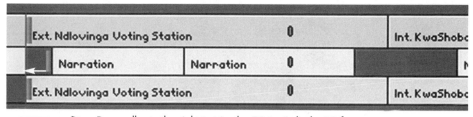

Drag roller to the right to trim the "Voting" clip by 30 frames.
Narration fill is shortened by 30 frames.

Figure 8.7

We can use the Single-Roller Trim to *add* to the head of the "Voting" clip.
This time we're dragging the rollers to the left to extend the clip by 30 frames.
Again, we put the single-roller on the black fill side of the narration.

Drag the rollers left to lengthen the clip. The Avid adds fill to the
narration track to keep the narration porperly aligned.

It took me a while to get the hang of this trimming in two directions business. Just remember that once you have the clip you want to trim, in order for
the other tracks to stay in alignment downstream of that trim, you have to add
or subtract from every track, or else you throw everything out of sync. Here's
another example, showing many tracks having their black fill adjusted, so that
the picture clip can be trimmed.

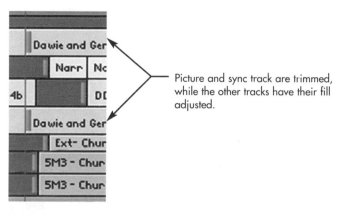

Picture and sync track are trimmed,
while the other tracks have their fill
adjusted.

Figure 8.8

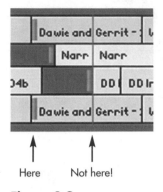

Figure 8.9

Watch Point

The transition the Avid shows you in the Trim Mode window when you click on the Review Transition button is called the *watch point*. It's easy when there are only two tracks and everything is straight cut, because then there is only one transition. But whenever you have transitions that aren't in a straight line, the Avid can select only one of the transitions to show in the Trim Mode window. The last track selected for trimming is the one that becomes the watch point. This isn't necessarily the one you want to watch. Look at the location of the position indicator in the example in Figure 8.9. It's on the roller for a sound effect. But the whole reason you're making a trim is to adjust picture and sync track. That's where you want the watch point to be.

To fix this situation, Shift-click on the roller at the transition you want. The roller disappears. Shift-click on it again. The roller reappears, and the watch point jumps to the right spot. Remember, the last spot you select is where the watch point will fall.

Practice this. See what happens when the watch point is wrong. Move the watch point so that the transition you want to trim is shown in the Trim Mode display.

MATCH FRAME

Sometimes when you're working in the Timeline, you want to see which clip a shot in the Timeline comes from. Or, you're wondering what comes before or after the section you spliced in. A quick way to open the entire clip is to hit Match Frame. Immediately, the entire clip will appear in the Pop-up Monitor or Source Monitor.

Match Frame command

The Match Frame command isn't on the standard keyboard. It's on a Fast menu on the Xpress.

And also on a Media Composer's Fast menu.

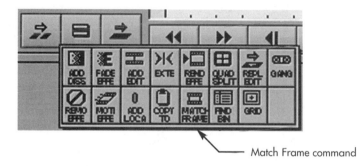

Match Frame command

Place the position indicator on the clip in the Timeline and press the Match Frame button. Match Frame finds the source clip for whichever track is selected. If you want to find the source clip for a clip of narration, make sure that's the track selected. If it's a picture, then make sure you select the video track.

SLIPPING AND SLIDING

Slip and *Slide* are power editing features that affect clips in the Timeline. They are unique versions of Trim Mode. These two features didn't come to the Xpress until late in 1999, with software version 3.0.

Slip

Slip is particularly handy. Say you have spliced a section of a master clip into the Timeline, and after playing the sequence, you see that the section of the clip you used isn't just right. Maybe you put your IN and OUT marks in the Source Monitor a bit too early. Without Slip, the only way to fix this would be to mark the clip in the Timeline and choose a new IN in the Source Monitor. Press Overwrite, and you've replaced the clip with a different section of the clip. If it still isn't right, try it again.

With Slip, you don't need to go back to the Source Monitor. You can change the clip in the Timeline. What you're doing is changing the IN and OUT at the

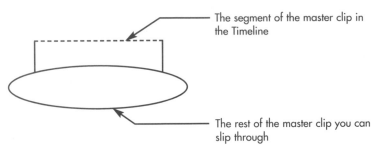

The segment of the master clip in the Timeline

The rest of the master clip you can slip through

Figure 8.10

same time. Think of Slip as working a bit like a conveyor belt. The whole belt is the master clip, and the portion of the belt you're seeing in the Timeline is the section you've spliced in.

You can change the section that's in the Timeline with Slip. As you slip through the footage, the length of the clip in the Timeline remains the same. When you slip, you are adding frames to the head of the clip in the Timeline, while trimming the tail by the same number of frames. Or you can trim frames from the head of the shot, while adding the same number of frames to the tail of the shot.

To get into Slip Mode:
• Press the Trim button and then double-click on the clip in the Timeline.
• Lasso the clip from the right to the left.

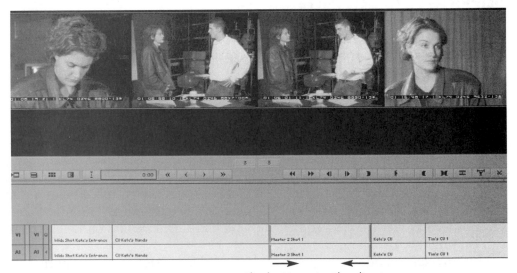

Slip the Master in either direction.

Figure 8.11

Single-trim rollers will jump to the cut points. The Source and Record Monitors will change to four screens (Figure 8.11).

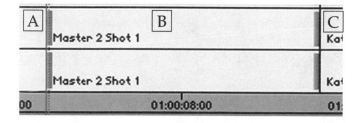

The two inner screens are the head and tail frames of the clip you are slipping—the Master Shot (Clip B). The far-left screen is the tail frame of Clip A, and the far-right is the head frame of Clip C. The frames of Clip B (the Master Shot) will change as you slip it. The frames of Clip A and C will not change at all.

You can use the Trim keys (<<, <, >, and >>) to move the clip, or click on and drag either roller. The frames that appear in the two inner screens will change as you slip.

Getting out of Slip is just like leaving Trim mode.

To leave Slip Trim:

• Click on the Timecode track.
• Press the Source/Record Mode button.

Slide

I have a hard time getting my head around Slide whenever I'm cutting both picture and sound. However, if I'm just working with blocks of sound, it works great. Then it functions just like the Lift/Overwrite segment button.

Slide is the inverse of Slip. It doesn't change any of the frames in the clip you're sliding (Clip B); instead it moves Clip B inside the Timeline, changing Clip A and Clip C.

As you drag either roller, Kate's CU will move toward the head or tail of the sequence. For instance, if you drag Kate's CU toward the head, Clip A gets shorter while Clip C gets longer. Kate's CU is unchanged (except that it has been relocated). You can also use the Trim keys to slide the clip.

To enter Slide Mode:
- Press the Trim button, and, while holding down the Option key, double-click on the clip in the Timeline.
- While holding down the Option key, lasso the clip from right to left.

SOME GREAT FEATURES NOT AVAILABLE ON THE XPRESS

Find Bin

Often, when you're working on a project, you want to know which bin a clip or sequence comes from. Say you're working in the Timeline, and you want to find which bin a clip comes from because there may be other clips you'd like to examine that are also in that bin.

1. Place the position indicator on the clip in the Timeline.
2. Press and hold down the Option key, and then press the Find Bin command. The bin will open with the clip highlighted.

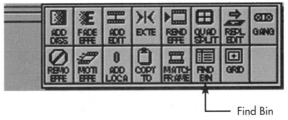

Find Bin

If you want to find which bin a sequence comes from, click the Record Monitor to activate it. Press the Find Bin button.

Replace

Replace does which you'd expect—it replaces material in the sequence with other material of your choosing. Let's say you have placed a clip in the Source Monitor, marked an IN and an OUT, and spliced it into the Timeline. Looking at it, you think another take would work better. Without replace, you would have to find the new take and overwrite it into the Timeline. Replace is different. Unlike overwrite, replace doesn't need IN and OUT marks. It can use the loca-

Figure 8.12

tion of the blue position indicators to do its work. I realize this is a new concept, so let's take a closer look at it.

Let's say we have footage of two people swimming. What's shown in the picture in Figure 8.12 is taken from "Swim" Take 1. You cut this into the Timeline. When you review the sequence, you think Take 2 might be better, because when the woman lifts her head out of the water we see more of her face in Take 2.

The most important action is the woman touching the wall and lifting her head, so I put the position indicator on that frame in the Timeline.

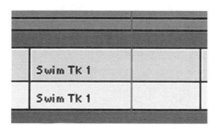

Then I go to the Source Monitor and get Swim Take 2. I play through the clip until I find the spot where she's lifting her head out of the water. I leave the position indicator there. Now, I hit the Replace command.

I have now replaced Swim Take 1 with a clip of the same length taken from Swim Take 2, but the part of Swim Take 2 that is overwritten is based on the location of the position indicators. The woman's head will lift out of the water at the same point in the sequence as it did when Take 1 was there. In this case, we are matching the action while replacing.

What's special about Replace is it can replace sound and picture even if

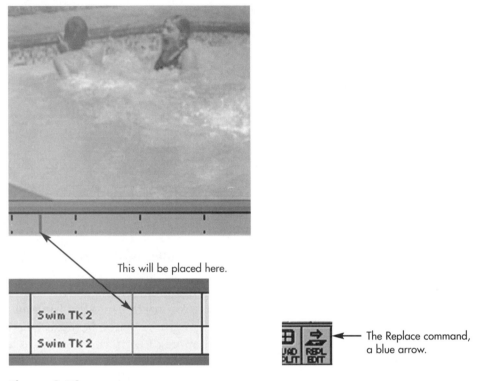

This will be placed here.

The Replace command, a blue arrow.

Figure 8.13

there is an overlap edit! It replaces sound based on the amount of sound used in the Timeline, even if there's more sound than picture (as might happen with an overlap) in the Timeline.

DO XPRESS USERS MISS THESE FEATURES?

If you work on an Xpress prior to version 3.0, you won't really care that you don't have Slide. You can use the Lift/Overwrite segment button to "slide" audio segments around, and that's where Slide is most useful. But you'll miss Slip. Replace isn't on any Xpress models yet and it's a great feature. Find Bin is another important command missing from Xpress models. It's not a big loss when you're working on a small project, but when you're doing a feature-length documentary or drama, with hundreds of bins, it's really helpful.

There are many other features and commands that come standard on Media Composer, yet aren't available on the Xpress. The ones we examined here are appropriate for a book aimed at beginning and intermediate users.

SUGGESTED ASSIGNMENTS

1. Go into Segment Mode by clicking the Extract/Splice button. Now move a clip (Shift-click to get sound) toward the head of your sequence.
2. Undo.
3. Move it again, but this time suppress the four-frame display by pressing the Shift key (MC only).
4. Undo. Leave segment mode.
5. Go into Segment Mode by clicking the Lift/Overwrite button. Move a clip to the head.
6. Undo. Leave segment mode.
7. Get into Segment Mode by clicking the Lift/Overwrite button. Move a clip of audio using trim keys. Undo.
8. Lasso three clips to get into Segment Mode.
9. Practice trimming in two directions.
10. Set the watch point to show the clip you want to "watch" in the Trim Mode display.
11. Select a video track and hit Match Frame.
12. Deselect the video tracks and select an audio track. Hit Match Frame.
13. Get into Slip Mode and slip a clip.

Media Composer Users

1. Choose a clip in the Timeline and use Find Bin to open its bin.
2. Use Replace to change a clip in the Timeline, using the position indicators to replace the material in the Timeline with the material in the Source monitor.

9

Titles

There are many different kinds of titles, and they serve different functions in a production. There's the main title of the show, and there are the opening and closing credits, identification titles (lower-thirds), subtitles, and copyright information. When you think about it, you really can't finish a project without adding titles.

The Avid used to come with a less-than-functional title tool, but that has changed. Now even the basic Xpress has a title tool that can handle almost all your title needs. Titles can be simple, such as white letters over a black or colored background, or complex, involving moving titles over a moving video image.

Figure 9.1 The Title window

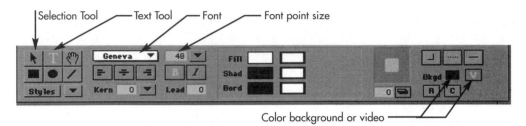

Figure 9.2

Usually you add titles when you're nearing the end of the editing phase. If you're still making a lot of changes to your sequence and you cut titles in, they can easily get out of sync and drift away from the images they belong to—and it's a real pain to put everything back together. Trust me on this. Wait to add titles as late in the editing process as possible. But since we're through editing "Wanna Trade" and possibly another short assignment, you can go back and add titles to them.

OPENING THE TITLE TOOL

If you're planning to add a title over a video image, normally you park the position indicator on that image in the Timeline and then open the Title Tool. That way, the background of your choice becomes the background that the Title Tool shows you. To open the Title Tool, go to the Clip menu and select New Title. The Title Tool will open, and you'll see the Title window.

CHOOSING A BACKGROUND

If you don't want a video image as the background for your title, click on the Color Background window. The green V will turn black. Black is the default background color, but you can hold the pointer in the Color Background window and a Color Picker will appear. Move the mouse through the colors to select the one you want for your background. You can also use the eyedropper to pick a color.

CREATING YOUR FIRST TITLE

Creating titles is fairly straightforward. I'm going to create a title to go over a specific shot of Nelson Mandela greeting voters. I click on the V so that the video image appears in the Title Tool window. To type the letters, make sure the T for Text Tool is green. If not, click on the T to make it active. Now click on the image

Selection handles.
Drag this right or left
to affect word wrap.

Figure 9.3

where you'd like the text to land. The cursor becomes an I-beam. As you type, the text will appear and flow to the next line. Don't worry—just type your text.

Geneva is the default font, and 48 is the default font point size. You'll find that 48 is often too large. Once you're through typing, click and drag across the letters to select them (two mirror-like lines form above and below the letters). Now select a smaller font size, and, if you like, a different font. I'm choosing Litho Bold. A font size of 24 will allow the words President Nelson Mandela to fit nicely on one line. You can delete letters, edit letters, type additional letters, change fonts and styles—basically do all the functions provided by most word-processing programs. *Kerning* allows you to change the spacing between letters. Select the text you want to kern, and pull down the Kerning menu, or type a number into the box. Negative numbers tighten the spacing. Positive numbers loosen the spacing. *Leading* changes the spacing between lines of text.

Once you're happy with what you've typed, you want to position the title in the frame. To do that you use the Selection Tool.

Click on the Selection Tool so that the arrow turns green. Now click on the title. A box with selection handles appears around the title. Now you can click and drag the entire title to a different area of the frame. In Figure 9.3, I've dragged my title to the part of the frame often called the "lower-third," where most identification titles are placed. When you're in Selection Mode, you can also make changes to the title's font, point size, and so on.

The selection handles also allow you to change the size of the box that the words fall into. If your words wrap around to a second line and you want them to all fall on one line, try dragging the right-hand selection handle—the one that's in the middle. Drag it to the right, and you'll see that your words have more room, so they fall onto one line. If you have too much unused space after your last word, drag the box to the left. That way you can align the text more easily within the frame.

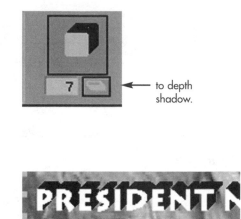

Drag the shadow to set
the direction and amount
of shadow.

Toggle this button to go
from drop shadow...

to depth
shadow.

Figure 9.4

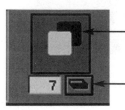

Figure 9.5   Drop shadow   Depth shadow

SHADOWS

You can add a *drop shadow* or *depth shadow* to your titles. Shadowing can often make the letters stand out from a busy background. To add the shadow in Text Mode, click and drag across the words to select them. Or, in Selection Mode, click on the title so that the handles appear. Then go to the Shadow Tools.

By toggling the Drop and Depth Shadow button, you change from one type of shadow to the other. By clicking on the shadow in the box, you can drag the shadow in any direction and increase or decrease the depth of shadow you'll add to your letters. The number will change in the Depth Selector box, to indicate how much shadow you are creating. Here, I've set the direction so that the shadow appears to the upper-right of the letters, and at a depth of 7. Really 7 is a bit too much, but by exaggerating the effect you can better see the difference.

SAVING TITLES

Titles aren't saved automatically. You must Save a title in a bin in order to use it.
Go to the File menu and select Save Title As...

File	Edit	Bin	Clip
New Title			⌘N
Open Bin...			⌘O
Close			⌘W
Save Title			⌘S
Save Title As...			

A dialog box will open, letting you select the bin that the title will be saved to, the hard drive partition, and the resolution. After clicking OK, the title will be saved in the bin you selected. If you're through creating titles, go to the File menu and select Close. If you want to keep creating titles, choose New Title in the File menu.

CUTTING TITLES INTO YOUR SEQUENCE

You can't edit titles directly into the sequence from the Title Tool. Once you've saved your title and closed the Title Tool, you must find the title in the bin. The icon for a title is different from the icon for a clip. The Avid treats titles a bit differently from regular clips. All titles are *effects*. An effect is something that needs computer power to make it appear on your screen. It must be rendered (created by the CPU). Here I've located the title in the bin. The title icon looks like one of those naval flags used to signal by semaphore. Double-click on it. It will appear in the Source monitor or Pop-up Monitor just like any other clip.

If you can't find the title and you know it should be in your bin, you need to go to the Bin menu, choose Select Bin Display, and make sure that the effects box is checked. If it's not, you won't find the title because, although its there, it hasn't been chosen for display.

Once you double-click on the title icon, your title will come up in the Source Monitor or Pop-up Monitor, as shown in Figure 9.6.

With the title in the Source Monitor or Pop-up Monitor, you're ready to splice it into your sequence. But wait. Where will it go? Since this title is supposed to be superimposed over the video of Nelson Mandela, we need to open a second video track. Go to the Clip menu and choose New Video Track. V2 will appear in the Timeline. Now you must patch the Source track to the V2 Record track, as shown in Figure 9.7.

Once you make the patch, V2 will be highlighted, and V1 will not. Make sure the video monitor icon is on V2. Remember, the Avid will monitor all the video tracks at or below the track with the video monitor. If the icon stays on V1, it won't monitor any tracks above it.

Now you're ready to cut the title in using "three marks make an edit." There are a few things you should know before you make the edit.

Figure 9.6

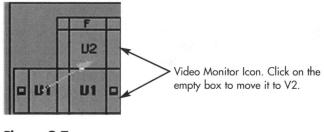

Video Monitor Icon. Click on the empty box to move it to V2.

Figure 9.7

The Avid generates about two minutes of title material every time you create a title. Since that's far more than you'll ever need, don't make your IN on the first frame in the Source Monitor. Instead, go in 40 frames and then mark your IN. That way you can have fades and trim available. Mark an IN and OUT and then look in the Source Tracking Monitor to check the I/O of your marks. Three seconds is a good length for most short titles. Now go to the Timeline and mark the IN where you want to cut the title into the sequence. It's best to use *overwrite* instead of splice. True, since this is the first clip you'll put on the V2 track, it doesn't matter now. But later on, when you add titles to a track that already has titles, only overwrite will keep those titles from getting pushed out of place.

As you can see, the title has been placed in the Timeline above the shot it will be superimposed over.

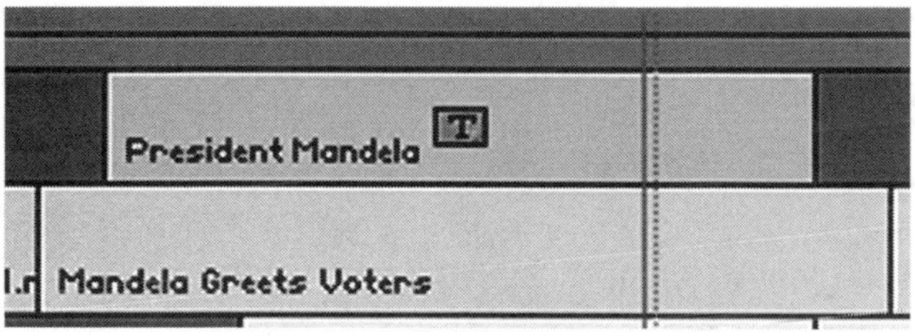

There's a tiny ball on the title icon, telling us that the title may need to be rendered. To see the title when we play the sequence, we may have to render it. You can see the title even before you render it, if you select Render On-The-Fly from the Special menu (MC) or Clip menu (Xpress). Now it will appear whenever you drag the position indicator through it. Of course, timing is everything, and to make sure the title is on for the right amount of time and looks the way we want it to, we'll render it.

RENDERING YOUR TITLES

Colored dots in the title's effect icon indicate that the title may need to be rendered.

To Render a single title:

1. Select the track containing the title.
2. Place the blue position indicator on the T icon in the Timeline.
3. Go to the Clip menu and choose Render at Position, or
   - Click the Render Effect button in the Composer Fast menu—Xpress.
   - Click the Render Effect button in the center Fast menu—MC.
4. When the dialog box appears, choose a target disk for the "pre-compute."
5. Click OK.

If you have a number of titles that need to be rendered, it's easier to render them all at the same time.

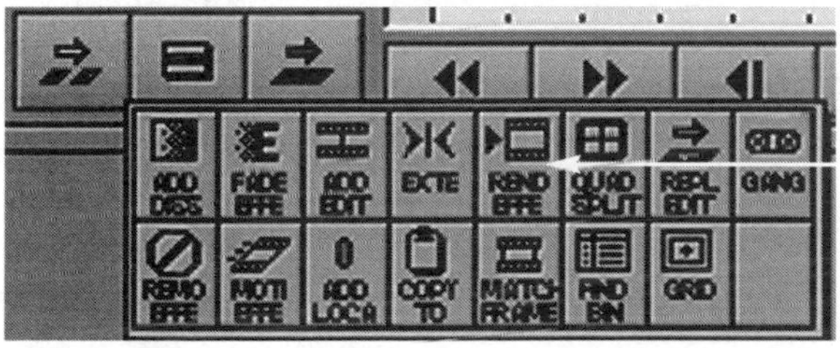

Render Effect button.

Figure 9.8

Rendering multiple titles:

1. Click the track selector to choose the track(s) holding titles you want to render.
2. Mark an IN before the first title and an OUT after the last title.
3. Go to the Clip menu and select Render In/Out.

Now that the title is rendered, we can play the sequence and see how it works. If it turns out that the title is on screen a bit too long use Dual-Roller Trim to trim the head or tail of the title. If it's not on long enough, use Dual-Roller Trim to extend the tail of the title.

That's it. We've created a title with drop shadow, placed it in the lower-third of the frame, saved it to a bin, opened it, cut it onto a new video track, and rendered it.

There's a lot more you can do with the Title Tool.

COLORED TITLES

You can change the colors of the letters, the color of the shadow, or both. You can even create a blend so that, for example, a title starts out dark and becomes lighter as it progresses. (Because this book is in black and white, you're going to have to practice the techniques on your Avid in order to see the colors.)

To turn a white title into a title containing color, select it with the Select Tool or, if you're in Text Mode, select the words by dragging. Now click on the Fill window (Figure 9.9). Press and hold the mouse on the Fill window, and a Color Wheel or Color Picker appears.

Drag through the colors until you select the color you want. Or you can click on the eyedropper and click inside the video frame to choose any color already inside the frame.

In Figure 9.9 I've selected the color red to "fill in" the title letters.

You can also select a color for the shadows. They don't have to be black. Select the title in the window, and then click and hold on the shadow window.

The Color Picker appears, and you drag through the choices until you select the one you want. Here I've selected a light red for the shadow. I've exaggerated the shadow by choosing a depth of 14 so that the change is more pronounced (Figure 9.10).

Click and hold here to open the Color Picker.

Figure 9.9

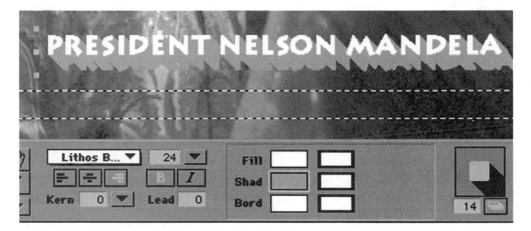

Figure 9.10

BLENDING A TITLE

Let's say the video background shifts from bright to dark so that a white title won't show up in the bright areas, and a dark title won't show up well in the dark areas. You can create a blend so that the title changes from one color to another color. When I click on the Fill window (Figure 9.11), two small windows appear to its right. Click and hold on the left window and select a dark color. Click and hold on the right box and pick a lighter color. Your choices appear in the respective box, and the mixture of the two appears in the Blend Direction box. You can change the direction of the blend by dragging the mouse inside this box. I've selected a dark gray in the left-hand box and white in the right-hand box.

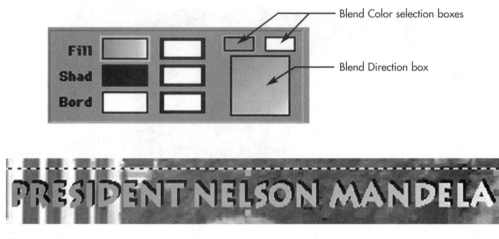

Figure 9.11

Figure 9.11 shows the resulting title. Notice how the letters go from dark gray to white over the width of the title.

CREATING TITLE STYLE SHEETS

After doing a lot of work to set up the title just the way you like it, it would be nice not to have to reinvent the wheel the next time you create a title just like it. Fortunately, the Title Tool has a Save As feature, which lets you create a *style sheet* so that you can set the same title parameters to any new titles you create.

To create a Style sheet:

- Click on the title or object you want to save as a style sheet so that it becomes a selection, and the arrow lights up in the tool box.
- Press the triangle next to Styles so that the Save As box appears.

- Choose Save As.
- The Style Sheet dialog box appears.
- Make sure that the parameters reflect your choices.

- Type a name in the text box.
- Click Done.

Once you have created several styles, your style sheets appear in the Save As window as choices.

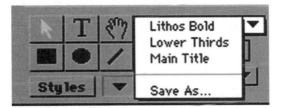

To apply a style, simply type a new title and then go to the Styles menu and select your choice. The parameters will be applied to the new title.

DRAWING OBJECTS

The Title Tool has drawing tools with which you can create boxes, circles, lines, and arrows of various shapes and colors. To give you an example of some of the things you can do with these tools, I've created a title that I want to superimpose over a shot showing swimmers in the ocean off Durban, South Africa (Figure 9.13). The white letters don't show up as well as I'd like, so I'm going to create a colored rectangle, which I'll place behind the title. First I'll select a color for the rectangle by clicking in the Fill and choosing an aqua blue color. Next I select the drawing tool that creates boxes (and rectangles). Because I want the rectangle to have rounded corners, I select the curved corner in the corner selection window.

When I drag the pointer across the title window, a blue rectangle with rounded corners appears.

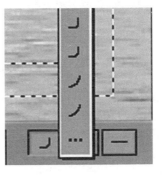

Drawing tools for boxes, circles and lines

Figure 9.12

Figure 9.13

Using the selector tool, I drag the rectangle on top of the title "Durban Waterfront." The title is no longer visible. I know—that's not good. But I'm not finished.

Now, I go up to the Object menu, which appears only when the Title Tool is open. I select Send To Back. This places the object that is in front—the blue rectangle—behind the title.

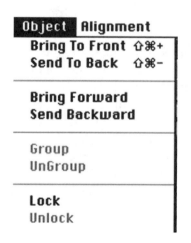

Now that's more like it. Our title is a lot more visible now that a blue rectangle surrounds it.

GROUPING AND LOCKING

If I were satisfied with this, I'd *Group* the title and rectangle, and then *Lock* them together. To group, choose the Selection Tool, and, while pressing the mouse, drag the cursor around the objects to be grouped. Then select Group from the Object menu. To lock them, select the object that is now a group, and choose Lock from the Object menu. Now you can't make inadvertent changes to your creation.

Figure 9.14

TRANSPARENCY

However, I'm not happy with the title and its blue rectangle. I think the rectangle would look better if it were less opaque, so that some ocean showed through. To set the transparency of an object, select the transparency tool for the object that you want to affect.

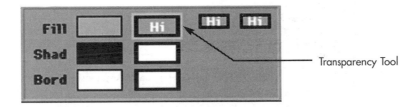

Transparency Tool

In this example, I've selected the Fill, which affects the transparency of my blue rectangle. To make the blue box more transparent, I must first place it in the foreground. I choose Bring To Front from the Object menu. Then I click and hold on the Fill transparency Tool. A slider appears, and as I drag it to the right, the blue rectangle will become more transparent. It now has a HI (high) degree of transparency. I need to send it to the back, using the Object Tool. There. Now, I'll group and lock it.

Figure 9.15

ALIGNMENT MENU

There's a second menu available once you've opened the Title Tool; it is called the Alignment Menu. You'll see that it has many items that help you position selected objects inside the frame. Using the selection tool, practice using the various alignment choices available in the pull-down menu.

LINES AND ARROWS

There are tools for creating arrows and lines of various thickness. These work with the line-drawing tool, and can be changed and manipulated just like the rectangle we created using the drawing tool.

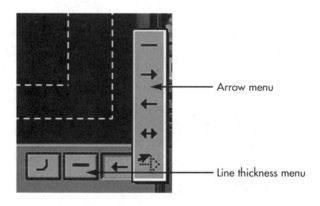

Arrow menu

Line thickness menu

OTHER BUTTONS

The Video Placement Tool is one tool I'd suggest you avoid using for now. It doesn't move objects within the frame; it moves the entire frame.

Stay away from this tool.

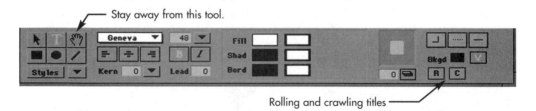

Rolling and crawling titles

On newer versions of Avid software there are two buttons on the tool bar for creating *rolling* (R) and *crawling* (C) titles.

ROLLING TITLES

Filmmakers have always called titles that move from the bottom of the screen to the top of the screen a "crawl." The many credits that appear at the end of films are usually handled by a lengthy crawl. Avid calls them rolling titles. They're not that difficult to create. The one oddity is that the speed with which the title "rolls" is determined by the size of the clip in the Timeline. To make the crawl go faster, you trim the clip. To make it go slower, you extend its length (size) in the Timeline.

To create a "rolling title:"

1. Select a background (black or video) by putting the position indicator over black or a shot in the timeline.
2. From the Clip menu, choose New Title.
3. Pick the Text Tool.
4. On the far right of Title Tool, click the "R" button—it turns green.
5. Choose your font and point size, and then click the text alignment box for "centered."
6. Type the text. As you type, the text might word wrap. Don't worry. Just keep typing. Press the return key at the end of each line of text.
7. Get the Selector tool and drag the handles to the left and right to make the text wide enough to prevent word wrap.
8. If the text goes onto more than one page (screen), drag the scroll bar that appears on the right-hand side of the title window to scroll through the text.
9. Select Close from File menu.
10. Save the title:
    * Select the target disk and bin.
    * Don't save with Fast Save.
11. Click OK.

The title is saved as a clip in a bin.

Cutting in Rolling Titles

Double-click the title clip to get the title to open up in the Source Monitor or Pop-up Monitor.

Mark an IN in the Timeline and overwrite or splice in the rolling title.

It will seem strange, but you use Trim Mode to change the speed of the rolling title. Drag the end of the crawl toward the tail (right), and the crawl slows down. Drag the end of the crawl toward the head (left), and the crawl speeds up.

The rolling title will always start with the first line off-screen. It will then appear at the bottom of the screen and move upwards. You can set IN and OUT marks in the Source or Pop-up Monitor to change the start and end points. For instance, mark an IN and you can get the rolling title to begin with the first line already on screen.

CRAWLING TITLES

Avid calls a title that move across the screen horizontally, a crawl. The text runs along the frame from screen-right to screen-left.

You create crawling titles the same way you create rolling titles, but you click on the "C" instead of the "R." You'll need to use the Selector Tool handles to keep the letters from word wrapping. For example, let's say you wanted the following title to crawl across the screen:

"Boston Celtics win NBA title. First time in fifteen years. Watch the News at Eleven for highlights."

To get this text to crawl as a single line, you'll need to drag the selector handle to the far right so that the text doesn't word wrap, as this sentence does. How to get this text to come true? I wish I knew.

SUGGESTED ASSIGNMENTS

1. Open the Title Tool and choose a font size of 24.
2. Type a title.
3. Click on the Selector Tool and drag the right-hand selection handle to make the title fit on the line.
4. Move the title around inside the frame.
5. Add a drop shadow. Increase and decrease the depth and direction of the shadow.
6. Change to a depth shadow.
7. Save your title.
8. Close the Title Tool and cut the title into your Timeline. If you need to, create a V2 track.
9. Render your title.
10. Open the Title Tool. Create a lightly-colored title. Add a depth shadow. Now create a blend for that title.
11. Close the Title Tool and cut this title onto V2.
12. Render it.
13. Open the Title Tool. Create a title. Draw a rectangle. Place the title on top of the rectangle.
14. Close the Title Tool and cut this title onto V2.
15. Render it.

10

Effects

I learned to make films before I ever worked in video, and I guess that's why it took me a while to take advantage of Avid's extensive effects. Effects are so expensive in film that you only use them when nothing else will work. Put in a few freeze frames and a strobe effect, toss in a flop in order to change screen direction, and suddenly you're writing checks for thousands of dollars to an optical house in New York or L.A. And then you wait weeks to see how those effects come out. When I started working in video, effects were certainly faster, but only marginally cheaper. Go into an online editing suite that has a sophisticated effects generator, and the bill you get when you're finished can grab your attention pretty fast.

It's different on an Avid. The effects are free, and you don't have to wait more than a few minutes—and usually much less—to see what they'll look like. It's true that if you're using the Avid as an offline machine, meaning you'll finish the project on film or at an online tape facility, you'll need to worry about your budget. But for all the projects you can finish on the Avid, don't worry. Use as many effects as the show demands.

Keep in mind that not every project benefits from a lot of effects. Scenes involving strong performances by talented actors are usually hurt by visual effects, because they steal the scene from the actors. Montage sequences that are music-driven or contain stunning cinematography are great candidates for effects, because the right effect heightens the mood and visual impact of the sequence. Rock videos, which are designed to be viewed many times, benefit from complex visual effects. Otherwise the video becomes stale after one or two viewings. Title sequences, show openings, and transitions between acts are usually polished with visual effects as a means of grabbing audience attention. Often, editors add a number of effects to the material coming right before and after a commercial break in order to separate the show's content from the commercial.

Some editors think of effects as "crutches," used to mask serious problems in the material. Others think they needlessly junk up a show. I think this is another area where the Avid comes in handy. Try it with, and try it without. You then can make your decision, based on what it looks like when you play the sequence. To evaluate the effectiveness of an effect, you must really watch. You must turn yourself into a critical viewer, which, as we've said before, is the editor's most important skill.

KINDS OF EFFECTS

There are two categories of effects. *Transition effects* are applied at the "cut point" or transition point in the Timeline. These effects change the way Shot A transitions to Shot B. A dissolve is an example of a transition effect. Instead of a straight cut, Shot A fades out while Shot B fades in, creating a melting of the two shots.

Segment Effects are applied to the entire clip or "segment" in the Timeline. You might have a shot in the sequence where your actor is facing screen left-to-right, and by applying a *flop*, the screen direction of the entire shot is changed so the actor is facing screen right-to-left. When you use a segment effect you are affecting a segment in the Timeline.

Segment effects can work on one video track, like the flop, or on several video tracks. For instance, you might have an image on V2 interact with an image on V1. In a multilayered effect, V1 is always the background layer, and V2 (and V3, V4) is layered on top of the background.

Many effects work as both transition effects and segment effects. They can be applied to either a transition or a segment.

Applying effects to a transition or segment is really quite simple. Getting them to do what you want is a bit more complicated.

EFFECT PALETTE

Let's take a look at the Effect Palette. Press Command-8 (Ctrl-8) or go to the Tools menu and select Effect Palette.

The left-hand column lists the categories of effects. Once you click on a category, a list of the types of effects your system offers is displayed in the right-hand column. Scroll through the category list, clicking on the different categories, and look at the many choices offered. For instance, under the Blend category, you see six different blend effects (Figure 10.2).

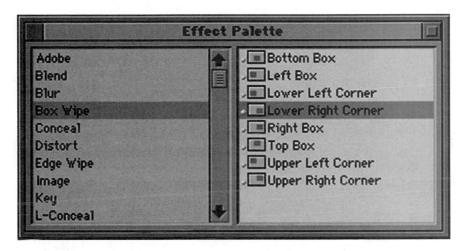

Figure 10.1   Effect Palette

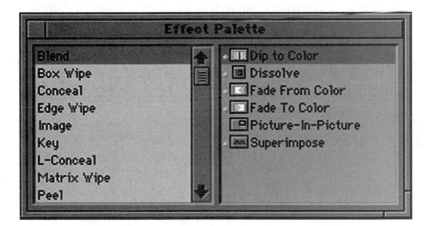

Figure 10.2

REAL-TIME EFFECTS AND COLORED DOTS

When you look at the effects, you'll see a colored dot next to some of them. Some dots are orange and some are green. Which effects have which dots depends on the Avid model you're working on. This whole dot business is fairly confusing and counterintuitive. Here's a quick guide that helps (I hope).

The effects with *no dots* are the most complex effects and will take a long time to render.

The effects with *green dots* are less complex; sometimes you'll be able to play them in real time, and sometimes you'll have to render them to see them.

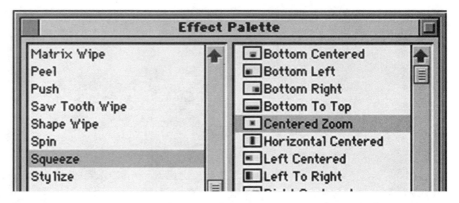

Figure 10.3

The effects with *orange dots* are the least complex, and you should be able to play them in real time (but don't bet on it).

When you apply an effect that has no dot, a blue dot appears in the Timeline.

Say what?

The dot-coloring scheme isn't Avid at its best. My experience is that unless you bought the most expensive system, you're going to have to spend a lot of time rendering to see the effects you've created.

APPLYING AN EFFECT

It's easy to apply an effect. Just click on the icon for the effect you want, and drag it from the Effect Palette to the Timeline. Release it when you've reached the transition or segment of your choice.

Let's try a transition effect. Let's use a squeeze effect. There are quite a few squeeze effects to choose from. Let's try a "Centered Zoom."

Here's Figure 10.4—the outgoing shot of a town, and Figure 10.5—the incoming shot of a map.

Figure 10.4

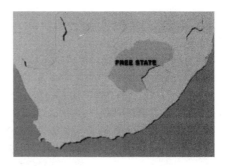

Figure 10.5

Now I'm going to click on the Centered Zoom icon in the Effect Palette, drag it onto the transition point in the Timeline, and release it. There. I've got a centered zoom squeeze between the two shots.

Drag the icon to the Timeline and release it.

Figure 10.6 gives you some idea what the effect looks like. The map starts out small and then gets bigger and bigger as it squeezes out the shot of the town.

To play the effect in the sequence, you'll probably need to render it. However, you can get a preview of what it will look like by going to the Clip menu and choosing Render On-The-Fly. Then, as you drag the position indicator through the Timeline, you'll see the effect. If you want to see it at normal speed, you need to render it.

RENDERING A SINGLE EFFECT

1. Place the blue position indicator on the effect's icon in the Timeline.
2. Click the Render Effect button in the Composer Fast menu, or choose Render from the Clip menu.
3. When the dialog box appears, choose a target disk.
4. Click OK.

Figure 10.6

Figure 10.7

Figure 10.8

Now let's try a segment effect. Scroll down the Effect Palette until you see the category "Image" in the left-hand column. Click on it. Now click on the effect called Flop. This effect changes the screen direction of a shot. Here's a shot showing South Africa's second black president, Thabo Mbeki, talking to South Africa's last white president, F. W. De Klerk.

To change the clip's screen direction, I simply drag the Flop icon onto the clip itself, not onto the transition, and presto, the screen direction changes.

When I went to render this flop, instead of going to the Clip menu, I went to a Fast menu, where you'll find several command keys that relate to effects. This Fast menu on the Xpress has several important effect command buttons. I pressed the Render Effect button.

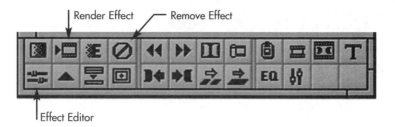

Figure 10.9 Fast menu

WAITING FOR EFFECTS TO RENDER

Some effects take a long time to render. When I rendered the flop, the computer took about five minutes to render it. Five minutes might not seem like a long time, but if you're really in a flow, and coming up with a lot of ideas, it can seem painfully slow—a bit like the world's longest traffic light when you're already late.

One strategy is to wait until you've created a number of effects and then render them all at once, while you go do something else. Lunch is one possibility.

RENDERING MULTIPLE EFFECTS

First, click the track selector boxes to choose the track(s) holding the effects you want to render.

1. Mark an IN before the first effect and an OUT after the last effect.
2. Go to the Clip menu and select Render In/Out.
3. When the dialog box appears, choose a target disk.
4. Click OK.

So far we've looked at some fairly straightforward effects. As you can see, it's not all that difficult to apply an effect to either a transition or a segment in the Timeline. Now let's look at more complicated effects that can be changed in significant ways by the use of the *Effect Editor*.

EFFECT EDITOR

Almost all effects have *parameters*, which are specific features that can be altered or adjusted. For instance, you might have one shot on the screen, and then a second image appears inside a box. The image in the box may start out small and gradually fill the frame, covering up the first image. There are a lot of parameters that you could manipulate to enhance this effect. You could, for instance,

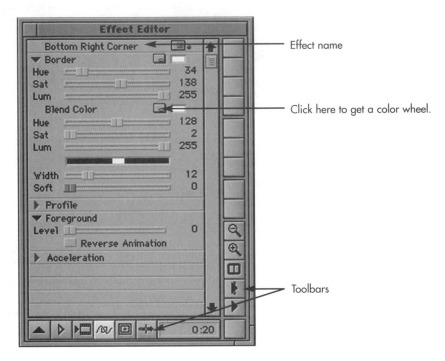

Figure 10.10   Effect Editor

give the box a border. You could give the border a color. You could create a path for the box to follow as it moves around the screen. You could have the box get bigger as it moves around the screen. These are all parameters that you can control with the Effect Editor.

Opening the Effect Editor

After you have applied an effect to the segment or transition in the Timeline:

1. Place the blue position indicator on the effect's icon in the Timeline.
2. Click the Effect Mode button on the keyboard or Fast menu.

You can also open the Effect Editor from the Tools menu.

It can be confusing at first, differentiating between the Effect Palette and the Effect Editor. Just remember that you select the effect from the Effect Palette. You control and manipulate the effect with the Effect Editor.

Let's examine the Effect Editor. The one in the figure below is for a peel effect called "Bottom Right Corner." At the top of the Effect Editor you'll see the name of the effect you are editing. In the middle area you'll see the *parameters* that can be changed. Triangle-shaped openers give you access to sliders, which control the amount or quantity of a particular parameter.

Each effect will have different parameters because each effect behaves differently. However, the effects within a category usually have similar parameters.

Notice also that the Composer/Record Monitor changes. Now the picture window beneath the monitor no longer shows the sequence, but just the segment that contains the effect.

Figure 10.11 shows the Effect Editor at work. The Peel effect has been applied to a transition between a map of South Africa and a group of South Africans.

Figure 10.11

Using the Effect Editor, I created a border, which makes the peel look like a page that's turning, and then I gave the border a cream color.

Here are some of the different parameters you'll encounter:

Border—Changes the color of the border, or box, that surrounds an image. You can also change the border's width and transparency.

Foreground Level—On most transitional effects, this represents the proportion of incoming to outgoing frames.

Foreground Level—On blends and key effects, it represent the video's opacity.

Reverse—This reverses the parameter you have set. Instead of a box starting out small and getting bigger, it will start big and shrink.

Acceleration—This controls the start and end of a move, so the move isn't too abrupt.

Scaling—Changes the size of the box. You can manipulate the width and height of boxes.

Effect Editor Tools

The tools that come with the Effect Editor help you work with each effect and control its parameters.

One of the most important tools lets you place *key frames*. Key frames enable you to change a parameter's look over time. For instance, you might place a box around an image and start that image on the far left of the screen. That's Key Frame Number One. Then you move the box a little toward the center of the frame and set the next key frame. Move the box some more and set another key frame. You could have the box go all over the place by setting multiple key frames. The number of key frames available on any given effect will depend on the type of software you have. Some effects might only have four key frames, while others might have unlimited key frames.

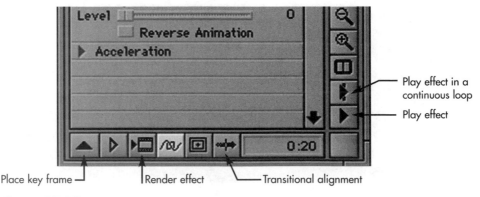

Figure 10.12

Figure 10.13 The image on V1 looks like this.

Figure 10.14 The image on V2 looks like this.

Let's work with a segment effect and use the Effect Editor and key frames to change the way a parameter works. We'll use the segment effect called Superimpose and work with the Level parameter.

For a superimposition to work, you need two images. First I add a second video track, V2. I simply go to the Clip menu and select New Video Track. I then splice in the second image onto track V2.

I next drag the Superimpose icon from the Effect Palette onto the V2 image.

Now I open the Effect Editor by placing the position indicator on the effect icon and pressing the Effect Editor command key on the keyboard or Fast menu.

Right now the effect gives me a superimposition of the image on V2 over the image on V1. The level is set at 50, meaning that the two images are blended evenly together (half and half, or 50%). If I play the image by clicking on the Play

Forward or Play Loop button, I'll see that the two images remain blended at this level throughout the length of the clip. That's not what I want. What I want to do is change the amount of superimposition over time. To do that, I will need to change the Level parameter (which affects the amount of V2's opacity) and set key frames in the effect's position bar, which will affect the Level changes over time.

First I drag the Level slider to the left, resulting in 0 opacity.

When I do that, the foreground image, V2, will not be seen at all. I want this to be the case at the beginning of the effect, so I set a key frame at the beginning of the effect's picture window.

To place a key frame, just drag and place the position indicator in the effect's position bar and click on the Key Frame button in the Effect Editor tool-bar, or on the key frame button on the keyboard (the same one you used for audio key frames).

Now I set a second key frame, further along in the effect's position bar, and then I move the Level slider to 25.

Now I place a third key frame, click on it to select it, and change the opacity to 75.

Now, the foreground image really starts to come through the background image.

Finally, I set the last key frame at the end and change the opacity to 100.

O Level   25 Level   75 Level   100 Level

Now I've created my effect. The image begins with V1 totally filling the frame—Level is set at 0. Over time, the image on V2 slowly takes over, as increasing amounts of opacity are set at those key frames, until finally by the end of the shot, the opacity is set to 100 and only the V2 image appears on the screen.

Figure 10.15
Begin with just V1.

Figure 10.16
V2 is supered over V1.

Figure 10.17
V2 takes over the screen.

Manipulating Key Frames

- After you have created a key frame, you can move it by holding the Option key and dragging it to a new position.
- You can change the parameter for any given key frame by clicking on it (it turns pink) and changing the parameters in the Effect Editor.
- You can delete a key frame by selecting it and hitting the Delete key.

EFFECT QUICK REVIEW

Steps for adding effects:

- Load a sequence into the Timeline.
- Open Effect Palette from the Tools menu (or hit ⌘-8).
- Choose the effect and drag it into the Timeline.
- Adjust the effect with the Effect Editor (keyboard or Tool menu).
- Render the effect.

DELETING EFFECTS

To Delete a transitional effect:

- Put the position indictor on the transition. Press the Remove Effect button from the Fast menu.
- Go to the transition and enter the Trim Mode. Press the Delete key.

To Delete a segment effect:

- Put the position indictor on the effect icon. Press the Remove Effect button from the Fast menu.
- Hit a segment button and select the segment. Press the Delete key.

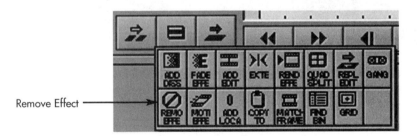

Remove Effect

ADDING DISSOLVES

Dissolves are so common that there's a Dissolve key on the keyboard and a Dissolve button on the Fast menu. The Dissolve button works a little differently from a dissolve that is dragged from the Effect Palette.

Add Dissolve Button

Dissolve Button

1.   Put the blue position indicator on the transition.
2.   Hit the Add Dissolve button.

A dialog window appears, giving you choices to control how the dissolve will look.
3.   Choose the duration. A 30-frame dissolve is the default length.
4.   Choose whether the dissolve is centered on the cut, starting on the cut, ending on the cut, or custom-designed by you.
5.   Choose the target disk.
6.   Click Add to place the dissolve on the transition, or choose Add and Render, to place it on the transition and have it rendered.

SAVING AN EFFECT AS A TEMPLATE

After doing all the work involved in setting the many parameters for an effect, you can save those parameters so you can use them again on another transition or segment in the Timeline. Simply drag the icon in the Effect Editor window to a bin. Rename it in the bin. You have just created a template. To place the template you created on a transition or a segment, simply click on it in the bin and drag it to the Timeline.

Drag icon to a bin.

There are two important effects that aren't found on the Effects Palette: freeze frames and motion effects.

FREEZE FRAMES

Freeze frames are given special status and are found in the Clip menu. Just follow these steps to create your first freeze. After you've done it once, you'll be able to do it in your sleep.

1. In the Timeline, go to the tail of the shot you want to freeze and put the position indicator on the last frame. Remember Option-Command-drag.
2. Select "match frame" (Fast menu item), and the clip will appear in the Pop-up Monitor or in the Source Monitor with the last frame marked by an IN.
3. Go to the Clip menu and choose Freeze Frame.
4. Select the length. Click OK. A new clip is created, labeled "Clip name" FF.
5. Mark an IN and an OUT.
6. In the Timeline, go to the first frame of the next shot (Command-drag the blue position indicator) and mark IN.
7. Splice in the freeze.

There will be no sound.

MOTION EFFECTS

This is a special effect that has its own button—this one is in the Pop-up Monitor's toolbar on the Xpress, or on the Fast menu on the MC.

Slow Motion/Fast Motion

1. Select a clip in a bin that you want to apply a motion effect to, and double-click to open it.
2. In the Pop-up or Source Monitor, mark an IN and an OUT to show the section of the clip you want to use for the effect.

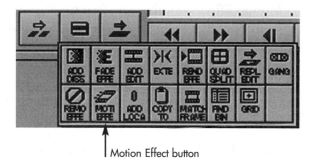

Motion Effect button

3. Press the Motion Effect button. A Motion Effect dialog box appears.
4. Fifteen frames per second and 50% are the default settings. The result-ing shot is twice as long, which is another way of saying it appears to be twice as slow, as normal.
5. Choose another setting, such as 8 FPS, to make it even slower. You can hit the Preview button to watch a clock's hand go around in a circle to simulate the speed.

When you click on Create and Render, the motion effect appears as a new clip in the bin. Now you open that clip and splice or overwrite it into your sequence.

Reverse Motion

This is useful, for instance, if you have a zoom that goes in, and you want to make the zoom go out.

1. Select a clip in a bin that you want to apply a motion effect to, and double-click.
2. In the Pop-up or Source Monitor, mark an IN and an OUT to show the section you want.
3. Press the Motion Effect button.
4. Put a minus sign (-) in front of the FPS or percent rate. Choose 30 FPS if you want it to be normal.
5. After clicking on Create and Render, cut the new clip into your sequence.

Strobe

1. Select a clip in a bin that you want to apply a motion effect to, and dou-ble-click.
2. In the Pop-up or Source Monitor, mark an IN and an OUT to show the section you want.

3. Press the Motion Effect button on the Pop-up Monitor toolbar.
4. Click on the Strobe Motion box and deselect the Variable Speed box.
5. "Update Every 5 Frames" is the default setting. This means every fifth frame is displayed, creating the strobe effect. Try 5 frames and then try another number. Click the Preview button to see the effect.
6. After clicking on Create and Render, cut the new clip into your sequence.

Here's what a title, slow motion effect, and freeze frame look like in your bin.

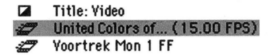

A WORLD OF EFFECTS

We could devote a whole book to effects. We've just touched the surface in this chapter. There's the whole subject of third-party plug-in effects, which I haven't mentioned. Nor have I discussed 3D effects, which come as a standard feature on many Avid models. To give you an idea about how much information is available, consider that the effects manual that Avid supplies to its customers is over 300 pages long.

SUGGESTED ASSIGNMENTS

Take the information provided in this chapter and apply it to as many effects as you have time to play with. Just drag the effect you wish to examine onto the Timeline, open the Effect Editor, and manipulate the parameters. Use key frames to change the parameters over time.

11

Saving Your Work

IF IT'S A COMPUTER IT WILL CRASH

Not too long ago there were articles in newspapers, weekly magazines, and online news sites about the convergence of television and computers, with companies arguing over whether we should be watching TV on a computer monitor, or viewing our favorite Internet site on the old RCA or Sony Trinitron. One scribe who favored the television monitor said he didn't want to be watching the Superbowl and have the system crash during a game-winning touchdown drive.

There is some truth to that observation. Computers do crash, they have bugs, and they are susceptible to viruses and other infestations. When you stop and think about it, those are problems we don't encounter on any of the other countless electronic products that surround us. My microwave doesn't crash, my television doesn't have bugs, and my CD player hasn't caught a virus, although I've loaded into it hundreds and hundreds of CDs.

That said, the Apple Macintosh Avid that I've been using for three years has been quite dependable. (Yes, the sound you hear is my knuckles striking wood.) It has never quit on me. It has only crashed about 30 times, and never have I lost more than about 10 minutes of work. Over time, it has developed some unattractive quirks. When I boot up, sometimes the screen resolution is incorrect. And sometimes it won't show me my titles in the Source Monitor. But given how much I've used it, and the service it has rendered, I figure it's one of the most dependable things in my life!

Another testimonial. The Avids I use to teach my digital editing classes have behaved beautifully. I've only had about three crashes in front of a roomful of students. That's an amazing record of performance. So, I'm a satisfied customer, and I don't hesitate to praise the machines whenever I'm asked. My point is that the Macintosh Avids are incredibly dependable, but they will crash. And when they do, you'd better be ready. Although there are people who doubt that the Windows NT Avids will achieve the same record of dependability, most NT users scoff at the idea. No matter which system you use, Mac or NT, I promise you, it will someday crash.

BACKING UP

If there is a system crash, hard drive glitch, or any number of horrors just waiting to befall you, *all* your work can be lost—unless you back up your work. By that I mean placing the information about your bins and sequences on a Zip or floppy disk. Here's how:

1. When you finish editing for the day, and after you save all your work, close the project and quit the application. You are returned to the desktop, or Finder.
2. Open the CPU's hard drive—the computer's hard drive, as opposed to the external storage drives; the C: drive on the NT machine.
3. Look for the folder called "Composer Projects" (Mac) or "Avid Projects" (NT).

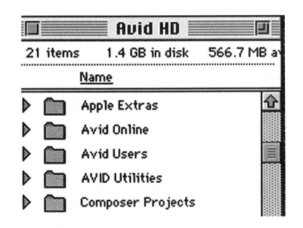

4. Open it.
5. Scroll through it until you find your project—the one you named.
6. Insert either a floppy disk or a Zip disk into the computer's CPU slot for that type of disk. (Make sure your disk is not carrying a virus!!)
7. When the disk appears on the desktop, drag the project folder containing your project's name onto the floppy or Zip disk (see Figure 11.1). The computer will automatically begin to copy to that disk.

That wasn't so hard. Remember to do it daily.

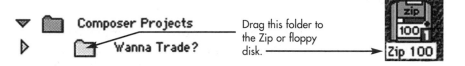

Figure 11.1

Examine the contents of the Zip disk named Avid Back-Up, which contains the "Wanna Trade" Project folder. Notice that there is one for April 14 and another for April 15. As I said, you should do this at the end of every editing session, and then rename the latest version with the current date, so you can easily find the one with the most recent changes.

Name	Size	Kind
▷ S. Kauffmann	—	folder
▷ Wanna Trade? April 14	—	folder
▷ Wanna Trade? April 15	—	folder

Avid Back-Up — 18 items — 62.8 MB in disk

All the project settings, sequences, and bins, including all your titles, effects, clips, subclips, and audio clip information—everything is copied to your backup disk. Open the most recent folder and you'll see that everything associated with the project has been backed up onto the Zip disk.

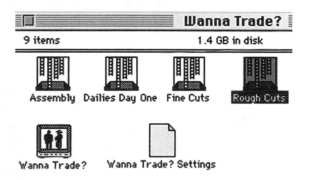

It's important to note that none of the media files—none of the digitized picture or sound—is copied to the Zip or floppy. Only the information the Avid has created about the project is copied. But that's usually all you need.

AFTER THE CRASH

If there is a bad crash and your project is missing or badly corrupted, or if some-one removes your project from the CPU, you can reload all your files onto your Avid. All you have to do is insert your floppy or Zip into the CPU's disk drive and drag your project folder to the Avid's Composer Projects folder (or Avid Projects folder). Launch the Avid program, and your project and all the clip infor-mation will be there. It will all be listed as "Media Offline," but you can easily redigitize the clips. And once you redigitize the clips, all the sequences that you've edited using those clips will be just the way you left them, like magic. We'll learn to redigitize your clips later in this chapter.

SAVING USER SETTINGS

You can back up your user settings the same way. All the user settings you made in the Settings area—how Trim Mode works, how the keyboard is configured, how the Composer Monitor looks, how auto save works, the color of your tracks in the Timeline—all these are all saved under your name in the Avid Users folder.

COPY USER SETTINGS TO A FLOPPY OR ZIP

When you are on the desktop or Finder (the application is closed and the CPU's hard drive is open), double-click on the Avid Users folder and then drag your user settings folder to a floppy or Zip drive (Figure 11.2).

Freelance editors love the ability to save user settings. They can bring a floppy disk to any Avid running the same version of the software, at any editing facility in the world. They need only drag their settings file to the Avid Users folder on the hard drive. When they launch the software, their name and all their user preferences will be there. Think of all the time they have saved themselves and their clients.

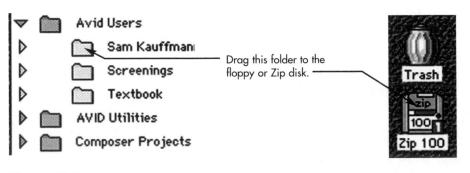

Figure 11.2

THE ATTIC

If you recall the work we did with settings, you'll remember that Bin Settings was one of the first settings we examined. There you told the Avid how often and when you wanted your work saved to the *attic*. The attic, you'll recall, is like an attic in a house, where old items get stored. In this case, the old items are previous versions of your work. If there is a crash, or if you lose a sequence, or something happens during an editing session, you can go to the attic and retrieve the last 30 versions, one of which is only 10 or 15 minutes old.

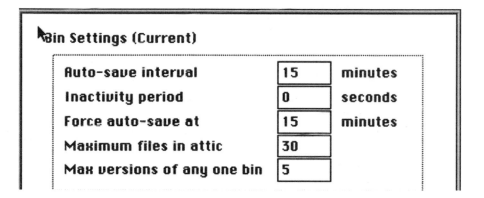

Perhaps you want to go back to a version you worked on three hours earlier. Whatever you're looking for, it's probably in the attic. You'll find the attic folder on the hard drive.

Double-click to open it, and you'll see all the files that have been saved. The Avid doesn't just save your sequences, but the entire bin.

Name	Size	Kind	Label	Last Modified
0051.bak.1	32K	MCXpress™ document	–	Wed, Aug 18,
BD HOUR THREE 75 CONS .bak.12	1.8 MB	MCXpress™ document	–	Wed, Aug 18,
BD HOUR THREE 75 CONS .bak.11	1.8 MB	MCXpress™ document	–	Wed, Aug 18,
BD HOUR THREE 75 CONS .bak.10	1.8 MB	MCXpress™ document	–	Wed, Aug 18,

Attic ƒ — 30 items — 1.4 GB in disk

RETRIEVING A FILE FROM THE ATTIC

1. In the Project window, close all of your bins.
2. Using WindowShade, move the Avid screens so you can open the CPU hard drive.
3. Open the Avid hard drive on the desktop.
4. Look for the Attic ƒ. Open it.
5. Scroll through it until you find your project—the one you named. Open it. You will see everything labeled as "bak.01" or "bak.02."
6. Look for the bin you want and, *holding the Option key*, select and then drag the bin onto the desktop. The computer will make a copy of the bin, leaving the one in the Attic just as it is.
7. Open the Project window by clicking anywhere on it.
8. From the File menu, choose Open Bin. Navigate until you find the "bak.01" bin you just created on the desktop. Click Open.
9. Now create a new bin. Call it "Restore."
10. Select the sequence you want from the "bak.01" bin, and then press the Option key while dragging the duplicate sequence to the new bin, "Restore."
11. Select and delete the "bak.01" bin.
12. Go back to the desktop and drag the "bak.01" bin to the Trash.

BACKING UP MEDIA FILES

There are systems that allow you to back up not just the master files, but also the media files. One system sold by Avid uses digital linear tape (DLT) drives and $1/_2$-inch cartridge tapes, capable of holding 20 gigabytes per tape. I once rented an Avid DLT storage device and purchased a couple of tapes in order to archive all the media that went into making an hour show. The tapes were $100 each! The transfer process is painfully slow, as you'd imagine, because you're transferring one heck of a lot of material. If I remember correctly, it took us over 12 hours. A few months later, I needed to put that material back onto my Avid hard drives, in order to make some changes. Frankly, I was disappointed. A lot of the material, both picture and sound, came back "offline," meaning I had to redigitize it. And a lot of the audio levels needed major work because they were all over the place.

The Avid Unity MediaNet, which is Avid's most advanced storage device, not only allows several Avid machines to share the same media, but also allows you to set it up to automatically back up any and all of your media files. For instance, if you had a system with 120-gigabytes capacity, you could use 60 of those gigabytes for media and the other 60 as backup. That way your media files would be 100 percent backed up. Or, you might use 80 GB for storage and 40 for backing up only the most critical media files, such as files that are graphics- and effects-intensive and can't be redigitized.

BATCH DIGITIZING OFFLINE MATERIAL—REDIGITIZING OFFLINE MEDIA

If your material goes offline (on purpose or by accident), or if you are going to digitize material that you logged, the process of batch digitizing is the same. Batch digitizing only works with material that has timecode—for example, Betacam SP or DAT tapes containing timecode.

Examine the accompanying bin in Frame View. There are two clips shown in Figure 11.3. The clip on the left is "offline." The clip information is there, but the media file has either been erased or was never digitized in the first place.

Batch digitizing is like digitizing. Before you digitize anything, you must have the source tapes in front of you. You also need to connect your equipment so that you can send your video and audio signals from the tape deck to the Avid. Take a look at Chapter 6, to review the steps you take to digitize. Once you're set up:

1. In the bin, select all the video or audio clips that you wish to redigitize.
   • You can lasso the clips or Shift-click the clips.

Figure 11.3

- You can first sort the bin to find all the offline material. Click on the offline column, and press Command-E.
- If all the clips in the bin were offline, you could press Command-A to select all.

2. When all the offline clips are highlighted, get the Digitize Tool from the Tools menu (Command-7).

3. Choose: Your target bin
    Your AVR or Resolution
    Tracks (V1, A1, A2, TC)

4. Go to the Bin menu (Xpress) or Clip menu (MC) and chose "Batch Digitize."

5. A dialog box will open. Click on "Digitize only those items for which media is currently unavailable." Then click OK.

Name	Scene	Take	Duration	Start
Kate's Entrance – Wide Shot	1A	1	46:14	01:16:02:0
Kate's Hands, Face – CU	1B	1	47:03	01:17:07:0
Master Shot – Kate & Tim	1C	1	1:45:25	01:19:45:2
Master Shot – Kate & Tim (P.U.)	1C	2	41:14	01:21:36:2
Tim's CU	1D	1	1:30:18	01:22:26:0
Tim's CU (tape out)	1D	2	1:26:14	01:24:02:0
Tim's CU	1D	3	1:34:06	01:25:46:1
Kate's CU	1E	1	1:25:27	01:27:29:1
Kate's MS	1F	1	28:23	01:29:10:0

Batch Digitize...

☒ **Digitize only those items for which media is currently unavailable.**

9 clip(s) selected.

Selection:

A1 A2 TC

Bin   Dailies –

BD-3 ▼

OK

The Avid will then ask you for the first tape. You should have all the source tapes nearby and insert them as the Avid asks for them. Once you insert Tape 0003, click on "Mounted."

Once the Avid begins to digitize the offline clips, you can watch the process in action. Once a clip is digitized, it is no longer highlighted, and so, over time, the list of highlighted clips gets smaller and smaller, until none is highlighted.

You can abort the batching process at any time. To abort, click on the Trash icon on the Digitize Tool.

Now you know *why* you must back up your projects and *how* to do it. You also know how to restore lost or missing projects, how to retrieve files from the attic, and how to redigitize offline media. And you've been told that one of these days, your beloved Avid is going to crash. Don't say I didn't warn you.

SUGGESTED ASSIGNMENTS

1. Open the CPU's hard drive and examine the folders it contains.
2. Find the Composer Projects folder or Avid Projects folder.
3. Find the Avid Users folder.
4. Back up your projects onto a floppy or Zip disk.
5. Back up your user file to a floppy or Zip disk.

12

Keeping in Sync

SYNC PROBLEMS

When I write about sync problems in this chapter, I have more in mind than just picture and audio tracks falling out of sync. To me, if a music cue is supposed to be heard as soon as a door opens, and instead it comes in two seconds late—it's out of sync. If you spend a lot of time getting narration, music or effects to land perfectly with a visual, and suddenly they don't—you're out of sync. If you have a lower-third title on V2 that says "Nelson Mandela," and when you play your sequence, the title comes up over a shot of a building, your title is out of sync. You have sync problems.

Getting out of sync can be a an editor's worst nightmare, especially if a client or producer is in the room. One second you're splicing shots, trimming transitions, building tracks, and working at a nice clip, and the next second you're lost. The sound is out of sync with the picture, the music comes in at the wrong moment, the titles land on the wrong shots—you don't know what's happened. And, as you try to solve the problem, the client is behind you, pacing back and forth, looking at the clock, and sighing meaningfully. It's not helping. If you haven't had this experience, you will, and if you have, I don't need to go any farther because you've been there.

Prior to the use of digital editing equipment, editors working in film experienced these sort of sync problems far more frequently than editors working on tape machines. Since film uses a "double-system," meaning the sound is physically separated from the picture, it's easy for the sound and picture to become separated. With a tape editing machine, the picture and sound occupy the same tape, so sync problems are less frequent. Of course, film editors *want* the separation between picture and sound because it means they possess far greater flexibility and creative control.

The Avid provides the same flexibility that a traditional film-editing machine provides, and with that flexibility comes sync problems. In fact, because you can easily add multiple video and audio tracks to your sequences, the Avid actually increases the potential for sync problems. When you're working with three video tracks and six audio tracks, a sync problem results in a confusing mess in the Timeline. Fortunately there are some tools that help you get back into sync quickly. And there are things you can do to keep from going out of sync in the first place.

THE SOURCE OF YOUR PROBLEMS

Before we talk about solutions, let's review the ways you can get out of sync. In other words, know your enemy. Know what can go wrong, and you'll be able to avoid the problem. Know what can go wrong, and you're in a better position to identify and fix the problem.

How did you get out of sync? Here are the three actions most often responsible for sync problems. They are what the police would call "the usual suspects."

- Single-roller trimming—adding material to or subtracting it from one track, but not the other(s).
- Splicing material to one track but not to the other(s).
- Extracting material from one track but not from the other(s).

Now that you know who they are, keep an eye on them. Stay alert whenever you're performing one of these three actions.

SYNC BREAK INDICATORS

If your audio and video were digitized at the same time, the Avid will lock the two together. If you go out of sync, *sync break indicators* will appear in the Timeline to show you exactly how many frames out of sync you've fallen. Numbers appear in the Timeline on the video and its associated audio track, indicating precisely what went wrong and by how much.

F						
U1	□	Master		Kate's CU	-9	Tim's CU	-9
A1	◁	Master		Kate's CU	9	Tim's CU	9

In the example here, I made the mistake of entering Single-Roller Trim Mode on just one track. I inadvertently added nine frames to Kate's picture, but not to her sound. The sync break indicator shows the sync break as well as the number of frames by which the entire sequence has been thrown out of sync. It also tells me in which direction I need to go to get back into sync.

To get back in sync, use the single-roller trim and add or subtract the number of frames indicated. Here, I need to either subtract nine frames from Kate's picture (-9) or add nine frames to Kate's sound.

MANY TRACKS MEAN MANY SYNC PROBLEMS

If you lose sync when cutting a sequence containing just a few tracks, you'll be able to restore sync without much trouble. But once you start adding tracks containing additional material into your sequence (such as narration, sound effects, and music), sync problems can become more frequent and more confusing.

Figures 12.1 and 12.2 show a sequence involving two video tracks and six audio tracks. The main visual material consists of an on-camera interview with a woman named Thandi Orleyn (TO). During her interview, I cut away to various visuals rather than having her "talking head" on screen the entire time. On track V2 there's a title; V1 contains Thandi's talking head plus the B-roll or cutaway shots; A1 holds the narration; A2 holds Thandi's sync audio; A3 holds the sync sound for whatever cutaway I used; A4 holds additional sound effects; A6 and A7 contain stereo music cues.

Let's see what happens if I get out of sync. To get out of sync I place the single-roller trim just on V1 and not on any other tracks, and trim (shorten) it by 50 frames. Immediately sync break indicators appear.

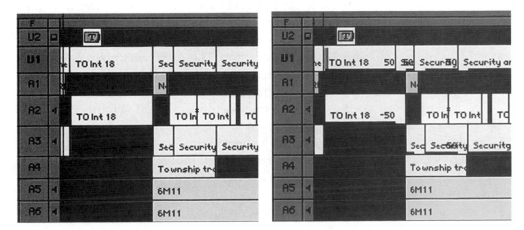

Figure 12.1   Before single-roller trim   **Figure 12.2**   After trim, showing sync break

Notice that the sync-break indicators show that Thandi's interview is out of sync by 50 frames. You can also see that the cutaways (Security) that were placed over her talking-head are out of sync (A3). But what you don't see is that the narration on A1, the sound effect on A4, and the music cue (6M11) on A5 and A6 are out of sync as well.

Why? Because sync breaks only work with pictures and sounds that were digitized together. The video and audio tracks containing material that you added later—the titles, narration, sound effects, and music—won't show sync breaks because they are independent of any video.

There are several ways to solve this problem. I'll show you one of the quickest methods.

LOCATORS

Locators are handy "tabs" that you can place on any and all tracks in the Timeline to show you that you are in or out of sync. You can also use them to leave neat little messages in the composer/record monitor.

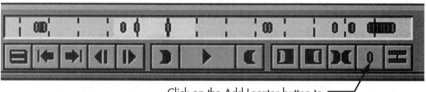

Click on the Add Locator button to place a locator.

If you click on the Add Locator command button, a locator will appear in the Timeline on whichever track is active. For sync purposes, you want to place the locator on all the tracks so the locators line up in a straight vertical row. In Figure 12.3 you can see that I have placed locators on every track that contains a clip. You must place the locators on each track, one at a time. I deselected all the tracks except V1, and then I hit the Add Locator button. Then, without moving the position indicator, I deselected V1 and selected A1 and pressed the Add Locator button again, and so on until all the tracks had locators.

Look what happens if any of my tracks get thrown off (Figure 12.4). The locators show me that they're out of sync with the other tracks.

You don't need to put locators everywhere in the Timeline. But I would suggest you place a vertical row of them every five minutes or so in your project. That way if you get out of sync, you don't have far to go before you have a checkpoint.

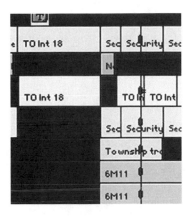

Figure 12.3 Tracks in sync

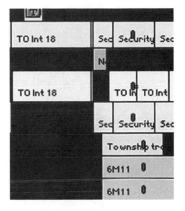

Figure 12.4 A4, A5, and A6 are out-of-sync

Locators can also tell you how many frames out of sync you are. By placing an IN at the first locator and an OUT at the second, and then checking the I/O (IN-to-OUT) in the tracking menu, you can see by how many frames A4, A5, and A6 have slipped.

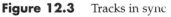

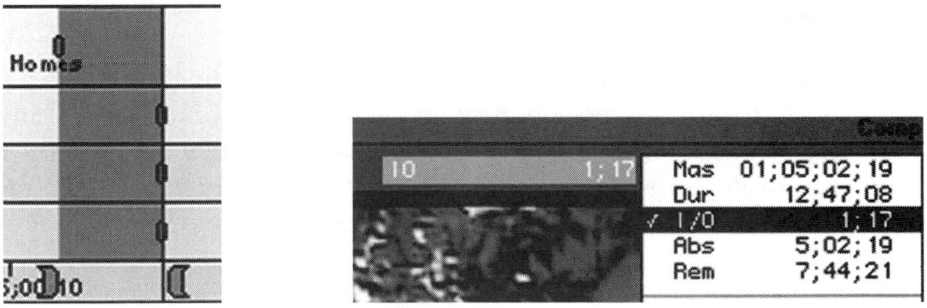

Figure 12.5 By placing IN and OUT on the locators, you can see how far your tracks have moved.

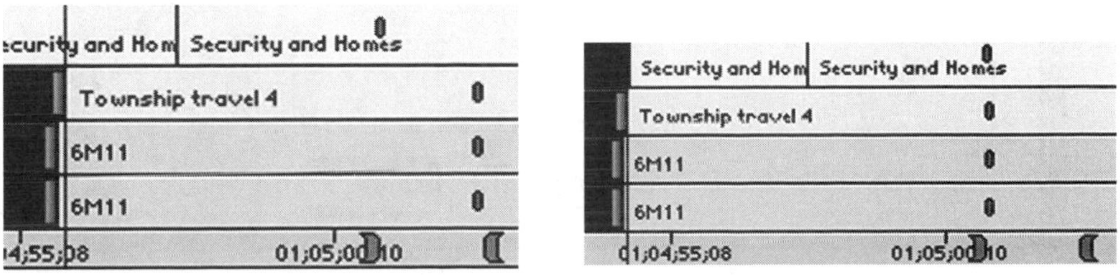

Figure 12.6 Drag the roller to the left and the locators line up again.

To get tracks A4, A5, and A6 back in sync, go into Single-Roller Trim Mode, place the single-rollers on the fill side of all three tracks and then drag them left (Figure 12.6). Now, it looks as if you should drag the single-rollers 47 frames to the left, because you see the I/O reads 1;17, or one second and 17 frames. That's 30 frames plus 17 frames, for a total of 47 frames.

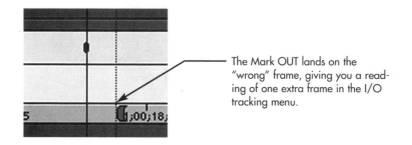

The Mark OUT lands on the "wrong" frame, giving you a reading of one extra frame in the I/O tracking menu.

But because of the way the position indicator lands on the locator whenever you set your mark OUT, it lands a frame past the locator. The correct number is always one less than indicated by the I/O, or in this case 46 frames.

Locator Information

While we're discussing locators, let's look at the message function that's part of this handy tool. To write a message, click on the track selector box containing the locator, so it's selected. Then drag the position indicator until it lands on the locator. When the locator appears in the Record/Composer monitor, click the mouse pointer on the red locator in the Composer/Record monitor. A message box appears. Just type your message in the box.

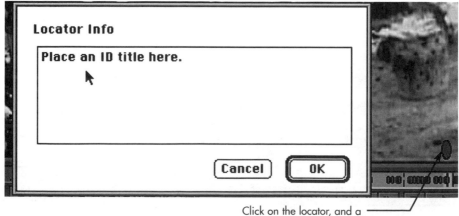

Click on the locator, and a message box appears.

Figure 12.7

Place an ID title here.

Figure 12.8

In Figure 12.8, I typed a reminder, "Place an ID title here." When I click OK, the message appears in the Record/Composer window whenever the position indicator stops on that frame in the Timeline. (Sometimes you have to use the one-frame step key to land precisely on it.)

Deleting Locators

If you want to delete the locator (and its message), click on the locator in the position bar (the window under the monitor). If it doesn't appear in the monitor window, step-frame until it does, and then press the Delete key.

EDITING TRICKS TO STAY IN SYNC

In Chapter 8, we examined the topic, "Trimming in Two Directions." Since this is a vital skill, let's take a moment to review it.

Trimming in Two Directions—A Review

If you have more audio tracks than just the sync track(s), and you want to add material (or trim material) using Single-Roller Trim Mode, you must trim all your tracks, in order to keep their relationship the same. If you just trim V1 and A1 (picture and sync sound), all the music and narration will fall out of sync.

- Go into Single-Roller Trim Mode and click/select all the other tracks downstream.
- Add the rollers on the "fill" or black side.
- Do this even if the rollers aren't all on the same side or going in the same direction.

• As you trim, Avid will add or take away black fill to keep all the tracks in sync.

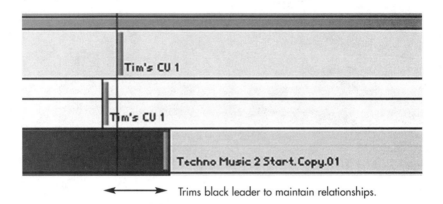

Trims black leader to maintain relationships.

In the example, when we drag Tim's CU on track V1 and his overlapped audio on track A1 to the left, we are adding to it, or making the shot longer. That would normally throw the music out of sync. But if we place a single-roller on the fill side of the music on track A2, then as we drag left, the Avid *adds* black fill, and sync is maintained. If we shortened Tim's shot by dragging right, the Avid would take away black fill to keep the music in sync. Remember, put the roller on the fill side of the music, not inside the music itself.

But what happens if you want to trim a shot in a sequence containing many tracks like the one in Figure 12.9. Let's say you're doing an hour show, and you have two video tracks and five or six tracks of audio. And let's say that the distance between where you want to trim and some of these other elements is too great to easily add rollers to them.

Figure 12.9

You can easily place your single rollers on V1, A1, A3, A5, and A6, but you can't even see the material on V2 and A4. Yes, you can change the Timeline view so that those elements come into view, but that takes time, and setting the watch point will take up even more time.

Add Edits in Black Fill

The solution is to hold the Option key while pressing the Add Edit key. As you recall, the Add Edit key will put an intentional edit or splice in a shot or audio. When you press the Option key, the add edit is placed in the black fill!

Press the Option key and .

When you hit Option-Add Edit, you won't see anything because the position indicator is in the way. Move the blue position indicator out of the way, so you can see the black lines representing the add edits in the black fill as in Figure 12.10.

Now, I'll enter Single-Roller Trim Mode, and the rollers will go right to the add edit lines (Figure 12.11).

Granted, I have to set one roller, the one for A2. Remember, the Option-Add Edit only puts the edits in black. But this is good. I don't want an add edit in the middle of Thandi's interview audio. Now trim to your heart's content and know that all your tracks will hold sync.

These add edit lines in the black fill can serve another function. During editing, they act as sync reference points, just as the locators do. If the lines don't line up, something has moved.

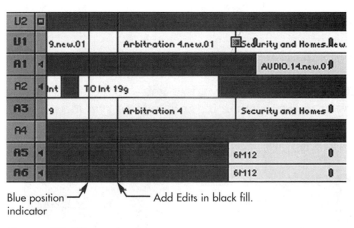

Blue position indicator ——— Add Edits in black fill.

Figure 12.10

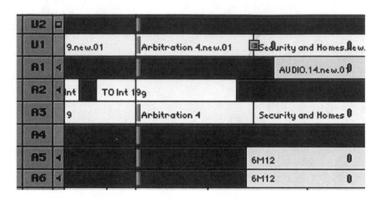

Figure 12.11

Deleting Add Edits

Media Composer users can easily get rid of these marks. Go to the Clip menu and select "Remove Match Frame Edits," which is another name for add edits. Xpress users don't have this command. The easiest way to delete them is to go into Dual-Roller Trim Mode (so you have dual-rollers on top of these edit lines in the Timeline), and hit the Delete key. MC users can do this as well.

With rollers in place, hit the Delete key.

SYNC LOCKS

Knowing how important it is to maintain sync, especially when you're getting toward the end of editing and the tracks are filling up with titles, visual effects, sound effects, and music, the Avid gives you a tool in the Timeline that enables you to lock your tracks together; it's aptly named *sync locks.*

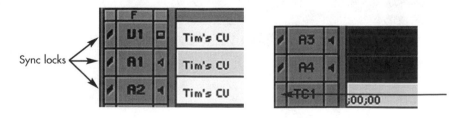

Sync locks

Click here to place locks on all tracks.

In the track selector area, there is a small block just to the left of the tracks. By clicking in the small box, you can place a sync lock on your track. You can lock two, three, or all of your tracks together. Click in the empty box in the TC1, or timecode track, and you'll place locks in all the boxes.

With sync locks in place on all tracks:

- The Avid will warn you if something you do is going to throw your tracks out of sync.
- If you lift a segment from one track, the Avid will cut it from all tracks.
- If you add a shot, the Avid will add fill on your other tracks to keep them in sync.
- In Single-Roller Trim Mode, the Avid will maintain the proper relationship with other tracks.

Figure 12.12 shows an example. V1 is the only track selected. I've marked an IN and an OUT in the Timeline, and I plan to press Extract to remove the tail of Tim's CU. Without sync locks on, what happens? I'm out of sync, because I'm removing material from one track, but not the others. But with sync locks on, the Avid will extract from *all* the tracks, even though they aren't selected. Try it and see.

Figure 12.13 shows another example. I've placed single rollers V1, A1, and A2, but I forgot to place trim rollers on A3 and A4. What happens if I trim Tim's CU? I'll throw the music cue 1M1 off, because I haven't trimmed in two directions. Right? Wrong. Because the sync locks are "on," the Avid will keep the A3 and A4 tracks locked together with V1, A1, and A2.

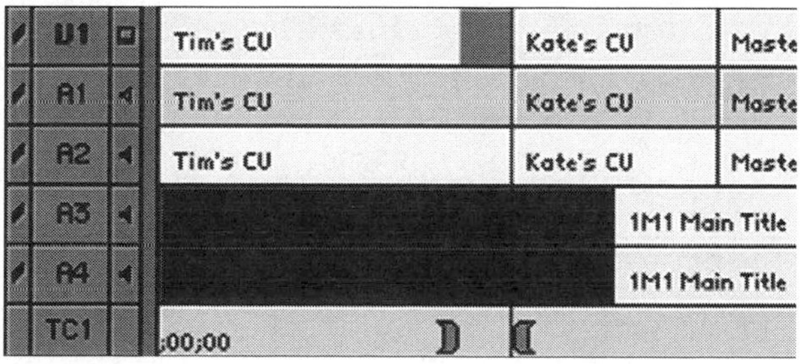

Figure 12.12

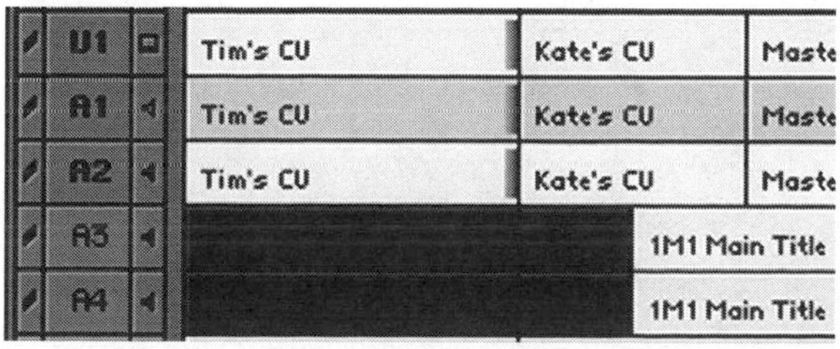

Figure 12.13   Even though there are no rollers on A3 and A4, they will get trimmed because the sync locks are on.

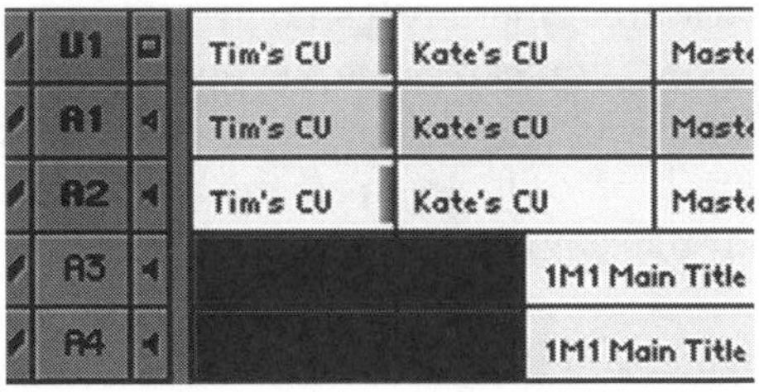

Figure 12.14

Don't believe me? Examine Figure 12.14. I shortened the tail of Tim's CU. The Avid shortened the black fill on A3 and A4 in order to keep the music cue in sync. The music stays right where it belongs on Kate's shot, even though I didn't "trim in two directions." The Avid's sync locks did it for me.

"Hey," you might say, "if this works so well, why did you spend so much time teaching us about trimming in two directions, and watch points, and placing add edits in fill, etc., etc., etc.?"

My answer is twofold. First, you need to know about all those other things in order to fully understand the value of sync locks, but mainly because sync locks don't always work. Another way to put it is that they work too well.

With sync locks, if the other tracks inline (vertically) with the tracks you are cutting are empty, the Avid adds or subtracts fill to keep your tracks in sync—and everyone is happy. But if the other tracks have material inline with the tracks you are cutting, the Avid cuts material from those tracks as well. This is a problem. Suddenly your narration and your music have disappeared. You're in sync, all right, but you've lost your narrator! Or a chunk of your music is missing!

Look at Figure 12.15. I've got sync locks on all tracks, and I'm going to extract some excess footage from the tail of Kate's CU. I mark an IN and an OUT, and hit extract.

Watch what happens with the sync locks turned on. Examine Figure 12.16.

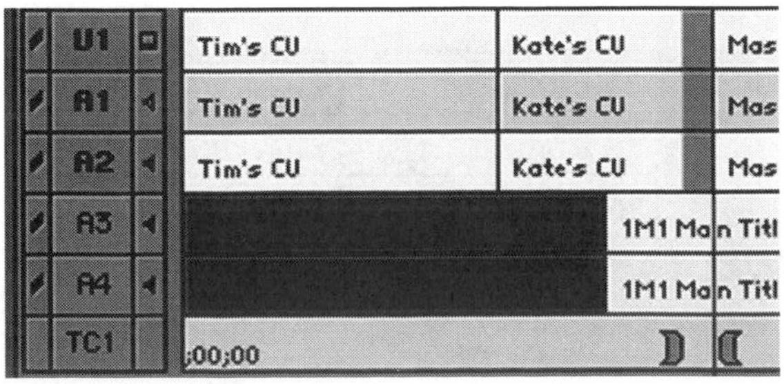

Figure 12.15

Whoa! A chunk of my music cue got extracted as well. I certainly didn't want *that*. Why did it happen? Because even though A3 and A4 weren't selected, they're sync-locked to the other tracks. Lift or extract from the other tracks, and the Avid will do whatever it takes to keep you in sync, even if it takes away important material.

Figure 12.17 shows another example. I've got single-rollers on Kate's picture and audio tracks, but not on the music cue. I want to extend the tail of her shot.

Look what happens in Figure 12.18 when I drag the rollers to the right to extend her shot (Figure 12.18).

Yikes! The Avid has added black fill in the middle of the music cue! That's not going to sound very good.

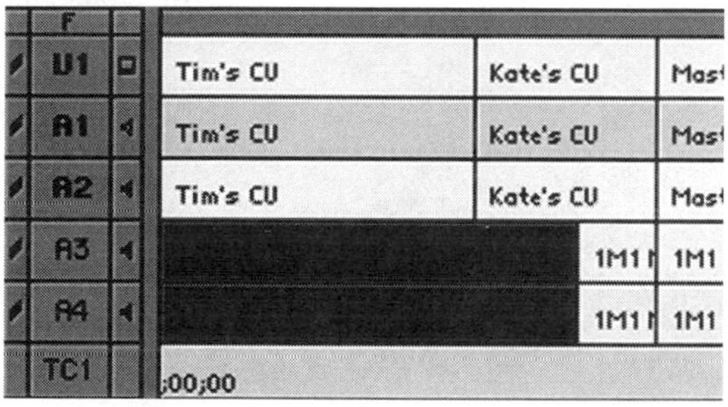

Figure 12.16

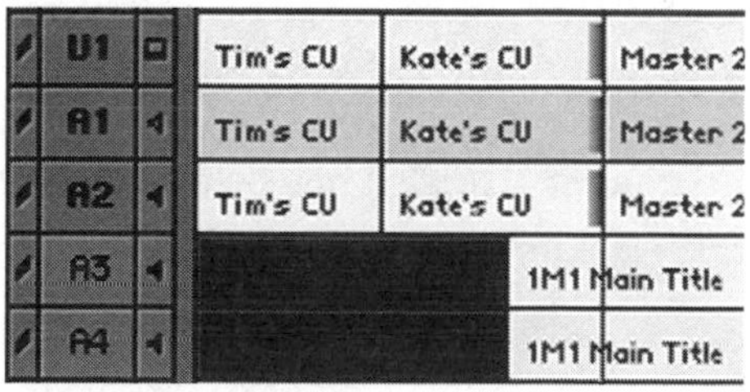

Figure 12.17

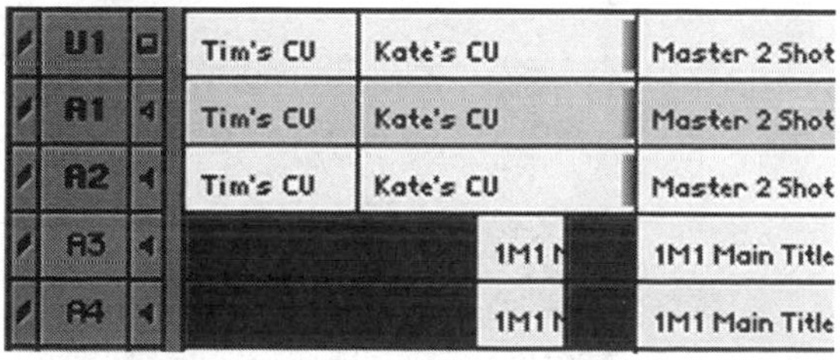

Figure 12.18

So, as you can see, sync locks work some of the time, but not all of the time. Remember, with sync locks on, the Avid will do whatever it takes to keep the tracks in sync.

If the other tracks inline (vertically) with the tracks you are editing are empty, sync locks can be fast and foolproof. But, if the other tracks have material inline with the tracks you are cutting or trimming, the Avid will blindly remove important material in its quest to keep you in sync.

I use sync locks whenever I have more than three or four tracks, and I want to splice a clip into the Timeline. That's when sync locks are great.

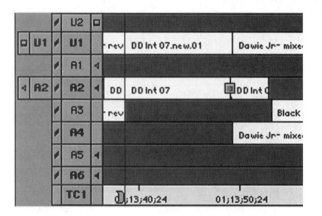

Figure 12.19

Here I want to splice in a shot at the mark IN (Figure 12.19). If I forget to select every single track before I splice, those forgotten tracks will get thrown out of sync. But with sync locks on, the Avid will make sure that all the tracks stay in sync.

I have cut in a clip named "Cur." It has been spliced in, and the other tracks have had fill added to their tracks in order to maintain the relationship between tracks (Figure 12.20).

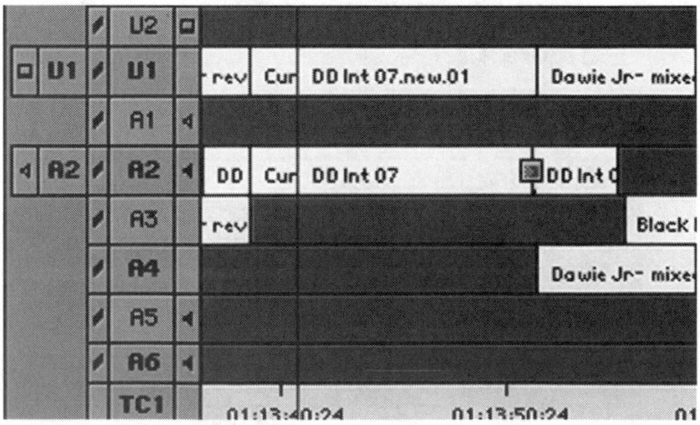

Figure 12.20

LOCKING TRACKS

Media Composer editors can "lock" their tracks to prevent accidental changes. Locking is different from sync locking. When you lock a track, no further editing can take place on that track. You can lock picture and/or audio tracks. Say you have several sync dialog tracks that are in sync with a video track, and you need to work on your music and sound effects tracks. You can lock the picture and dialog tracks. Now you don't have to worry about accidentally changing your video and dialog tracks while you work on your music or effects tracks.

To lock tracks:

1. Select the tracks you want to lock and deselect the others.
2. From the Clip menu choose Lock Tracks. A padlock icon appears in the track lock indicator space.

Because you're beginning to take advantage of all the Avid has to offer, you're in danger of going out of sync. You're adding video tracks for titles and effects. You're adding tracks to hold music and narration. Once you go beyond cutting just a few tracks, sync problems can really cause you heartache. We've spent a lot of time on the subject of sync, because losing it can be so painful.

My best advice is to keep it as simple as you can for as long as you can. Don't add titles, music, and sound effects until you've reached a fine cut. Tell the story first. Otherwise you'll spend your time repairing sync, rather than editing.

SUGGESTED ASSIGNMENTS

1. Place a single-roller (Trim Mode) on one track and not the other. Drag left and look at the sync break. Leave Trim mode. Now go back into Trim mode and fix the sync break.
2. Place a row of locators on your tracks.
3. Leave yourself a message, using the locator message function.
4. Delete the locator.
5. Put a row of add edits in black fill.
6. Use single-roller trim to add or delete material to all your tracks.
7. Delete the add edits.
8. Place sync locks on your tracks. Try extracting material. Try single-roller trimming. Try splicing a clip into the Timeline.

Media Composer Users

1. Place locks on one or more tracks. Try editing the locked tracks.

13

Importing and Exporting

For those of you who have imported and exported various files before, this chapter may seem a bit simplistic. Accept my apologies. It's just that I'm not worried about you. You simply need to be shown how to use Avid's import and export tools, and off you'll go. This chapter is aimed at those of you who have never imported or exported files before, and who think the whole business sounds incredibly difficult. I've streamlined and simplified the process as much as possible so you'll be able to master it, if you give it a try. Don't worry that you have no files to import, because you do; there's one sitting inside your computer, waiting patiently for you. It's called SMPTE Color Bars.

TYPES OF FILES

Because the Avid deals with digital information, just about any digital information can be brought in or sent out of the Avid. Here are several examples.

- Using Adobe Photoshop, you could create an opening title that combines text with a special blurring effect. You could save that title as a graphic file, import it into one of your bins, and then cut it into your sequence.
- You could create an image or sequence of images in the Avid, export it as a file to a program like After Effects, make changes to create a special look, and then reimport it into a bin and cut it into your sequence.
- You could take an audio clip that has sound problems and export it as a audio file. You could then bring it to a sound facility with Pro Tools™ for audio sweetening, and reimport it back into the Avid.
- You could import CD tracks from your computer's CD player.

You can import and export many kinds of graphic files, picture files, animation files, and audio files. Here is a partial list:

Graphic and Animation File Types
   PICT
   Alias PIX animation
   Quick Time
   OMF Interchange
   Photo CD
Audio File Types
   Audio Interchange File Format (AIFF)
   Sound Designer II
   OMF Interchange
Shot Log Files
   FLEx File
   ATN File
   FTL file

IMPORTING

In order to import, there must first be a file to import. It can be located on the Avid hard drive, on a floppy disk, or on a Zip disk that you've inserted into your CPU.

To import, simply select Import from the File menu. If the word Import is dimmed on the menu, it's because a bin has not been selected. Click anywhere in the bin that you want to import the file to. After you select Import, an Import dialog box opens. I've included the boxes for Windows NT and for the Macintosh as well (Figure 13.1 and Figure 13.2).

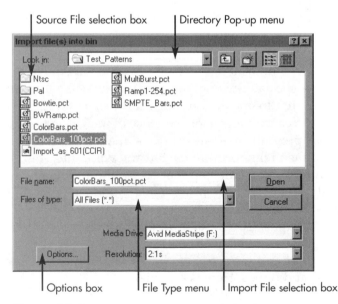

Figure 13.1 Windows NT Import dialog box

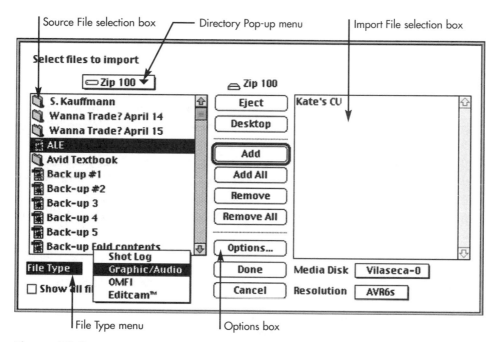

Figure 13.2 Macintosh Import dialog box

Import Dialog Box

As you can see, although they appear to be quite different, the Mac and NT Import windows offer the same choices.

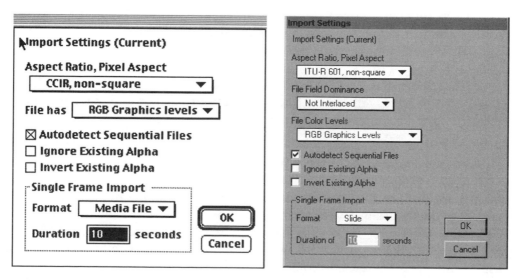

Figure 13.3 Mac Options

Figure 13.4 Windows NT Options

Let's trace the steps I take to import a PICT file called "Kate's CU." Importing a File:

1. First I select a bin by clicking on it.
2. Then I choose Import from the File menu. See Figures 13.1 and 13.2.
3. I select the file from the Source File list, by navigating through the desktop or hard drive. I double-click on disks and folders in the list to open them, and I scroll through them to locate the file I want.
4. Once I find it: On the Mac, I click on it and then hit Add to send the file to the Import File selection box on the right-hand side. On the NT, I simply click on it so it's highlighted.
5. I select the File type from the pop-up menu. Because it is a PICT file, I choose Graphic/Audio.
6. I click on Options, and a box opens. See Figure 13.3 and Figure 13.4.
7. I choose CCIR, non-square in the first window. On the NT machine, I choose ITU-R 601, non-square (the newer name for CCIR 601).
8. On the NT machine, I choose Not Interlaced in the File Field Dominance box.
9. Choose RGB Graphics Levels.
10. In the Single Frame Import box, I choose Media File (not Slide) as the Format, because I want it to act just like a master clip. In the Duration box, I select how long the clip will be. If I want the graphic to turn into a 10-second clip, I leave it at 10. If I want it to be longer or shorter, I change the number.
11. I click OK. The Options box closes.
12. Back in the Import tool, I choose a media disk or drive to store the media.
13. Because it's a graphic, I select a resolution in the Resolution box that matches the resolution of my sequence.
14. When I'm finished, I click Done (Mac) or Open (NT).

I look in my bin. There it is, saved as a master clip that is 10 seconds long.

Now that I've walked you through an import, let's examine what some of the choices and settings we made actually mean.

COMPUTERS VS. TELEVISION

Most of the problems associated with importing files into the Avid stem from the fact that you are creating your files on a computer, and while the Avid is a computer, it doesn't behave like one. It behaves like a digital television set. A computer and the Avid deal with images differently. The main differences involve aspect ratio, pixel shape, and color.

Aspect Ratio

Aspect ratio refers to the dimensions of a rectangle. In our case the rectangle is a picture image, film or video frame, or screen size. You determine a rectangle's aspect ratio by dividing its width by its height. (A square has an aspect ratio of 1:1, because the width is the same as the height.) Look at any standard television screen. It's not a square; it's a rectangle. The frame is wider than it is high. On a standard analog television set, the aspect ratio is 4:3. Filmmakers are more familiar with the number 1.33:1, which comes from dividing 4 by 3.

The new standard for high definition television (HDTV) presents an even wider frame, with an aspect ratio of 16:9.

In the computer domain the image is usually described in terms of pixels: the number and shape of the pixels that make up the image. Graphic artists often work on a computer creating images that have a frame of 648 (width) by 486 (height) *square* pixels. Divide 648 by 486 and you get an aspect ratio of 4:3, or 1.33:1.

The Avid's frame in pixel terms is slightly different because it comes from Avid's video capture board. It is 720 (width) by 486 (height), *nonsquare* pixels. When you do the math, you see that instead of an aspect ratio of 1.33:1, you get an aspect ratio of 1.48:1 (720 divided by 486). This never made sense to me. Why would a video capture board give you an image that didn't match the 4:3 standard for all analog television screens? The answer lies in the pixel shape the Avid creates. It's not shaped like a square. It's tall and thin.

Square pixel   Avid's non-square pixel

If those nonsquare pixels were square, like the ones a computer generates, the aspect ratio would be wrong. But because the pixels are horizontally *squeezed*, 720 of them take up the same space as 648 square ones. So Avid's 720 × 486 nonsquare pixels provide the same aspect ratio as a computer's 648 × 486 square pixels, namely 4:3.

Color

At this level you don't need to know that much about the different ways the Avid and a computer monitor handle color. Just remember that computer color is referred to as RGB color, whereas the Avid's color conforms to a digital standard known as CCIR 601 or ITU-R 601.

Now, armed with this information, let's look again at the Options box on the Macintosh (Figure 13.5). You see that the Avid is asking for information about your file so it can properly translate it into the Avid's format.

The first window you'll see is labeled "Aspect Ratio, Pixel Aspect." The window has a triangle which, if you drag, will reveal three choices: (1) CCIR, non-square, (2) Maintain, square, and (3) Resize, square.

CCIR, non-square takes graphics with the correct aspect ratio, no matter what the pixel shape, and makes them fit the Avid's CCIR, non-square standard. So if the title you created in Photoshop has the right aspect ratio for the Avid, but has square pixels, select this option and it will import nicely.

Maintain, square keeps the graphic just the way you designed it, with no change in size. For instance, you might not want it to fill the Avid's frame, and if that's the case this will keep your image shape just the way it was created.

Resize, square forces the graphic to fit the Avid's frame no matter what. Often the Avid places a black border around your image to make it fit.

"File has" deals with the color issue. If the file you are importing was created on a computer, then it probably has RGB Graphics levels. If it came from a videotape or video camera, select CCIR Video levels.

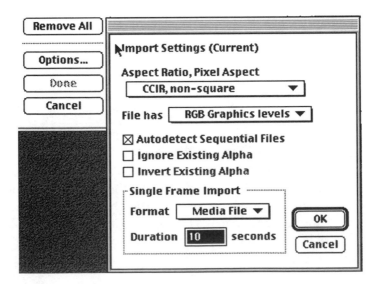

Figure 13.5

File Field Dominance

If you look at the Options dialog box that comes on the Windows NT machine (see Figure 13.4), you'll see a choice not found on the Macs I've been using. It's called File Field Dominance. The choices are Non-Interlaced, Even Field Dominant, and Odd Field Dominant.

The Windows NT Avids all use a Meridien video capture board, while my Mac Avid uses an ABVB board. The Meridien board captures two-field video differently from an ABVB board, and that is why there's a File Field Dominance selection. Any Macs that come with Meridien boards will have this choice as well. The ABVB Avid has odd field dominance, whereas the Meridien has even field dominance. Remember, a video signal is made up of two fields, one containing all the odd lines and the other containing all the even lines. The Meridien wants the even line first. When you're working with graphics involving the ordering of fields, you should set the field dominance to match the Avid you're going into—even for Meridien, odd for ABVB. (PAL ABVB and PAL Meridien are both Odd Field dominant.) If the file you are importing doesn't deal with fields, for example a PICT file, then Non-Interlaced is the correct choice.

IMPORT PRACTICE

Let's create a title using Adobe Photoshop, import it, and cut it into a sequence. It's true that Avid has a title tool, but you might not be able to spend as much time on the Avid as you can on your home or office computer. Or perhaps Photoshop has an effect that your Avid doesn't have. Whatever the reason, it's handy to be able to import graphic files from programs like Photoshop.

Importing a Photoshop File

When I open Photoshop, the first thing I do is set the aspect ratio in the New File dialog box. Remember 648 × 486 pixels is correct for most graphic applications, but the Avid uses non-square pixels. Therefore we must slightly distort the image in order to get the image to come out correctly once it's imported into the Avid. First, set the Photoshop image at 720 × 540 pixels (Figure 13.6).

Figure 13.7 shows the title I created. After placing the text, I created a drop shadow. Then I applied a Blur effect to the shadow. Now, I go to the Image menu and select Image Size. In the dialog box, I change the pixel size from 720 × 540 to 720 × 486. This will squash the letters, making them appear shorter. This looks wrong, but when I import the graphic into the Avid, the letters will be squeezed, making them appear thinner, because of Avid's non-square pixels. The result is perfectly proportioned letters.

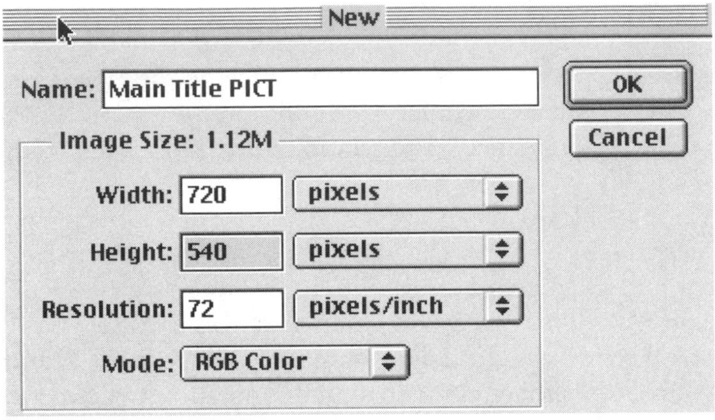

Figure 13.6   Adobe Photoshop's New File dialog box.

Figure 13.7

Adobe Photoshop saves your work as a Photoshop file, but many Avids can't import those files. So I dragged down the format menu and selected PICT File, which is one of the file formats the Avid can easily import (Figure 13.8). (If PICT File is gray, it means you haven't flattened your layers. Go to Layers and select flatten. When you choose Save As, PICT File is now available.)

Save this document as:

Main Title

Format: Photoshop

Photoshop

Photoshop 2.0
BMP
CompuServe GIF
Photoshop EPS
Filmstrip
Doc: 4.15M/24   JPEG
                 PCX
Help With Quick   PDF
Keyboard & Map   PICT File
Main Title   PICT Resource

Cancel
Save

Figure 13.8

I name the file "Main Title PICT" and save it onto my Zip disk, which I then eject from my home computer and carry to the Avid. Once the computer is turned on, I insert the Zip disk so it appears on the desktop. I then launch the Avid software and, once I'm in my project, I select a bin. Now I go to the File menu and choose Import. I navigate through the directory window until I find the Main Title PICT file. I click on it and press the Add button, and it appears in the Import File selection box.

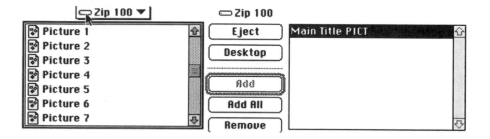

I then select the media drive and resolution. Finally, I click on the Options... button and select the settings, as shown in Figure 13.9. I know that CCIR, non-square and RGB Graphics Levels are the correct settings for this file. I click OK.

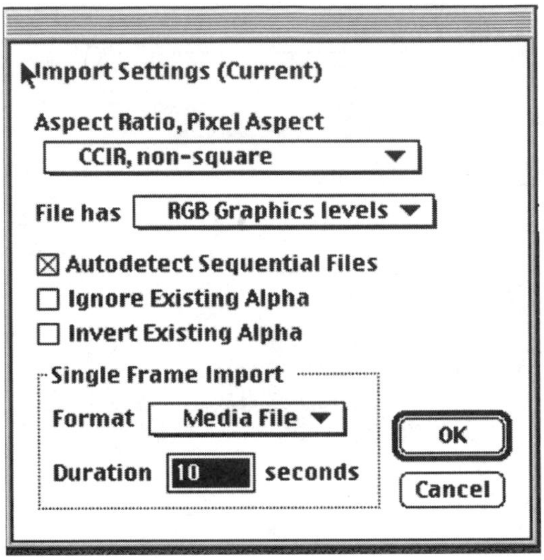

Import Settings (Current)

Aspect Ratio, Pixel Aspect

CCIR, non-square ▼

File has RGB Graphics levels ▼

☒ Autodetect Sequential Files
☐ Ignore Existing Alpha
☐ Invert Existing Alpha

Single Frame Import

Format Media File ▼   OK

Duration 10 seconds   Cancel

Figure 13.9

Back in the Import window, I click Done. The window closes, and the Avid creates a media file in the drive I chose. When the import process is completed, I look in my bin and there it is.

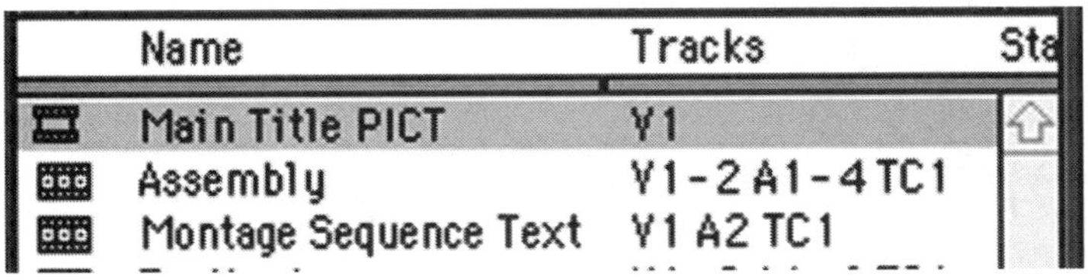

Name	Tracks	Sta
Main Title PICT	V1	
Assembly	V1-2 A1-4 TC1	
Montage Sequence Text	V1 A2 TC1	

Now I double-click on the clip icon. It opens either in the Source Monitor or Pop-up Monitor. I mark an IN and an OUT. Then I mark an IN in the Timeline and splice the title into my sequence.

	U2			
U1	U1		Main Title PICT	Kate's CU
	A1			Kate's CU
	A2			Kate's CU

Importing Color Bars

Let's import something else. Normally, when you send a sequence to videotape (which we'll do in Chapter 14) you put SMPTE Bars at the head of the tape, so a video engineer can use them as a reference in order to properly set up the playback monitor and tape recorder. Let's import the SMPTE Bars that come bundled with the Avid software. This file is already loaded on your computer.

1. When you are in your project, click on a bin.
2. From the File menu, select Import. The Import window opens.
3. Navigate the Source Files until you get to your computer's internal hard drive. You are looking for the Supporting Files folder, and inside that the Test Patterns folder.
4. When you locate the folder, double-click on it and look for a file called SMPTE Color Bars, or SMPTE_Bars.pct (NT).
5. Select it and add it to the Import file selection box.
6. Select File Type as Graphic/Audio. If you're using version 6.x, select PICT.
7. Select the Media Drive and Resolution.
8. Click on Option.
9. Choose CCIR, non-square pixel or ITU-R 601.
10. On a Meridien-based machine choose Even Field Dominant.
11. Click on the "File has" or the "File Color Levels" window, and drag the menu to select CCIR Video levels. This choice is correct because the file was created on video, not on a computer.
12. Choose 60 seconds.
13. Click OK.
14. In the Import window, click Done/Open.
15. In your bin you will find a clip called Color Bars. Double-click to open it and cut it into the head of your sequence.

IMPORTING OTHER FILE TYPES

If you look at the Import window (Figure 13.2) on page 241, you'll see that there are three file types besides Graphic/Audio. In Chapter 15, we'll learn about Shot Logs. OMFI stands for Open Media Format Interchange and is designed to help you import files that were created on different computer platforms and across many different applications. Editcam™ is for importing footage shot on a special video camera manufactured by Ikegami.

There are lots of different files you might want to import. Now that you know the parameters, you should be able to import just about any file successfully. As with anything else discussed in this book, you'll only learn through practice and experimentation. Try importing different types of files and playing with the many options. Keep a written record of what settings work. If you have a file you want to import, there's a way to do it. Just keep trying.

EXPORTING

There are hundreds of computer applications that can change, alter, sweeten, and enhance your Avid-generated picture, sound, or both. And there are lots of outlets for the work you create on the Avid, including the Web and CD-ROMs. To take advantage of all these applications and avenues for distribution, you need to understand the basics of exporting.

Here are three situations in which you might want to export frames or sequences from the Avid:

- Create a newsletter or flyer to advertise your project. You could export a still frame from a sequence, retouch the image in a program like Photoshop, and then place the retouched photo in the flyer or newsletter that you've designed using page layout software.
- Export audio tracks for sweetening in Pro Tools. You could then reimport the sweetened tracks back into the sequence.
- Export part of a sequence to Adobe After Effects, make changes, and reimport it into the Avid.

Preparing to Export

There are several things you should do to make sure your export goes smoothly:

1. If you are exporting a sequence, make sure you duplicate the sequence before initiating an export. Create a new bin for the duplicate and export it. If anything goes wrong, you have an original to return to.
2. If you want to export a sequence, load it into the Record/Composer Monitor.
3. Make sure you render any and all effects that exist on the track(s) you are exporting.
4. If you're exporting more than V1, make sure the video track monitor is on the highest level.
5. Make sure the material you want to export is selected.

    - If it's a frame, mark the frame by placing the position indicator on it.
    - If it's one or more tracks, click on the track selector panel to select the ones you want, and deselect the ones you don't.
    - If it's part of a sequence or clip, place IN and OUT marks.

6. Go to the Export settings in the Settings list (click on Settings at the top of the Project window). If you want to select parts of a sequence or clip by placing a mark IN and a mark OUT, select Use Marks. If you want to choose tracks by clicking on them individually, click on Use Enabled Tracks. If you want to use the entire sequence, deselect Use Marks and also deselect Use Enable Tracks.

Export Settings (Current)

☐ Use Marks
☒ Use Enabled Tracks
☒ Use Both Fields

Destination Size (width x height)

Once you have selected the frame, clip, or sequence to export, go to the File menu and choose Export. The Export dialog box opens.

EXPORT DIALOG BOX

If you're using the latest software, you'll probably see a dialog box appear. The newer Avids assume that you have already set up your Export options and saved them as an Export template. Since you haven't, click Customize. The Export Settings dialog box appears (Figure 13.10); this one is from a Windows NT Avid. It's similar to the Macintosh Export dialog box in Figure 13.11.

As you can see, there are several different types of files, and each type offers one or more menus containing more choices and settings.

Yikes!

To be honest, there are so many choices, combination of choices, and settings available to you that if I go through all of them, you'll be terribly confused. Instead, I'm going to walk you through a couple of useful exports, so you can get the basic idea.

To really learn about exporting, you need to be familiar with the software application you are exporting to. Often you'll be exporting files for tweaking in applications such as Pro Tools, After Effects, Photoshop, 3D Studio Max™, and countless others. Get guidance from the graphic artists, sound engineers, and animators living in your area, who work with the software application on a daily basis. Ask them to walk you through the settings and options required for a successful export for each specific application.

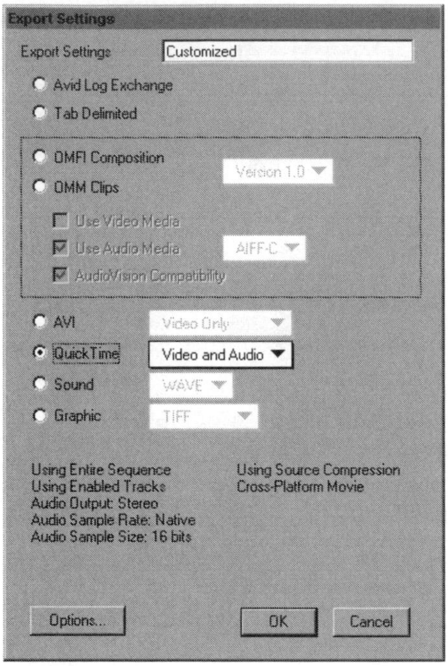

Figure 13.10   Windows NT Export Settings dialog box

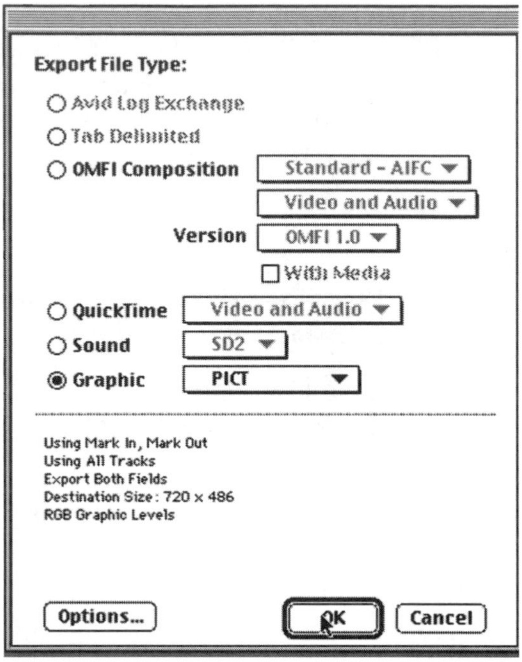

Figure 13.11   Mac Export dialog box

EXPORT PRACTICE

Let's do a couple of simple exports.

Exporting a Frame to Photoshop

It's fairly easy to export a frame of your project taken from either a clip or a sequence. You save it as a PICT file, and open it up in a program like Adobe Photoshop. Once in Photoshop, you have access to hundreds of tools, filters, and masks to make your frame take on a new life. Here are the steps:

1.   Digitize at the highest resolution possible.
2.   Place the sequence containing the frame you want to export into the Record/Composer Monitor and park the position indicator on the exact frame. The Timeline should be active.
3.   Then go to the File menu and choose Export.
4.   Click Graphic and then choose PICT file.
5.   Click the Options button.
6.   In the dialog box, click Use Marks (Figure 13.12), click Use Both Fields.
7.   Choose Destination Size as 720 × 486.

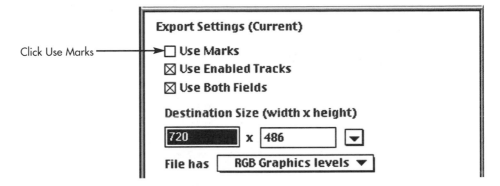

Click Use Marks

Export Settings (Current)

☐ **Use Marks**
☒ **Use Enabled Tracks**
☒ **Use Both Fields**

Destination Size (width x height)

720   x   486   ▼

File has   RGB Graphics levels ▼

Figure 13.12

8. Choose RGB Graphics levels.
9. Click OK.
10. You can save it to either a 1.4-MB floppy disk or a 100-MB or 200-MB Zip disk. You'll need about 1.2 MB for the file, so you can only fit one file onto a floppy.
11. Once in Photoshop, you'll need to unsqueeze the image. Go to the Image menu, select Image Size, and change the pixels to 720×540.

Avid software versions 8.x and higher have templates for the most common export settings. A pop-up menu on the Export dialog box lists the choices available. You'll find a template for Adobe Photoshop. Just select it and it will choose the correct settings for you. This is a nice feature. In fact there are templates for all sorts of applications including Adobe After Effects, Matador™, Elastic Reality™, and perhaps the foremost desktop audio application, Pro Tools. This brings us to the topic of exporting audio files.

Exporting Audio

The newer versions of Avid's software work with three different types of audio files: Audio Interchange File Format (often called AIFF-C), Wave Format (WAVE), and Sound Designer II (SD2). If your Avid offers AIFF-C, that's the format you should chose when starting a project because it's the easiest to transfer to another application or system. In the Project window go to General Settings and choose AIFF in the Audio File Format window before you digitize any audio. WAVE is a Windows-based format, and SD2 is a Macintosh-based format.

Although the Avid is capable of fairly sophisticated audio manipulation, it's not as sophisticated as Pro Tools, or other dedicated digital audio workstations. And although you may be a great editor, sound mixing is probably not your specialty. Sometimes it's worth going to a professional sound mixer—someone who does this sort of work every day. Not only can a professional solve your

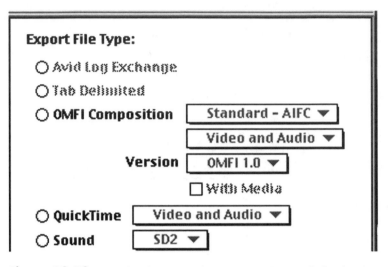

Figure 13.13   Media Composer version 7.1, Export dialog box.

sound problems, but he or she can set perfect levels for any number of distribution formats, including videotape, DVD, and film magnetic and optical tracks.

Because Pro Tools is one of the most common audio workstations, we'll review the steps you should take to export your audio to Pro Tools. After you digest these instructions, speak with your sound engineer to discuss each step, in case he or she wants you to do something different.

The basic idea is that you will be sending the audio's master files and the audio media files to a drive, which you will disconnect from your Avid and carry to the Pro Tools workstation. You could also attach a Jaz drive to your computer, and carry the Jaz cartridge to the workstation. Because audio take up far less space than video, a Jaz drive can probably hold your master files and media files.

1. Make a duplicate of your sequence. Create a new bin, labeled Pro Tools Sequence, and place the duplicate in the bin.
2. Delete the video track(s), by selecting them and deselecting all audio tracks. Hit the Delete key.
3. Make sure all your audio effects are rendered and all your tracks are enabled (selected).
4. Consolidate the sequence onto a spare drive using 30-frame handles. (See Chapter 14 for an explanation of consolidating.)
5. Select the sequence in the bin, and choose Export from the File menu.
6. The latest software versions have templates for moving files to various applications. Choose Pro Tools AIFF-C Embedded and then click OK.
7. If your system doesn't have templates, select the OMFI Composition radio button in the Export window.
8. Choose Standard - AIFC. See Figure 13.13.

9. Choose Audio Only.
10. In the Version pop-up window select OMFI 2.0.
11. Select With Media. NT users select the box Use Audio Media.
12. Click OK.

Save the resulting export document onto the same drive on which you con-solidated your media. Remove this drive from the system and bring it to the Pro Tools facility.

I've just outlined the steps you would take to bring an audio files to a Pro Tools facility for audio sweetening. There are many different Avid systems and versions of software, and there are differences in the way they handle files, so I can't guarantee this will work exactly as I've described. If you think you'll be going to a Pro Tools workstation, talk to the sound engineer in charge of the facil-ity. Use this as a guide to help you better follow the engineer's instructions.

Avid publishes a book called *Avid Products Collaboration Guide*, and it lists the Import and Export settings for hundreds of applications. No doubt the facil-ity will have a copy and can let you know which settings will work best when moving files from your particular Avid to its particular application.

EXPORTING OTHER FILE TYPES

If you look at the Export dialog box, you'll see that there are quite a few file types. In the chapter on film, we'll learn about Avid Log Exchange™ and Tab Delimited™. OMFI stands for Open Media Format Interchange, and it helps you send mostly audio files to lots of different applications. In the NT dialog box you'll see a couple of choices not found on earlier software versions (Figure 13.14). One is called OMM clips. OMM stands for Open Media Management, which is a media management system created so users can share media though the Web and other networked sources.

AVI™ is Microsoft's version of QuickTime™, Apple's highly successful video compression system.

QuickTime is used by both PC and Mac users to bring Avid sequences to Web pages and to CD-ROMs, or for manipulation by applications like After Effects. We've discussed only one of the files in the Graphic window: PICT. There arc scores of other supported file types. You may find that "PICT sequences" is a better choice for exporting sequences than QuickTime. It depends on the appli-cation you're exporting the material to.

Exporting is more complicated that importing because there are hundreds of applications you could be exporting to, and only one application—your Avid—that you're importing to. Just as I did with importing, I've tried to make exporting as simple as possible. I've accomplished this by employing an old trick; I left out most of the difficult and confusing material.

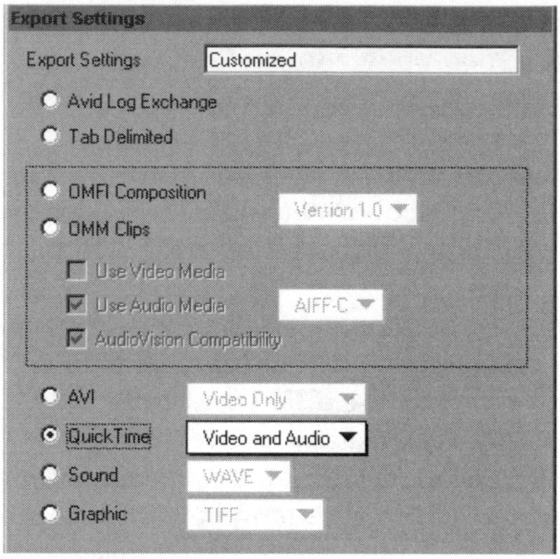

Figure 13.14

To become expert at exporting, you need to learn about the applications you're exporting to, such as After Effects, Photoshop, and Pro Tools. The more applications you master, the more valuable you are to your client or employer. Or, if you're editing your own projects, the fewer outside vendors or freelance people you'll need to hire.

SUGGESTED ASSIGNMENTS

1. Import Color Bars from the Avid Test Patterns folder.
2. Import a file created in Photoshop. If you don't have a file, borrow one from a friend. Ask him or her to save it as a PICT file.
3. Cut it into a sequence.
4. Export a frame from a sequence.
5. Open the file in Photoshop. If you don't have Photoshop, ask a friend who does to open it for you.

14

Finishing

I think successful video and filmmakers are product-oriented. Let's face it, a lot of people start films and videos, but only the truly dedicated finish them. It's easy to give up, to run out of steam, to take a never-ending break from a project. Making a film or video is a lot of hard work, and often you do it for little reward. I think the reason some people finish their projects, while others abandon theirs, is that they love having a product. They can't stop until they hold something in their hands, whether it's a videotape, film, or DVD.

"Here," they say, "is my project. Come look at it."

They're the ones I admire, no matter how many problems appear on the screen. They did it. They finished. It's an accomplishment worthy of our praise. Let's be like them. Let's learn how to finish a project on the Avid.

PATHS TO THE FINISH LINE

There are three paths that lead to a finished project.

1. You can output your sequence to videotape, after redigitizing it at your Avid's highest resolution.
2. You can create an Edit Decision List (EDL) and take your tapes to a tape facility for an online editing session.
3. If your project originated on film, you can create a Cut List so a negative cutter can conform your camera negative to the Avid sequence, and from that you make a 16mm or 35mm print.

Chapter 15 is devoted to path number 3. It takes you through all the steps involved in getting a print of your film. In this chapter, we're going to concentrate on outputting your sequence to tape right from the Avid. We'll briefly touch on the steps you go through to get an EDL.

FINDING ROOM ON THE HARD DRIVES

Most people digitize their footage at a low resolution, such as AVR 3s or 20:1, for editing purposes. Once they finish editing and want to output to tape, they redigitize their footage at a finishing resolution, such as AVR 77, 2:1, or even 1:1.

As we'll see shortly, this isn't all that difficult a task, since the Avid handles most of the work automatically. The difficulty comes in finding space on your hard drive to accommodate the high-resolution material. Usually, by the time you're ready to output your project, all your drives are full. If you can rent, borrow, or purchase additional drives, then by all means, do so. But if you can't, and you must use the drives you've got, then you need to make space. Something has to be tossed out, or at least taken offline, if you're going to clear enough space on the drives. Sometimes you have to make difficult decisions about what to throw out. You'd probably like to keep the low-resolution sequence online, in case you need to cut another version later on, but you might not be able to. Some of the decisions are easy; you're delighted to toss out some of the stuff on your drives. For instance, getting rid of unreferenced precomputes is a pleasure, once you know what they are. Unreferenced precomputes are the mohair sweaters of the digital editing world—they take up space and you never use them.

Deleting Unreferenced Precomputes

Briefly, a precompute is the new media the computer creates when it renders an effect or a title. If, while editing your sequence, you change or delete some of your titles or effects, those old precomputes don't get deleted. They remain on the hard drive, taking up valuable space. These hidden hard drive hogs are called unreferenced precomputes. It's frightening how many of them you'll find, and amazing how satisfying it is to blow them away.

Why are they still there? Why, when you delete unwanted effects, does the Avid hold on to the precomputes? One reason, I'm told, is so you can use Undo to change your mind. The Avid knows you pressed the Remove Effect key, but it worries that you might change your mind 30 minutes later and press Undo. If it didn't hang on to the precompute, it couldn't perform the Undo. You also may want to remove the effects from Sequence #5, but keep them for sequences 1 through 4. Since the Avid doesn't know what you want, it holds onto the unreferenced precomputes. Fine. I understand all that. However, I do think Avid should rewrite the software so that you can determine a length of time, in days or weeks, by which unreferenced precomputes are automatically removed from your system. You shouldn't have to keep tracking them down, like some Arnold Schwarzenegger wannabee.

You'll use the Media Tool for this mission. Go to the bin that holds all your sequences and shift-click all the ones you still use.

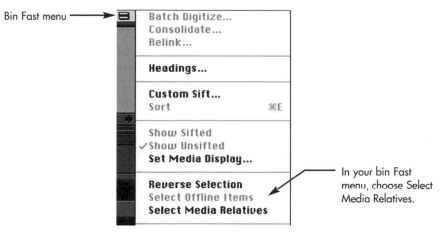

Bin Fast menu ⟶

Batch Digitize...
Consolidate...
Relink...

Headings...

Custom Sift...
Sort   ⌘E

Show Sifted
✓Show Unsifted
Set Media Display...

Reverse Selection
Select Offline Items
Select Media Relatives

In your bin Fast
menu, choose Select
Media Relatives.

Figure 14.1

1. In the Tools menu, open the Media Tool.
2. In the dialog box, check the boxes Current Project and Precompute Master Clips. Deselect all other choices.
3. Now, go back to the bin that contains your sequences. Make sure the sequences you care about are highlighted. If not, shift-click to select them. Go to the bin Fast menu (Figure 14.1) and choose Select Media Relatives. The precomputes which are connected to your sequences are selected in the bin *and* in the Media Tool.
4. Go to the Media Tool window and click on the title bar to activate the window. All the precomputes associated with the selected sequences are highlighted. They're the ones you want to keep.
5. Go to the Media Tool's Fast menu and choose Reverse Selection. Now all the unreferenced precomputes are revealed.
6. Press the Delete key. In the dialog box, make sure only the precomputes are selected.

Delete Media Files

Selected 0 digitized clip(s).
☐ V   Delete 0 video file(s).
☐ A1   Delete 0 audio file(s).
☐ A2   Delete 0 audio file(s).
☐ A3   Delete 0 audio file(s).
☐ A4   Delete 0 audio file(s).

Selected 496 precompute file(s).
☒ V   **Delete 438 video file(s).**
☒ A   **Delete 109 audio file(s).**

[Cancel]   [OK   ]

Check it out. There are nearly 500 unreferenced precomputes lurking about in this project. Press OK and they're gone.

Consolidating Your Sequence

As satisfying as it is to get rid of all your unreferenced precomputes, your drives are still quite full with all the low-resolution footage you digitized when you began the project. If you consolidate your sequence, you can keep the footage you used in your sequence, while the footage you didn't use gets placed offline.

Let's say you have a 20-minute project, but you digitized three hours of footage. The two hours and forty minutes of material you didn't use is taking up valuable storage space. When you consolidate your sequence, you are keeping what you used and getting rid of the media files—the actual digitized footage—that didn't make the cut. Consolidating removes the outtakes. Consolidating can free up vast amounts of space on your drives.

1. Open your sequences bin and select your sequence, so it's highlighted.
2. Xpress users, go to the Bin menu and choose Consolidate. MC users, go to the Clip menu and get Consolidate.
   A dialog box appears:

```
┌─────────────────────────────────────────────────────┐
│  Consolidate                                          │
│                                                       │
│     ☒ Delete original media files when done.          │
│                                                       │
│     ☐ Skip media files already on the target disk     │
│                                                       │
│                                                       │
│     Target Disk:  [ Media F ▼ ]                       │
│                                                       │
│     0 Clip(s) selected                                │
│     ┌───────────────────────────────┐  ┌──────────┐  │
│     │  1 sequence(s) selected.       │  │    OK    │  │
│     │  ▸andle Length: [3̶0̶] frames    │  └──────────┘  │
│     └───────────────────────────────┘  ┌──────────┐  │
│       ☐ Consolidate all clips in a group edit. │Cancel│ │
└─────────────────────────────────────────────────────┘
```

3. Select the box "Delete original media files when done." Deselect the box "Skip media files already on the target disk."
4. Select a Target Disk or click on a Target Volume(s).
5. Choose a Handle Length. Handles are frames before and after each transition point. Handles allow you to tweak your sequence, even after

you've consolidated it. The amount you can lengthen a shot is determined by the number of frames you choose as a handle length. The default is 60 frames, which gives you more flexibility but takes up more hard drive space. If I'm tight on space, and don't think I'll make many changes, I'll select 30 frames.

6. Click OK.

Consolidating a sequence allows you to select a drive for the consolidated material. In Chapter 13, when we discussed exporting, we mentioned that if you were going to export the audio tracks in your sequence to Pro Tools, you needed to first consolidate your sequence, because consolidating allows you to move your media files to a target disk—the one you'll carry to the Pro Tools workstation.

Checking for Space

You can check to see if you have enough room on your hard drives to digitize your project at your chosen AVR, or compression. Put your sequence in the Timeline, choose the Digitize tool, and set it to AVR 77, 2:1, or 1:1. Next to the name of the drive you'll see a time display, showing you how many minutes are available at the selected resolution. Check the other drives connected to your system for space. Add up the total minutes and see if you have enough. You can also check space by choosing the Hardware Tool in the Tools menu.

Blowing It All Away

You may find that all your efforts have not created enough space on your drives to redigitize your project at the highest resolution. If that is the case, you'll need to take all your video offline. Once done, when you play your sequence, the Record/Composer Monitor will display the dreaded words "Media Offline." Don't worry. Soon you'll be redigitizing it to AVR 77 or 1:1, and your sequence will look so beautiful, you'll never miss the old, low-resolution version.

Deleting Your Low-Resolution Media

1. Go to the Tools menu and select the Media Tool.
2. In the dialog box, checkmark all the boxes except the last one— Individual Media Files.
3. Click on the Media Tool and press Command-A. This will select every clip in your project.
4. Press the Delete key.
5. In the Delete Media Files dialog box, checkmark the box "V"—Delete video file(s) (Figure 14.2).

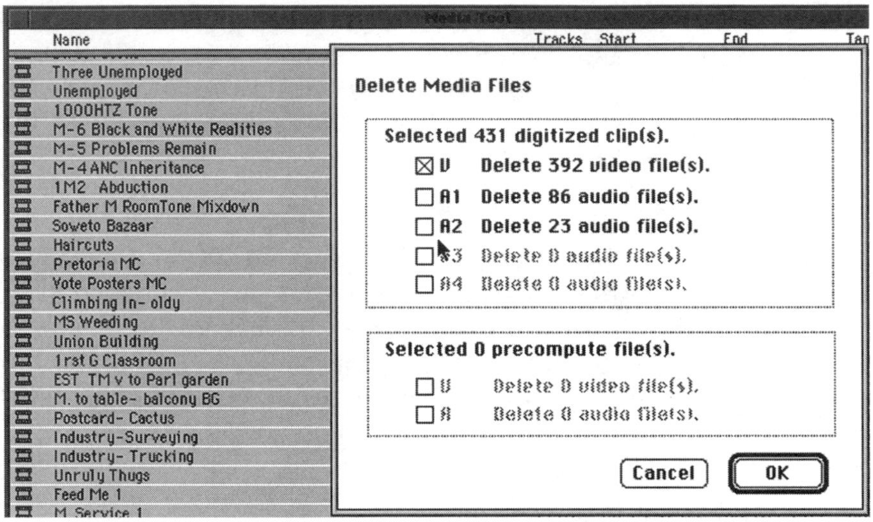

Figure 14.2

6. Make sure you deselect all the "Delete audio file(s)" choices. Do not delete your audio!
7. Hit OK.

Now, your drives will be practically empty, giving you plenty of room for redigitizing the clips in your sequence at the finishing resolution of your choice.

PREPARING TO REDIGITIZE YOUR SEQUENCE

There are several steps you need to take before you start to redigitize.

1. Make sure you have all your source video tapes with you.
2. Go to the Project window and click on the Settings button. In the scroll list, double-click on "Digitize." Click on the box that instructs the Avid to go to the next drive as the selected drive becomes full.
3. Create a new bin and call it "Online."
4. Duplicate your final sequence (select it and hit Command-D) in its original bin and drag the duplicate copy to the new Online bin.
5. Name the duplicate sequence "Online Sequence."
6. Delete all the audio tracks in the duplicate. To do this, place the Online Sequence in the Record/Composer Monitor so the tracks appear in the Timeline. Select the audio tracks and deselect the video tracks. Hit the Delete key.
7. Close all your bins except the newly created Online bin.

REDIGITIZING YOUR SEQUENCE

In order to redigitize your sequence at a higher resolution, you'll need to hook up your videotape deck. See Chapter 6 for suggestions on how to do this. Remember to open the Video Tool and set it to component, composite, S-video, or Serial digital. Once you're connected:

1. Select the sequence in the Online bin (it should be the only one there).
2. Bring up the Digitize Tool (Command-7).
3. Choose the target drive (the darkest one on the drive menu).
4. Select the finishing resolution—AVR 77, or Resolution 2:1 or 1:1.
5. Select Batch Digitize from the Bin menu (Xpress) or Clip menu (MC). If it is grayed out, click on the sequence in your Online bin.
6. In the Batch Digitize dialog box, deselect the option "Digitize only those items for which media currently is unavailable."
7. Choose a handle length of 30 or 60.
8. Click OK.

The Avid will ask you for the first tape, by name. Feed it the tapes as it asks for them. The process takes a while, but it's exciting to see the footage looking so sharp after all the time you've spent at a lower resolution.

When the redigitizing is complete, you'll see that you need to restore the audio tracks that you deleted earlier.

REPLACING YOUR AUDIO TRACKS

1. To get your sound tracks, open the bin that contains the final sequence—the one at the low resolution.
2. Xpress users, double-click on the sequence so it becomes a Pop-up Monitor. MC users, drag the sequence icon to the Source Monitor.
3. Go to the very first frame of the offline sequence. Mark IN. Go to the very last frame and mark OUT.
4. Now, make your Timeline active and go to the very first frame of the Online Sequence. Mark IN.
5. Now you're ready to splice the sound tracks into your Online Timeline. To do this you will need to create new audio tracks—as many as there are source tracks.
6. Select the audio tracks and deselect your video tracks. Now hit the Splice button. All your audio should splice into the Timeline.

RECREATING TITLE MEDIA AND RENDERING EFFECTS

Your sequence probably will not play because you may still have all those titles that you created at a lower resolution, while everything else is at a higher resolution.

1. Select all your titles by selecting the video tracks and marking an IN and an OUT in the Online Timeline.
2. Go to the Clip menu and choose Recreate Title Media. Your titles will be recreated at your new resolution.

You will need to render those recreated titles and effects again. Select each track and mark an IN and an OUT. From the Clip menu, choose Render In/Out. All your effects will be re-rendered.

CHECKING AUDIO LEVELS

Before you output the final sequence to tape, check your sound levels one last time. Get a pair of isolating headphones that prevents you from hearing anything other than what's coming through the earpieces. Open the Audio Tool and set the Input/Output toggle to O, so you're monitoring the levels you are sending out.

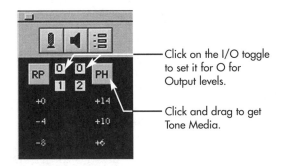

Click on the I/O toggle to set it for O for Output levels.

Click and drag to get Tone Media.

Figure 14.3

OUTPUTTING TO TAPE

Now your sequence is just as you wished. It looks and sounds perfect. You're itching to get it onto tape, but first there are a few things you need to do to get ready.

Prepping your sequence:

You should import SMPTE Color Bars and cut them into the beginning of your sequence. Chapter 13 walks you through the process. Make sure you import the file at the correct AVR and that you bring in at least 60 seconds. Cut them into your sequence. If you sync-lock all your tracks before you splice in the bars, everything will stay in sync.

Now cut in a reference head tone at 1000 hertz to go with the SMPTE Bars. To create this tone:

1. Get the Audio Tool from the Tools menu.
2. Click and hold on the PH box in the Audio Tool (see Figure 14.3). A menu will open. Select the last option in the menu, "Create Tone Media."
3. In the dialog box, set the reference tone to a desired decibel, and choose the length of tone in seconds. A tone of –14 dB is the default setting, which works nicely. You need a length to match your SMPTE Bars—60 seconds.
4. Click OK.
5. The 1000-Hz tone appears in your bin as a clip. Overwrite it into your sequence so it lines up with the Bars. Now you have "Bars and Tone."
6. Put in 15 seconds of black (fill) on all your tracks between the Bars and tone and the first frame of your show. You now have one minute and fifteen seconds of material before your show starts.

Connecting the Avid Cables to the Tape Deck

If you've just finished redigitizing your sequence to the highest resolution from your source tapes, you're going to have to switch the video cables around. You were sending video signals out from the tape deck to the Avid, and now you need to connect the cables from the Avid's Video Out to the tape deck's Video In. You also need to send audio from the Avid's Audio Out to the videotape deck's Audio In.

If your Avid facility has some sort of patching panel, you may not need to touch any cables at all. Just select the right buttons.

Manual Recording or Crash Recording to Tape

The simplest method of recording to tape is called manual recording. You don't need to be a video engineer to get it to work. You simply set your video deck to record, and play your sequence.

With your Online Sequence in the Timeline, and the cables hooked up and patching connected:

1. Put a brand new tape in the deck.
2. Pack the tape. To do this, fast-forward the tape and then fast-rewind it.

3. Set the Remote-Local switch on the video deck to Local.
4. On the video deck, press either Pause/Play/Record or Stop/Record, so you can monitor without recording.
5. Play the sequence and monitor the audio levels on the video deck's audio meters, adjusting the input pots on the tape deck.
6. Check the picture on a monitor attached to the tape deck.
7. Once you are satisfied with the levels, park the blue position indicator at the head of your sequence in the Timeline.
8. When everything is set, press Play and Record together, count 10 seconds, and then play your sequence on the Avid.

There. You're finished. Congratulations.

DIGITAL CUT

A more complicated method of sending the sequence to tape involves the use of timecode and the serial control. Using the Digital Cut Tool, you can get a frame-accurate recording using timecode. The Avid acts as the edit controller for the video deck.

To employ this method, you must use a master videotape that has been *blackened*. A blackened tape is one that has had a "black" video signal and time-code striped onto the entire tape. With timecode already on the master tape, the Avid can control the tape deck. The advantage to this method, compared to a manual recording, is that you can make changes to the master tape without re-recording the entire sequence. You can go back later on and do an insert edit.

For instance, I once recorded a sequence to a master tape, and then later, while playing back the master, noticed a bad sound level halfway through an hour-long show. Instead of having to redo the entire tape, I went to the Timeline and adjusted the audio. Then, using the Digital Cut Tool, I inserted the "corrected" audio onto the master tape.

You can purchase a blackened tape from a tape facility. Obviously, it costs more than a blank tape. Or, you can set your deck's timecode and blacken a tape yourself. Ask the owner of the deck how to set up the deck to do this, as each deck is configured differently.

Starting Sequence Timecode

The Avid sets each sequence you create to start at 1:00:00:00. Most television stations want the show's first frame to start at this timecode. But if you add 60 seconds of Bars and tone before the beginning of your show, and fifteen seconds of black fill before the first frame, as you should, then the show's first frame will be

1:01:15:00. You need to change the sequence's starting timecode. Go to the Settings window and select General. You can set the starting timecode to whatever you want and the next sequence you create will start with that timecode. Type 58:45:00 in the box. Type colons if your show's timecode is non-drop-frame and semi-colons if it's drop-frame. (Look at your sequence, or see Chapter 15 "Types of Timecode" on page 277.) Return to your online sequence, select all your tracks, mark an IN at the first frame and an OUT at the last frame and then copy it to the clipboard. Go to the Clip menu and create a new sequence. Now open the clipboard monitor, mark an IN at the first frame and an OUT at the last frame, and then splice your show onto the Timeline of this new sequence. Your new sequence will have a starting timecode of 58:45:00. Name this new sequence, "Online for Television."

When you order your blackened tape, instruct the tape facility to stripe the tape so the timecode they lay down starts at 58:30:00. Then, the timecode on the tape will lock up with the timecode on your sequence, and you can perform a digital cut using "Sequence Time." If the need arises, you can insert material onto the master tape at a later date. Make sure to tell the tape facility whether your sequence contains semi-colons for drop-frame timecode, or colons for non-drop-frame timecode.

To perform a digital cut:

1. After connecting the cables from the Avid to your timecode deck, place the deck's Remote/Local switch on Remote.
2. Load your online sequence into the Record/Composer Monitor.
3. Choose Digital Cut from the Clip menu (Xpress) or Output menu (MC). The Digital Cut Tool opens.
4. Select all the tracks you wish to record. If you're recording more than just V1, make sure the video track monitor is on the highest level.
5. Select the box Entire Sequence.
6. Select the box Record to Tape.
7. Select Sequence Time in the menu window.
8. Press the Record button on the Digital Cut Tool (Figure 14.4).

The Avid cues up the tape and begins recording your sequence to tape.

If you want to insert material at a later date, deselect the box Entire Sequence, place IN and OUT marks in the Digital Cut Tool's Deck Control window, and select which track(s) you're inserting. Now when you press the Record button, the Avid will cue up to the insert points and do an overwrite, replacing the old with the new.

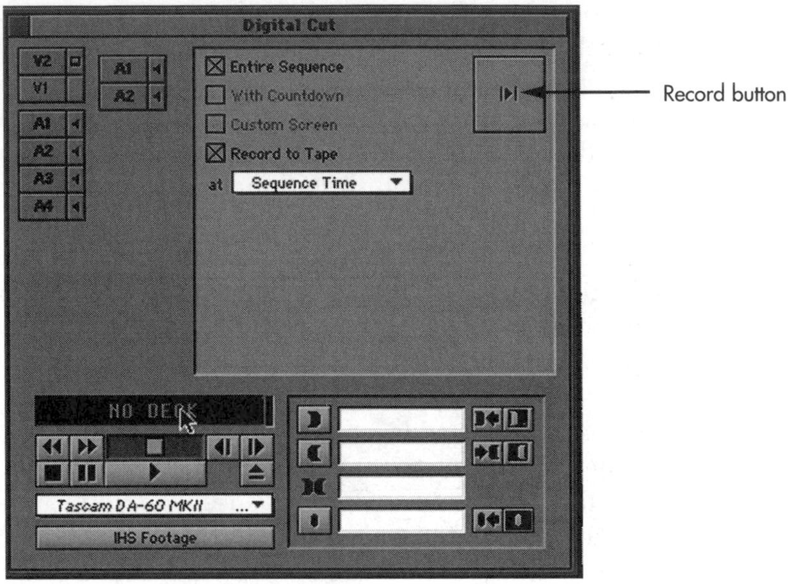

Record button

Figure 14.4

EDL (EDIT DECISION LIST)

You can use the Avid as an offline editing machine, and then have an online tape house put your show together using the Avid sequence as a guide. In theory it's simple. Give them your Edit Decision List and your source tapes, and they can finish your program using a sophisticated video tape system and edit controller, such as those manufactured by CMX, Grass Valley Group, Ampex, and Sony. They will deliver your show to you on the tape format of your choice, whether it's Digital Betacam, D1, D5, Digital-S, or Betacam SP.

The Avid will print out and put onto disk all your editing decisions, in a form that can be read by many different edit controllers. Your first step is to ask the online facility what format they need. The Avid will support many different types, but since so many of them are incompatible, you must provide the right one. An EDL for a Sony 9500 won't do your tape house any good if they have a CMX machine.

To get an EDL:

1. Put your final sequence in the Record Monitor so it is active.
2. Open the EDL Manager. The EDL Manager main window opens.

   • If you're an Xpress user: Go to the desktop, search through the Avid folders, and find the EDL Manager icon. Double-click on it.
   • If you are an MC user: Go to the Output menu and choose EDL.

3. Choose Format floppy from the File menu.
4. Insert a floppy disk in the computer's CPU. In the dialog box that opens, select the correct format for the edit controller you'll be using.
5. In the EDL format window, select your format, such as CMX_340 or GVG_7.0_7.0.
6. Click on the arrow between the icon of the edit controller and the UPDATE box. Your sequence will be brought into the EDL Manager, and it will display your EDL (Figure 14.5).
7. From the File menu choose Save As . . . and save it to your floppy disk.

In fact, the whole process is often a bit more complicated than I've explained it here. There are many issues having to do with the format of the floppy disk, the proper naming of files, and so on. The information here is intended to show you how to open the EDL Manger so that you can have a productive conversation with your online editor.

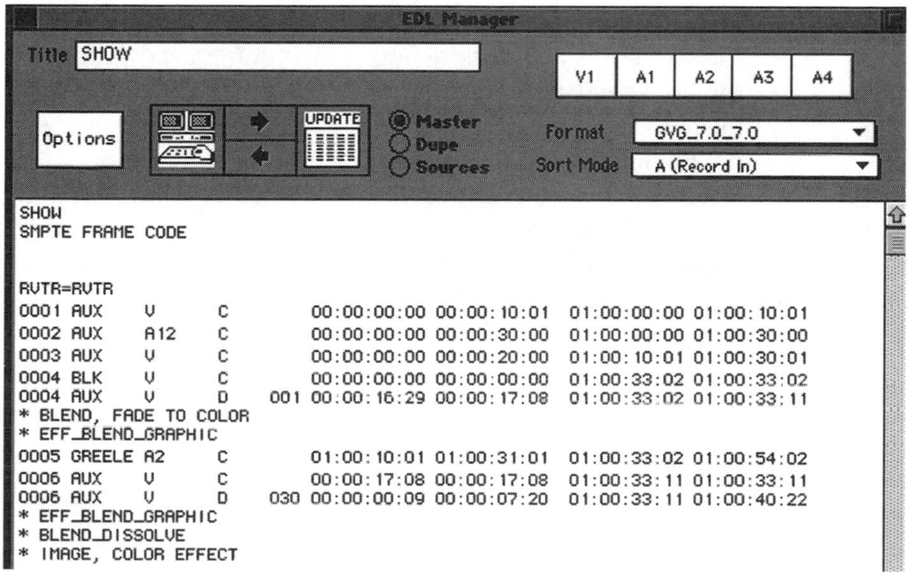

Figure 14.5

If there aren't too many visual effects, it's not that difficult for the online tape facility to reproduce your sequence based on an EDL. But if your sequence is made up of many multilayered effects that took a lot of time to render, chances are the online facility will be hard-pressed to recreate them accurately. And you might find that the whole process is quite expensive.

Part of the reason Avid came out with the Meridien board, with its 1:1 uncompressed video feature, was to reduce or eliminate the need for EDLs and online editing sessions. If you can get uncompressed resolution right from your Avid, you don't need to go to an online tape facility. And all the effects you created while editing your sequence will appear on the master tape when you do a digital cut, at no extra charge.

SUGGESTED ASSIGNMENTS

If you are in a classroom setting, sharing media files with other students, it's difficult to practice the space-saving steps explained in this chapter, because you may wipe out someone else's media. If that is the situation:

1. Go through each of the space-saving steps, examining the dialog boxes and windows, but stop short of actually pressing the final OK or Delete button.
2. Output your sequence to tape.

If you are working alone, on your own system, and have finished editing a sequence:

1. Select the sequences and then delete your unreferenced precomputes.
2. Select the final sequence and consolidate it.
3. Select the final sequence, duplicate it, create an Online bin, and strip out the audio tracks.
4. If you have space, redigitize this sequence to a "finishing" resolution.
5. Splice in your audio tracks.
6. Recreate your titles and render all effects.
7. Output your sequence to tape.

15

Finishing on Film

This chapter is designed to help those of you who want to use a Media Composer or Xpress to cut a film project that will result in either a 16mm or 35mm projection print. The information about Avid's matchback software will be particularly useful to editors who don't have access to an Avid Film Composer or to a Media Composer with 24-frames-per-second capabilities.

WHY FILM?

The main problem with video as a medium of distribution is that there are just so many video formats and standards in use around the world. There are three "standards" to deal with: SECAM, PAL, and NTSC. And each standard has at least fifteen different tape formats. None of them plays on any other format's tape machines. What a mess.

The great thing about a film print is that there is only one standard and only a couple of formats. A 16mm or 35mm print can be shown at festivals and theaters anywhere in the world, from Afghanistan to Zimbabwe, from Sydney to Cannes. However, making that film print can be a challenge.

FILM AND THE AVID

Currently there is no way to digitize film directly into the Avid. Instead you must first transfer the film to videotape. Once your film is on tape, you can digitize it, using the Digitize Tool, just as you would any other videotape.

THE FILM-TO-TAPE TRANSFER

After you have shot your footage, you take the exposed film to a laboratory for processing. Once the film has been processed, it has an image, either negative or positive. You then take your processed film to a telecine facility (many labs have them), for a film-to-tape transfer. The film's individual frames are projected or scanned onto videotape. There is a variety of systems in use today, ranging from film projectors beaming the film's image onto a video camera, to highly sophisticated machines using a flying spot scanner, capable of incredible image manipulations. Many flying spot systems cost over $500,000. The film is transported on rollers that never touch the image surface, so your film won't get scratched or damaged. A flying spot scanner can also transpose a negative image to a positive one. So, if you shoot negative film, as most people do, you don't have to make a positive print of your film to get it transferred.

FINISHING ON FILM OR FINISHING ON TAPE

Television commercials, rock videos, and many episodic television dramas are shot on film, but the finished product is a videotape. If the end result of your film project is a videotape, then once the film is transferred, you no longer need the film. And, to be honest, you don't need to know much about the film-to-tape process.

However, if you plan to make a projection print of your film, which is currently the case for all feature films and many student film projects, then you need to pay a lot of attention to the film-to-tape transfer. Why? Because after cutting your project on the Avid, you will then ask a negative cutter to go back to the original film and conform that film to match your Avid sequence. Think about it. The negative cutter must be able to locate hundreds of strips of film and splice those strips together in the right order and at the right length, based on an edited sequence that was digitized, not from that film, but from a video copy of that film! Needless to say, the process is far from straightforward. You can help the negative cutter do the job correctly, and save yourself a lot of money, if you know how the process works.

HIRE A NEGATIVE CUTTER FIRST

Usually filmmakers finish editing their film, and then they go in search of a negative cutter. That's not a good idea when cutting your film on an Avid. The negative cutter can help you even before you send your exposed film to the lab. By the end of this chapter, you and your negative cutter will speak the same language. In fact you'll probably know more about the overall process than most negative cutters. Still, I urge you to contact a negative cutter even before you send your film for processing.

THE $64,000 QUESTION

The key question when editing a film project on the Avid is this: Which frame of film was placed on which frame of video during the film-to-tape transfer? Everything depends on that. The Avid can tell you which frame of video you edited. That's easy. The difficult part is figuring out which film frame that video frame represents. What's the big deal, you ask? Film runs at 24 frames per second, and video doesn't. And that, as they say, is a problem.

THE 2-3 PULLDOWN

Film intended for projection in a theater is shot at 24 frames per second. Videotape travels at different speeds, depending on the country you live in and the tape standard that country has adopted. In the United States we use the NTSC standard, and NTSC tapes travel at approximately 30 frames per second. Transferring film onto tape in a NTSC country is a bit tricky, as you can imagine. How do you transfer 24 frames of film onto 30 frames of video? And secondly, how do you do it in a way that will allow a negative cutter to go back to the film and cut the correct frame?

Fortunately, it's not that difficult to get 24 frames to fit nicely onto 30 frames. Each frame of videotape is made up of two fields. (Each field contains half the frame's total lines, which are scanned horizontally. Odd lines are scanned first, then even lines to give the total image.) During the transfer process, the telecine machine places four frames of film onto five frames of video, using the two fields to make the math work. Examine Figure 15.1.

The first film frame, called the A-frame, goes onto the first two fields of the videotape. The second frame of film, called the B-frame, goes onto three fields. The third film frame, the C-frame, goes onto two fields, and the fourth film frame, the D-frame, goes onto three fields. Two fields then three fields, two fields then three fields, and on and on like that. Hence the name "2-3."

As you can see in Figure 15.1, four film frames are transferred onto five video frames. If you do this six times (6×4 film frames = 24, or one second, and 6×5 video frames = 30, or one second), you have a second of film and a second of video.

Look closely at this diagram. Notice that each frame of film (A, B, C, D) is transferred differently. The A-frame is the only one that is transferred onto a single frame of video, all by itself. The C film frame is like the A film frame, in that it covers just two fields, but the C film frame is transferred onto two different video frames. B and D are transferred onto three fields, but the way each goes onto those three fields is different. If you transfer 10,000 frames, each frame is either A, B, C, or D.

The way the four film frames are placed on the video is called the frame "pullin," and is critical to the process of identifying which video frame holds which film frame.

Film Frames

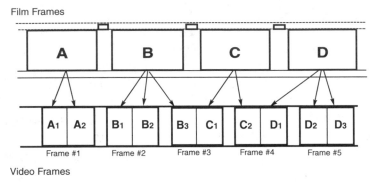

Video Frames

Figure 15.1

IT'S REALLY 29.97

Another complication arises from the fact that NTSC video doesn't actually run at 30 frames per second. It used to, but with the development of color television, many decades ago, the frame rate of NTSC videotape changed to 29.97 frames per second.

It turns out that the difference between 30 and 29.97 is .1 percent. So what film-to-tape transfer facilities do is actually slow the film down by .1 percent when doing the film-to-tape transfer. The film is slowed down from 24 fps to 23.976 fps. The difference between 23.976 and 24 fps is .1 percent. The film's running speed is "pulled down" during transfer. You just learned about the 2-3 part, and now you know about the pulldown part. Combine them together and you have the film-to-tape transfer process known as "2-3 pulldown."

KEYCODE AND TIMECODE

Knowing that we can accurately transfer from film to tape doesn't entirely solve the problem of identifying which frame of videotape contains which frame of film. In the beginning of this textbook we discussed the timecode system that video uses to identify each and every frame. Using a system based on clock time, every video frame has its own unique number. Film has a corresponding system using *key numbers*, which look something like this: KL74 0246 8805, where the two letters indicate the film's manufacturer and the film type, the first six digits identify the film roll, and the last four digits provide the footage count on that roll. Strictly speaking, *keycode* is a machine-readable bar code version of the key numbers, but most people just say keycode when referring to the numbers as well as the bar code version. Keycode isn't placed on every frame of film. In 16mm, for instance, the key numbers are placed every 20 frames. (There are 40 frames in a foot of 16mm film, so every half-foot.) But even though there isn't keycode on every frame, it's easy to identify each frame by counting the frames in between the keycode. Computers are good at this sort of counting, and during the transfer from film to tape, not only is the keycode read by a *keycode reader*, but the frames in between the keycode are counted and given numbers. Those numbers are called the frame "offset."

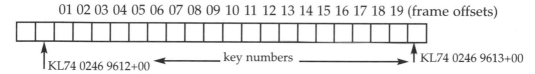

01 02 03 04 05 06 07 08 09 10 11 12 13 14 15 16 17 18 19 (frame offsets)

KL74 0246 9612+00 ◄———— key numbers ————► KL74 0246 9613+00

Since the film has keycode and the videotape has timecode, during the film-to-tape transfer, you place the keycode information onto the videotape, together with the tape's timecode information. But there's one more crucial piece of information needed—the frame pullin. Remember that the 2-3 pulldown process places four frames of film (A, B, C, or D) onto five frames of video. Each frame of video must contain this pullin information. Each video frame must say, "I've got an A-frame," or "I've got part of a B-frame," or "I've got the other part of the B-frame," in order for the negative cutter to know which frame of film that videotape frame holds.

During the film-to-tape transfer, a machine locks together each frame's keycode information, timecode information, and frame pullin information. Because this information is critical, it is "burned" onto the videotape so all the information is visible whenever the tape is played. As you can see in Figure 15.2, the timecode information is displayed on the left and the keycode, with frame offset (count) and pullin, is displayed on the right. This frame of film is 6 frames past the frame containing the keycode number KL 0246 9612. And it is a C pullin.

01:16:31:18 . 1   KL74   0246   9612·06C

Figure 15.2   A video frame displaying the timecode, keycode, frame offset, and pullin

PROBLEMS WITH THE TRANSFER

It's easy to accurately burn the timecode onto the tape. But, as Figure 15.3 illustrates, the device that reads the keycode is some distance from the telecine's film gate, and problems do crop up. If the film is not threaded properly in the telecine machine, the keycode can be off. This should not happen, but it does.

IDENTIFYING THE FIRST FRAME WITH A PUNCH

As I said before, it's critical for the negative cutter to know which video frame holds which film frame. The pullin (A, B, C, D) helps us know which film frame landed on which video frame. But for this to work, we need a place to start, so everyone knows which is the first frame.

After processing the film, your lab should punch a hole in the frame containing the first visible keycode number at the head of each camera roll. The telecine facility then lines up that punched frame so it is an A-frame pullin. All the timecode and keycode numbers, all the frame offsets, and all the pullin letters have that punch as a common reference point.

As the film is transferred, the keycode numbers are sent to a box which burns them onto the videotape. Part of the process involves a controller, such as a Time Logic controller, which keeps the timecode locked together with the keycode coming from the keycode reader.

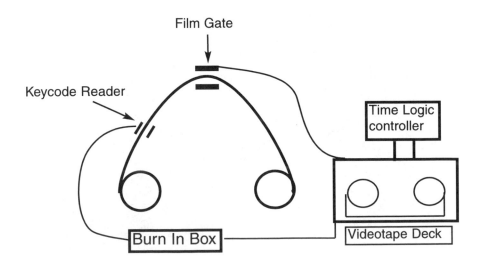

Figure 15.3   The Telecine Process

CHECKING THE NUMBERS

Errors do occur. So it is a good idea to check the accuracy of the transfer. Do the keycode numbers on your tape match the keycode numbers on the negative? One way to find out is to ask your negative cutter to go through the negative rolls and create a Key Code Log. Have the negative cutter fax the log to you and then check to see if the numbers on the negative match those displayed on the Avid. On big-budget features, a workprint is often made, so the editor or assistant can check the numbers without having to pull the negative out of the vault.

TYPES OF TIMECODE

Speaking of timecode, there are actually two kinds of timecode: non-drop-frame and drop-frame. As you know, videotape used to run at 30 frames per second, but when color was introduced, the rate was changed to 29.97. Because of that slight difference, whenever non-drop-frame timecode is used, a show's running time and its timecode time can be off by several seconds during an hour-long show. To solve this problem, drop-frame timecode was introduced. No frames are actually dropped, but some frame numbers are dropped to make up for the difference between 30 and 29.97. Video engineers prefer drop-frame because an hour show equals an hour of timecode. But the film industry uses non-drop-frame, and you should always specify non-drop-frame when given a choice.

How do you tell the difference? The Avid can tell, almost as soon as you feed a tape into the deck during digitizing. Non-drop-frame will display colons: 01:23:54:21, whereas drop-frame will appear with semicolons. The same timecode would appear as 01;23;54;21.

WORK ORDER TO YOUR LAB

As mentioned earlier, you should speak with your negative cutter before taking any film to the lab to be processed and transferred to tape. The negative cutter can offer suggestions as to how he or she wants the camera rolls prepared. The main points you would stress in your work order to the lab and transfer facility are as follows:

- Prep negative for video transfer. Punch head of each camera roll at the first visible key number at a "0" frame. Punch tail of each camera roll at a "0" frame.
- Perform a 2-3 pulldown starting with the A-frame at head punch of each camera roll. Use non-drop-frame timecode.
- Transfer original camera negative to Beta SP tape with timecode, keycode, and "A" frame reference burned onto tape. Please place the burn-in at the bottom of frame.

- Provide a log file on a 3.5 floppy disk with a hard copy.
- Transfer each camera roll as a nonstop transfer.

THE MATCHBACK PROCESS

There are any number of negative cutters in New York City who could take a video copy made from your sequence on the Avid, and using the numbers on the screen, look at each cut point and then go to the negative film and conform it perfectly. Using just the video copy, they could "match back" the film to the video copy of your sequence.

But most negative cutters outside of New York use the videotape and an Avid generated *Cut List*. A Cut List is like an Edit Decision List, but with keycode numbers instead of timecode numbers. Avids with matchback software can generate a list of all the edit points, showing the keycode number and pullin for each transition point. Avid now calls its matchback software FilmScribe™.

Unfortunately, neither the Avid nor FilmScribe can read the keycode, offset, and pullin information when you digitize the videotape. You must input that information yourself. Only then can the matchback software produce a Cut List.

There are two ways that you can feed the keycode information into the Avid: typing each number by hand, or importing the numbers into your bins from a disk provided by the transfer facility. Guess which one is easier. Good. Now, guess which one is cheaper.

TELECINE LOG FILE

If the price is right, you should ask the transfer facility to make a Telecine Log File. This is a file containing all the timecode, keycode, and pullin information pertaining to your film-to-tape transfer. It contains all the information you, the Avid, and your negative cutter will need to conform the film to the Avid version. It eliminates the need for logging each take on each camera roll. A FLEx file is perhaps the most common type, and it is created whenever the transfer facility has used a Time Logic machine during the transfer. If an Aaton system was used, the file will be an ATN file, and if an Evertz was used, the file will be an FTL. Some transfer facilities charge a lot of money for the Telecine Log File. One New York transfer facility was asking over $100 for each one, and there's one for each tape. Others charge you no more than the price of the floppy disk. Shop around. Bargain.

You need to convert these log types to Avid log format. Fortunately, the Avid gives you a utility, already installed in your computer, to do this. Usually the files come from the telecine facility on a PC disk, but don't worry if you are using a Mac, since they can read PC disks these days. I've only imported FLEx files, so it's the file most often discussed in this chapter.

Steps for importing a FLEx file:

1. Insert the disk containing the FLEx file into the CPU's floppy drive.
2. Open the disk and drag the file onto the desktop.
3. Look for the Avid Log Exchange in the Avid Utilities folder on the hard drive.
4. Open (double-click) the Avid Log Exchange (ALE) utility. There are two columns—one for input and one for output.
5. Select: Input - FLX   Output - ALE. Select CLEAN and RELAXED.
6. Deselect the Log Audio tracks, keeping only Log V for video. Click CONVERT.
7. A window appears. Scroll through the window until you find your FLEx file (on the desktop).
8. Click on OPEN. Your file will be converted to ALE.
9. Quit the Avid Log Exchange utility.
10. Launch Avid.
11. Create a New Project, give it a title, check off Matchback, and select 16mm or 35mm.
12. Once you're in the project, create a new bin.
13. Name the bin "Dailies - Day 1."
14. Open the "Dailies - Day 1" bin and choose Import from the File menu.
15. In the Import window, select the File Type and choose Shot Log.
16. Scroll through the directory until you find your file—ALE. It's on the desktop.
17. Add it to the right-hand column.
18. Click Done.

You should see all the clips in the Dailies - Day 1 bin with the Start and End timecode. Go to the Bin menu, choose Headings, and select Camroll, KN Start, KN End, KN Duration, Pullin, Scene, Take, and Start.

Now digitize the takes. Just select all the clips in the bin and batch digitize (Clip menu—MC; Bin menu—Xpress).

If you don't have a log file, you can enter the information by hand. It's not as fast, nor as much fun.

LOGGING KEYCODE BY HAND

1. In the New Project window, name the project by its title. Then select Matchback, and then choose the 16mm or 35mm option.
2. Click OK.
3. Create a New Bin and give it a name: "Dailies - Day 1."
4. In the Bin menu or the Bin Fast menu, select Headings.

5.   Select: Camroll, KN Start, KN End, KN Duration, Pullin, Scene, Take.
6.   Open the Digitize Tool. When it asks for a tape, insert the videotape and click New Tape. Then name the first tape "Tape 001."
7.   Place the Digitize Tool into the Log Mode and enter start and end keycode for each take. To do this you find a point before the clapstick and mark IN, go to the end of the take and mark OUT, hit Log, and then enter the keycode information in the bin by typing in the heading "Keycode Start."
8.   The Keycode should look like this: KL 236892 0512 +00A.
9.   Type the letters and numbers without spaces, and the Avid will set spaces.
10. Hit the Tab key and enter the Pullin frame in that column. (A will probably be there already. If it's not an A-frame, type the right letter.)
11. The Avid will supply the Keycode End.

To avoid having to enter keycode numbers for *each* take, you can create what's known as the *Phantom Master Clip*. Sounds like a low-budget horror film.

PHANTOM MASTER CLIP

1.   On the videotape, go to the hole punch at the head of the first camera roll and in Log Mode, mark an IN. Write down on a piece of paper the keycode number at this punch frame. You should see the camera roll's first keycode number, plus 00 frame, and an A-pullin. Go all the way to the end of the camera roll, where there is still visible picture and keycode, and mark OUT. Hit the Log button. Now you've set the timecode information.
2.   Now type the keycode information, which you wrote down on the paper, in the bin heading "Keycode Start."
3.   Type the letters and numbers without spaces, and the Avid will set spaces.
4.   Hit the Tab key and enter the pullin frame in that column. (A will probably be there already.)
5.   Avid will supply Keycode End.

Now you can play the tape and log your individual clips or takes, choosing IN and OUT points with the Digitize Tool. The Avid will provide the Keycode numbers, which it gets from the phantom master clip, automatically. You can either log and then batch digitize the takes, or digitize each one as you go along. Be careful not to digitize the phantom master clip! Just digitize the clips inside of it.

Sometimes the keycode numbers in the bin will be correct, but the pullin may be listed as an X-pullin. I asked Avid's Tom Ohanian (Chief Avid Editor) about this X-pullin, and he said, "You don't need to futz with the pullin. As long as the master clips have the correct key number that they obtained from the phantom master, you're all set."

Keep in mind that every camera roll has different keycode, so you have to enter keycode information, not by the videotape, but by the camera roll. A videotape might contain three or more camera rolls.

SOUND AND THE AVID

When you record your field tapes on either a Nagra or a DAT recorder, you set those machines to match the film camera's speed of 24 frames per second. To do this, you use a Nagra set at 60 Hz, and a DAT set to record at 30 frames per second, non-drop-frame. Remember that your film was slowed down in the telecine from 24 to 23.976 frames per second. It was slowed down by .1 percent. For your audio to sync up with the film, it needs to be slowed down as well. It needs to be played at a speed that is .1 percent slower than normal, in order to be in sync with the picture that's already inside the Avid.

(The Film Composer and several expensive Media Composers with 24-frames-per-second options are exceptions to this. With those models, you don't need to slow down the audio, because the film is sped up inside the Avid to 24 fps.)

For a hefty fee, your transfer facility will sync up the field audio tapes from the Nagra or DAT and lay the audio in sync with the picture on your videotape. That way, when the videotapes are delivered to you, you can digitize picture and sound together. You no longer have to deal with all the issues of slowing down the sound, or syncing up the rushes. They've done it all for you. Needless to say, it's quite expensive.

You can save a lot of money by doing the syncing of the field tapes yourself.

Many students and low-budget filmmakers use analog Nagras to record sound for their films because they're reliable and inexpensive (relatively speaking), and they provide great sound. You could slow your Nagra down by .1 percent and transfer the sound into the Avid by using a device that slows the Nagra down to 59.94 Hz (.1 percent). The one problem with this method is that the sound transferred into the Avid has no timecode. If your audio goes offline, you can't batch digitize the audio back into the Avid. Instead, you must redigitize and then resync and re-edit all your sync sound.

NAGRA 4.2

The best method for those of you using the popular Nagra 4.2 is to transfer all your field tapes to a DAT machine which will lay down timecode on the DAT tape. Now your audio has timecode and can easily be redigitized if it goes offline. You still must slow those DAT tapes by .1 percent when you digitize them.

TIMECODE NAGRA AND TIMECODE DAT

If you recorded your field tapes on a Nagra equipped with timecode or on a timecode DAT, then you still must slow the tape by .1 percent. But since these tapes already have timecode information, you can transfer them directly into the Avid without first transferring them to DAT. Remember, if you're doing a film project that's going to be projected at 24 fps, field tapes *must* be recorded at 60 Hz for analog Nagras and 30 NDF for machines with timecode.

SLOWING DOWN THE AUDIO DURING DIGITIZING

When you digitize the audio tapes, you slow them down as you play them into the Avid. I've used a Tascam DA-60mkII DAT deck to do this because it's easy to set the pitch to –.1 percent. Because it's a timecode machine, the Avid's Digitize Tool can control the deck, just as it would a videotape deck.

I set up a separate bin for each audio tape, and digitize the clips into that bin. I usually don't digitize the audio as individual takes, but as larger master clips. Once the audio is in the bin, I'm ready to sync up the sound takes to the picture takes.

SYNCING RUSHES

Syncing picture and sound is a time-consuming endeavor. Usually you have a lot of takes on a camera roll and each one has to be synced by hand. Of course the process is the same if you are on a KEM or Steenbeck. Usually film projects hire assistant editors to do the syncing. If you have 50 rolls of film, and you've had your fill of syncing after just three rolls, you might think about finding an assistant editor.

There are probably six or seven ways to sync your sound to your picture clips. The one outlined here seems as straightforward as any, and takes advantage of the Avid's AutoSync feature.

1. Create a new bin and call it "Synced Takes." Now create a second new bin and call it "Sync Subclips."
2. Open the bin with the picture clips: "Dailies - Day 1."
3. Open the first clip to be synced: Scene 1 Take 1.
4. In the Source/Pop-up Monitor, find the first frame where the clapstick closes. If there was sound, it would "crunch" here. Mark this frame with an IN. Go to the end of the take and mark an OUT.
5. Make a subclip of this by holding the Option key and dragging the picture to the "Sync Subclips" bin. (You should see the subclip symbol.)
6. Press the Caps Lock key so you can use "digital scrub" to hear the sound.

7. Locate the audio clip for the first scene: Scene 1 Take 1. Open it.
8. In the Source window, find the first full frame of "CRUNCH." Use the Step one-frame button to locate it precisely. Mark an IN.
9. Go to the end of the take and mark an OUT.
10. Make a subclip of this audio by holding the Option key and dragging the audio to the "Sync Subclips" bin. (You should see the subclip symbol.)
11. Now you have two subclips in the bin, each with an IN point referenced to the clapsticks. Shift-click so both subclips are selected. Go to the Bin menu and choose AutoSync.
12. A dialog window appears. Select the "Inpoints" box and click OK.
13. A third subclip is formed—combining sound and picture locked in sync. Drag that to the "Synced Takes" bin.
14. Hit Command-S to save what you have done.
15. Play it in the Source/Pop-up Monitor to check sync.
16. If there is a problem with the sync, delete it, and the subclips you used to make it, and try it again.
17. Now sync up the next take in the same way.

It's slow going at first, but after you do it a while, it'll get a lot faster.

EFFECTS

Fades and dissolves are the only effects that I recommend you add to your sequence. You can do wonderful things with the Effect Palette, but each effect you add to your sequence will cost you hundreds, if not thousands, of dollars to recreate on film. Fades and dissolves can be created when you make a 16mm or 35mm print. A single fade or dissolve only adds about five dollars to your laboratory bill. All the other effects available on the Avid will cost you serious, eye-popping, wallet-breaking money.

When placing fades and dissolves in your Timeline, choose them by seconds and parts of seconds, and then translate that into video frames. For example, choose a 30-frame fade-in if you want a one-second fade to go into your film. Choose a 45-frame fade if you want the fade to last a second and a half.

ADD EDITS

Once you've finished cutting your film on the Avid, go through and delete any Add Edits that might appear on your Video track. You don't want them to throw off your Cut List.

SMPTE LEADER AND BEEP

You need a SMPTE Leader at the head of your film, and so the negative cutter wants to see one at the head of your Avid sequence. The easiest way to accomplish this is to digitize a SMPTE Leader (ask your lab to splice one onto the negative before the transfer, so it's on your videotape) and then cut it into your Timeline. Take out any Bars and tone you might have added to your sequence. The Picture Start frame on the SMPTE Leader must be the very first frame in your sequence. The 8, 7, 6, 5, 4, 3 will follow until the single frame of 2 appears. After the 2-frame, there is a precise amount of black: 47 film frames on the leader. The very next frame (48 frames after the 2) is the first frame of your picture—whether it is a shot, a title, or a fade-in of a shot. Once the SMPTE Leader has been cut into your Timeline, splice in a single frame of 1000-Hz tone (the beep) into your audio tracks in sync with the number 2 on the SMPTE Leader.

The Picture Start frame becomes the 0 point of your footage on the Avid, and if you have cut the SMPTE Leader in correctly, the first frame of your show (48 frames after the 2) would be listed in the Cut List as starting at 4 feet and 32 frames (4 + 32). Look at the Cut List on page 286. When you get your first Cut List, check this. If your first shot doesn't start at 4 + 32, recut the SMPTE Leader until it does.

CUT LISTS AND VIDEO COPY

Once you have a final sequence, it's easy to get a Cut List. After loading your sequence into the Record/Composer Monitor, open the Cut List Tool (Figure 15.4). MC users will find the tool in the Output menu, and Xpress users should go to the Tools menu.

1. Load your sequence into the Composer/Record Monitor.
2. Move the mouse to the Get Sequence window and click on it.
3. Select the video tracks you want to include. Usually select just V1, unless you have multilayered effects and the money to pay for them.
4. Select the Lists by clicking on the buttons. The Avid generates four lists; the negative cutter especially needs the Assemble and Optical Cut Lists, so make sure you choose those two.

    The Avid regards simple fades and dissolves as opticals, when in the film world, those are effects that the negative cutter can set up for you when doing the A&B Rolls. A true effect, like a freeze frame, would require that the negative cutter pull the shot from the negative camera roll and have it sent to an optical house. If you have a true optical, then

Click on the Fast menu to view and save Cut List.

Click here to get the sequence that is in the Record or Composer Monitor.

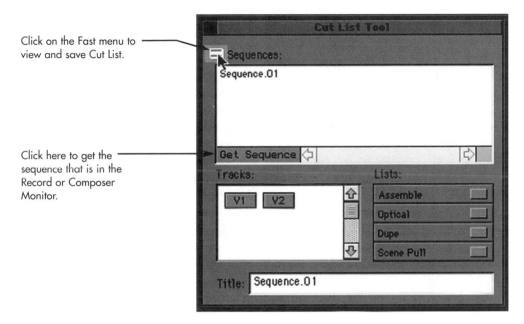

Figure 15.4

the negative cutter would need the Pull List as well as the Assemble and Optical lists. The Dupe List shows you where you have used any footage or frames more than once. That is a big problem, because there's only one frame in the negative. If you have dupes, find out where they are and use some other footage, or be prepared to pay for optical printing.

5. Now go to the Fast menu and choose View Cut Lists. View them.
6. Now go to the Fast menu and choose Save Cut Lists. Save them to a floppy or Zip disk.

Back at your office/apartment, insert your floppy and open the lists with any popular word-processing program. The resulting columns of numbers and text are easier to read when you set your page orientation to horizontal, rather than the standard vertical page setup. You may have to fiddle with the columns, using the Tab key to line things up. Once they look good, print them. The negative cutter will also need a video copy of your finished project, showing the time-code and keycode burn-in clearly visible (no mask). Some want a VHS copy, and others want Beta SP. Ask.

Armed with Cut Lists, the video copy of your film, and the negative camera rolls, the negative cutter can now conform and A&B Roll your film.

"MATCHBACK SHORTENED THE TAIL OF THE CLIP BY 1 FRAME"

Look at your Cut List and you'll probably see a message saying, "Matchback shortened the tail of the clip by 1 frame." Because the Xpress and most Media Composers aren't true 24-frames-per-second machines, when you make a cut to your sequence, that cut point corresponds to a video frame, and that video won't always conform to a film frame. (Look at a C-frame for an example of this.) Since you can't split a film frame in half, the Avid will adjust the length of a clip by shortening or lengthening it by one film frame to get things to work out. You can be out of sync by a frame, but that will be made up, or corrected, at the next cut point.

Cut List

Footage	Duration	First/Last Key	Address TC	Cam Roll	Sc/Tk	Clip Name
1. 0+00 4+31	4+32	NO EDGE NUMBERS				ACADEMY LEADER
2. 04+32 20+06	16+15	Opt 1-0000+00 Opt 1-0050+06				OPTICAL #1
3. 20+07 25+23	5+17	KL 74 0246-8770&19 KL 74 0246-8781&15	01:04:54:29 01:05:03:29	1	2B/1 CU HANDS	
4. 25+24 28+38	3+15	KL 74 0246-8795&18 KL 74 0246-8802&12	01:05:15:23 01:05:21:11	1	2B/1 CU HANDS	

Matchback shortened the tail of the clip by 1 frame.

MIX AND OPTICAL SOUND TRACK

After you've locked your picture and done your sound work, you can do a sound mix on the Avid. Check your levels by playing your tracks with the Audio Tool open, set to Output. Use isolating headphones as you watch your levels. Once you're happy with everything, you can send your final mixed tracks to DAT. The DAT becomes your Mixed Master. Now you're ready to make the optical sound track, either a 16mm mono track, or a 35mm stereo track.

Most people suggest that you not speed up the sound yourself; let the sound house do it when they make your optical track. Remember, you slowed the sound down by .1 percent to conform it to the telecine process, which slowed the film down. Rather than speeding it up yourself to match the 24-fps film print, let the sound facility do that for you. Transfer your sound to DAT set at 30 ndf with the pitch shift off. Then send the DAT to them with instructions that say that

"The DAT tape is referenced to video," or that it is "recorded at 59.94." They will speed it up .1 percent so it will sync up with your film print. Remember to ask for a B-wind optical track.

CHECKING SYNC

If you are nervous about sync—and who wouldn't be—try the following. Have the lab make a silent answer print from the A&B Rolls. Then have the sound facility make a magnetic film track (mixed mag) from your DAT.

If you have access to a magnetic film recorder and a DAT recorder, you could make the mag track yourself. Make sure you set the pitch shift button on the DAT player to +00.1 percent when you transfer from the DAT to magnetic film.

Once you have the "sped-up" magnetic track and the silent answer print, get on a Steenbeck and check out the sync. Obviously, it should all be in sync. If it isn't, you can at least figure out why, before you have an optical track and a married print made.

IT WORKS

For the past two years, I've taught a class called Film Production III. Undergraduate students in the class use Avid Xpress machines with matchback software to cut their senior thesis films. Six of the sixteen films produced in that class have been made into 16mm prints, and all six have won recognition at film festivals. The steps I've outlined here are the same steps my students used. In fact, we worked together, often by trial and error, to come up with them.

NEXT STOP CANNES

Is it simple? Not exactly. But then, what in life that's worth doing ever is? Don't be afraid to ask for guidance from your negative cutter, film lab, transfer facility, and sound studio. Remember, you're paying them, not the other way around. Keep at it, and soon you'll have a print that you can show anywhere in the world.

Bon chance.

16

Present and Future

WHERE DO YOU GO FROM HERE?

If you want to make videos and films, then go make videos and films. You now know enough about the Avid to edit your own projects, and what you don't know, you can figure out. However, if you want to be an Avid editor, this book is a beginning, not an end. I'll be the first to admit that this book doesn't cover every Avid command or examine all of Avid's capabilities. Far from it. I've tried to give you all the information you need to efficiently edit your projects, but there is certainly more to learn. There are several excellent books on the market that I urge you to read. *The Avid Handbook* by Steve Bayes covers, in great detail, many areas that I have treated lightly. It's for advanced users, but you're fast becoming one. *The Avid Digital Editing Room Handbook* by Tony Solomons is particularly helpful for those of you hoping to edit feature films on an Avid. *Digital Nonlinear Editing* by Thomas A. Ohanian provides the complete history of nonlinear editing, tracing it's growth from tape and laserdisc machines to the full-featured systems of today. His chapter on digitization and compression explains the heart of nonlinear digital editing. *Avid Media Composer Techniques and Tips* by Steven Cohen is aimed at Media Composer users. Steven is a feature film editor and a member of the prestigious American Cinema Editors (ACE). His chapter on groups and multiple cameras is particularly helpful. Although it's not a book on nonlinear editing, I highly recommend *The Filmmaker's Handbook* by Steven Ascher and Edward Pincus. This book covers nearly every aspect of video and film production and will answer just about any question you might have about moviemaking.

Last but not least, I recommend the various user manuals that Avid supplies when it sells a system. Much of my understanding of Avid's products comes from these manuals, which are clearly written and come with lots of illustrations. Unfortunately, you have to buy an Avid system to get them, which is one reason I wrote this book. This book might seem expensive, but you didn't have to shell out $30,000 to get it.

INFORMATION ON THE INTERNET

Like all modern companies, Avid has a well-maintained Web site. To visit it, go to www.avid.com. You'll find lots of hype as well as information about new products and upgrades. There are a number of user groups on the Internet that discuss digital products like the Avid. Try www.wwug.com. One of the most helpful ones I've encountered is called the Avid-L. The vast majority of Avid-L subscribers are professional Avid editors, living and working all over the world. Most of the postings are by editors seeking specific help for problems they're having on real projects. And the answers come from experienced editors who've encountered similar problems and are offering suggestions, workarounds, and quick fixes. You can learn a lot just by following the postings over time. These editors owe no allegiance to Avid, and are just as likely to blast the company for its missteps as to praise it for its achievements.

To subscribe to the Avid-L Digest, which is a compendium of the day's postings, send an e-mail to: majordomo@calvin.edu. In the body of your e-mail (where your text goes) simply write: Subscribe Avid-L Digest. To post a message or ask a question, send an e-mail to Avid-L@calvin.edu.

GETTING A JOB AS AN AVID EDITOR

If you want to be an Avid editor, I suggest that you find an entry-level position or internship at an editing facility that uses Avids, and works on the sorts of projects you're interested in. I know it's wrong to generalize about people, but it's been my experience that editors are the most down-to-earth and helpful people in the film and television industry, and many enjoy sharing their knowledge. Once you get a foot in the door, seek out a mentor and ask her or him to teach you what she or he knows in exchange for loyal and dependable assistance. Ask if you can get on a machine after-hours and try your hand at cutting the day's work. Employee turnover at some post houses can be amazingly fast, and you may find yourself moving up the ladder quickly. You need to demonstrate four things: Your reliability, your proficiency with the equipment, your ability to please clients, and your creativity; you'll find the order of importance varies from company to company.

OTHER AVID PRODUCTS

Avid now offers a full range of products on both Macintosh and Windows NT platforms, and several graphic-intensive systems on Silicon Graphics computers. The move is away from the ABVB video capture board and toward the Meridien system, which offers uncompressed video, both digital and analog input and output, and a rack-mountable In/Out box so you can plug just about any kind of video deck into the system.

Avid divides its products into three groups, touting these as three "solutions": the Media Composer line of products, the Avid Symphony™, and SOFTIMAGE | DS™.

The Media Composer line (and I'll toss the Xpress into this group) is designed for mainstream picture and sound editing. If you're cutting a documentary or narrative film, a Media Composer is for you. The Avid Symphony is for "finishing" projects. Symphony looks and behaves like a Media Composer, but offers more visually sophisticated tools to make the finished show look even slicker. SOFTIMAGE | DS products are for graphic- and effects-centric programs. Television commercials, station promos, bumpers, and music videos would benefit from the tools that make up the SOFTIMAGE | DS. Another way of putting it is to say, if you're interested in content, you want a Media Composer, and if you're more interested in the "look," head for SOFTIMAGE | DS.

The Avid Symphony is an important product. It's like a super Media Composer, and it's designed for productions that must meet the most exacting video standards. Many broadcast and cable networks will not accept programs that are finished on ABVB-based Avids because even at the highest resolution, AVR 77, you're working with compressed video. These networks flatly refuse to accept tapes that contain compressed video, even if the images are uniformly gorgeous. Until Avid offered uncompressed video, producers were forced to create EDLs and go to expensive online tape facilities for a tape-to-tape finish. EDLs are fine to a point, but effects involving many video layers are hard to reproduce. Now people can bring their Media Composer shows to the Avid Symphony and not only get uncompressed video but also get all their most complex effects recreated perfectly. And the Symphony has visual effects not found on Media Composers.

TELEVISION'S FUTURE

One difficulty facing Avid, its customers, and you, relates to the future of television. We are already in the digital television (DTV) age, but there is no single format or set of standards for this DTV. Basically, as long as the signal is digital, it's OK. Most networks and television producers plan to offer a picture that is much wider and has much greater resolution than we're used to seeing. One such format is called high-definition television or HDTV. The shape of the television screen will be 16:9 rather than 4:3, and it will look more like a movie theater screen than the analog television set you grew up watching. In addition, the frames-per-second rate will likely change from the current 29.97 fps, with its interlaced signal, to 24 fps progressive, or 24P. However, it'll be a few years before most folks actually buy one of these television sets, so producers will want to produce a version of a show for the new television and a version for the old.

To give producers flexibility, Avid is offering features such as "Pan and Scan," so you can create images with different aspect ratios from the same tape, and frame rate independence, so you can switch between 23.97, 24, 25, 29.97, and 30 frames per second to meet the requirements of formats such as NTSC, PAL, and HDTV. The idea is that you come into the Avid with one format and leave with many different formats, so your show can be played on any television in the world.

When it comes to storage, formats like HDTV require many times more space than the analog television shows of the twentieth century. The standard 4:3 aspect ratio signal with its 720 $\times$ 486 pixel matrix uses about 22 megabytes per second. HDTV, with its 16:9 aspect ratio, is made up of 1920 $\times$ 1080 pixels and uses about 120 megabytes per second, or about 7 gigabytes per minute! An hour show would need at least 420 gigabytes.

AVID'S FUTURE

I'm an Avid user and a fan as well. Overall, I think they make great products. A lot of my former students work at Avid, and I like and admire all the people I know who work there. That said, Avid is a big corporation, and like all corporations it has only one mission—to turn a bigger and bigger profit every year. Most economists will tell you that, in theory, this quest for profits will serve you, the customer, perfectly well. They argue that if the corporation isn't doing right by you, you won't buy its product. Therefore the company has to follow the wishes of its customers.

You have to wonder if Avid was trying to test that theory in 1999. That was the year Avid made its move to the Windows NT platform.

When Avid announced, with great fanfare, their extensive plans for Windows NT Avids at the 1999 National Association of Broadcasters (NAB) annual convention, a lot of Avid customers got terribly upset. Based on what Avid said about its big plans for Windows NT systems and its meager plans for Apple Macintosh systems, they thought Avid was going to abandon the Mac platform. They felt they were being forced to move to a Windows NT system if they wanted to get the latest software and the top-of-the-line machines. And the prices Avid offered to those who wanted to make the move from their Macs to NT machines were exorbitant. It almost seemed as if Avid was punishing people who had bought Macintosh Avids.

This was strange behavior, indeed, especially when you consider that Avid hardly had any customers who hadn't bought Macintosh Avids. Naturally, these 50,000 or so people felt betrayed. Lots of them lashed out at Avid on various forums, including the Avid-L. Many wrote that they had grave concerns about the stability and dependability of Avids on Windows NT machines. It's hard to tell whether this concern came from dyed-in-the-wool Mac-lovers (of whom there are substantial numbers), who hate Bill Gates, Microsoft, and the whole PC universe, or from people who knew what they were talking about. I do know some of it was the result of bad feelings. Avid made a terrible mess of the move to NT machines by giving little or no thought to the impact it would have on Mac users. Loyal customers felt confusion, fear, and anger. Is that how a successful company treats 98 percent of its customers? Not exactly.

It got so bad that Bill Miller, Avid's Chairman and CEO, sent out a letter of apology. "In particular," he wrote in a letter dated July 21, 1999, "we are responding to the fact that during the past few months, we have succeeded in confusing many of you about our plans for the Avid Media Composer on Macintosh. Judging by the emails we've received and postings we have seen on various forums, we've also made some of you pretty angry in the process." The heart of the letter stated that Avid was, in fact, not abandoning Macintosh at all. Mr. Miller promised us that Avid is pouring tons of money into the Avid Macintosh product line.

As bad as they handled it, Avid probably made the right decision to move to Windows NT. Having all your eggs in one computer basket (Apple) isn't smart business, especially given the unpredictable nature of the computer industry. I live in Massachusetts and without even thinking about it, I can rattle off the names of three companies that were once computer giants, all based within 30 miles of my home. All three are gone—history. You might not remember them but Wang, Digital Equipment Corp., and Data General were *huge* global players.

Another point to consider when analyzing the move to Windows NT is this: there is a lot of great software that isn't available on Macs—only on Windows machines. Given the thousands of programs that run successfully on PC computers, it's hard to believe Avid software won't perform as well on a PC as it does on a Mac.

Avid makes a great nonlinear editing system, but over the years they have alienated a lot of their customers by selling expensive products and then squeezing their customers even more by offering costly product support and exorbitant software upgrades. The way Avid handled the move to Windows is just another example of Avid's insensitivity to its own customers.

And now Avid is starting to feel the heat. New and relatively inexpensive nonlinear editing systems are suddenly making a splash and real competition has arrived. This competition couldn't come at a worse time for Avid, since they have nearly saturated the market for mid- and high-end systems, and must compete with low-priced products like Final Cut Pro™ for the expanding low-end market. Avid has a big lead in the race, but it has often stumbled in the past and long-term success is far from certain.

One positive sign came in October, 1999, when Avid announced significant management changes. Avid CEO Bill Miller is gone and the new management team seems to place customer satisfaction higher on its priority list than Mr. Miller's team ever did.

Avid has long enjoyed a reputation as a company with a big brain, but it has often appeared to posses small ears and tunnel vision. To continue to be successful, Avid must learn to listen to you, the Avid editor. I hope they do—you are Avid's future. Don't be afraid to tell them what you think. If you do and they pay attention, they'll be around a long time, and your investment in time and money will pay off.

Index

About the CD-ROM...

This CD-ROM contains all the video and audio clips for the scene, "Wanna Trade." It will mount on a Macintosh Avid (ABVB) and a Windows NT Avid (Meridien). The audio was sampled at 44.1K. If your Avid has an external Pro Tools Audio I/O, select the 44.1 setting on the 48/44.1 switch.

For installation instructions, refer to the Readme file found on the disc.

Beyond providing replacements for defective discs, Butterworth-Heinemann does not provide technical support for the contents of this CD-ROM.

Send any requests for replacement of a defective disc to: Focal Press, Customer Service Dept., 225 Wildwood Avenue, Woburn, MA 01801-2041 or email **techsupport@bhusa.com**. Be sure to reference item number CD-0421X.

OTHER AVID SYSTEMS

For those of you using Macintosh Avids with the Meridien capture board or the Avid XpressDV on IBM, the Focal Press website contains instructions for downloading and installing the scene "Wanna Trade." For the support material for these Avid systems, please visit www.focalpress.com/companions.